Confederate Naval Cadet

Confederate Naval Cadet

The Diary and Letters of Midshipman Hubbard T. Minor, with a History of the Confederate Naval Academy

HUBBARD T. MINOR
edited by R. Thomas Campbell

McFarland & Company, Inc., Publishers
Jefferson, North Carolina, and London

FRONTISPIECE: Midshipman Hubbard Taylor Minor, CSN.

LIBRARY OF CONGRESS CATALOGUING-IN-PUBLICATION DATA

Minor, Hubbard T.
Confederate naval cadet : the diary and letters of
Midshipman Hubbard T. Minor, with a history of
the Confederate Naval Academy / Hubbard T. Minor ;
edited by R. Thomas Campbell.
p.   cm.
Includes bibliographical references and index.

ISBN-13: 978-0-7864-2645-4
ISBN-10: 0-7864-2645-4
(softcover : 50# alkaline paper) ∞

1. Minor, Hubbard T.—Diaries.
2. Midshipmen—Confederate States of America—Biography.
3. Confederate Naval Academy—History—Sources.
4. Patrick Henry (Ship: 1861–1865)
5. Confederate States of America. Navy—History.
6. United States—History—Civil War, 1861–1865—Naval operations.
7. United States—History—Civil War, 1861–1865—Personal narratives, Confederate.
I. Campbell, R. Thomas, 1938–
II. Title.
V438M55A3   2007   973.7'57092–dc22 [B]   2006036982

British Library cataloguing data are available

Cover photograph: The CSS *Patrick Henry* (*Official Records of the
Union and Confederate Navies in the War of the Rebellion*)

Manufactured in the United States of America

McFarland & Company, Inc., Publishers
Box 611, Jefferson, North Carolina 28640
www.mcfarlandpub.com

Acknowledgments

Confederate Naval Cadet has been, off and on, several years in the making. During this period of time many people and organizations have provided information and offered encouragement. To all of these, I am extremely grateful.

Several individuals and institutions deserve special thanks. In no particular order they include: Herbert O. Funsten, titleholder of the Minor Family Papers, which reside in the archives of the Virginia Historical Society, Richmond, Virginia; Dr. Richard Sommers of the U.S. Army Military History Institute in Carlisle, Pennsylvania; and E. Lee Shepard of the Virginia Historical Society.

Also deserving my thanks are Bob Holcombe of the Civil War Naval Museum in Columbus, Georgia, the folks at the National Archives in Washington, D.C., and the Museum of the Confederacy in Richmond, Virginia.

In addition, my wife Carole garners an honorable mention as my editor and critic. She also deserves special thanks for spending many hours deciphering Hubbard Minor's handwriting.

To all of the above I am deeply indebted.

Contents

Preface

The Civil War diary of Hubbard T. Minor is located in the archives of the U.S. Army Institute at Carlisle, Pennsylvania. Actually, there are three diaries, here combined into one. I have personally inspected the handwritten diaries and have carefully transcribed them to create this book. Together, their entries give a day-by-day account of Minor's activities while he was a cadet at the Confederate Naval Academy and while he was stationed aboard the ironclad CSS *Savannah* at Savannah, Georgia, near the end of the war.

Preceding the diary text are three chapters providing information to help the reader better understand the times and adversities under which Minor served as a midshipman in the Confederate States Navy. Chapter 1 recounts the operations of the 42nd Tennessee Infantry Regiment during the time of Minor's army service, which preceded his assignment to the academy. Chapter 2 provides information about the Confederate Naval Academy. Chapter 3 offers biographical sketches of several of the principal instructors that Minor encountered at the school. The remaining text, except for a few of my own thoughts in Chapter 5, consists of Minor's diary entries and letters.

Hubbard T. Minor, Jr., was born near Spotsylvania Court House in Virginia on July 7, 1845. When war erupted, Minor joined Company E of the 42nd Tennessee Infantry, commanded by Colonel William A. Quarles. The 42nd Tennessee was captured at Fort Donelson, Tennessee, and after the regiment was exchanged, saw duty on the Mississippi River at Port Hudson, Louisiana, where Minor enlisted.

It was not until July 6, 1863, that he was transferred to the navy and assigned to the Academy on the school ship CSS *Patrick Henry* located below Richmond. One of the requirements of a cadet upon entering the

Academy was to keep a written record of his duties and activities, to be presented at the time of his examination. Minor's work is a product of this requirement and is one of only two diaries to have survived. His notes and views on academy life are very descriptive; nor is he shy about recounting his many forays into the entertainment arenas of Richmond and Savannah.

One of the practices of the Naval Academy was to rotate its cadets out among operational units for field experience. After five months of classroom and shipboard instruction, Minor was transferred to the Savannah Squadron in December of 1863. Here he was assigned to the CSS *Savannah* under the command of Captain Robert F. Pinkney. During this assignment Minor was chosen to accompany the raid on the USS *Water Witch* on June 3, 1864, in which the Union vessel was captured and he was slightly wounded. He presents a long and detailed account of this action. On December 6, 1864, as General Sherman's forces close in on Savannah, Minor describes an expedition against enemy shore batteries on Argyle Island in which he participated.

As part of the editing process, I have inserted, where chronologically appropriate, several letters written by Minor to his cousin, Lieutenant Robert D. Minor, CSN.

The continuing narrative of Minor's diary describes the evacuation of Savannah, his arrival and service at Charleston, the retreat to Richmond, and finally, the end of the conflict. With the war over, he returned home and enrolled at the University of Virginia for the fall semester of 1865. In 1867, he married his Savannah sweetheart, Annie Lamar. By 1870 they had two children, Harriet and Lamar. Tragically, however, in that same year Annie died, and four years later Minor was dead at the age of twenty-nine.

The Minor diary is a significant piece of Civil War literature. It affords us a fleeting but realistic view of what life was really like for a young man thrust into the midst of America's most deadly conflict. I am grateful and humbled to be able to bring his ordeal to light.

Introduction

In the summer of 1863, a most unusual but remarkably successful institution began its operation in the beleaguered Confederate States of America. It was unusual in that it was inaugurated during the midst of a violent war in which the country it represented was struggling for its very existence. It spite of the war that waged all around it, the Confederate Naval Academy managed to successfully supply several classes of well-trained officers to the Southern navy.

In all the historical chronicles that have been preserved from the American Civil War, none presents a more admirable account of courage and perseverance in the face of enormous odds than that of the Confederate States Navy and its naval school. The Southern navy, formed by an act of the Confederate Congress on February 20, 1861, literally began life with nothing. There were no ships and no sailors. There were no shipyards capable of constructing warships and few artisans versed in the science of shipbuilding. Even if vessels could have been built, the timber for their hulls was still growing in the Southern forests, and the iron for their machinery was still buried deep in the ground. In addition, the new nation of seceded states was threatened with an imminent invasion by a much superior power. It was, therefore, a most challenging position that Stephen R. Mallory assumed when President Jefferson Davis appointed him Secretary of the Navy the following day.

Mallory's appointment was one of the best ever made by President Davis. It was through Mallory's vision and perseverance, his imagination and courage, that a Southern navy and a naval school for future officers were eventually created.

Although the acquisition and construction of warships was Mallory's main challenge, the assembling of a professional officers' corps also

3

loomed as a formidable task. Although many senior naval officers were resigning and offering their services to the fledgling Southern navy, there was still a dearth of junior grade officers. These, Mallory determined, would have to be recruited and trained locally. The greatest deficiency was in the quantity and quality of the lowest officer grade (but a very necessary one) of midshipmen. Already the Secretary's thoughts were turning to that splendid university on the Severn River, the U. S. Naval Academy at Annapolis. While chairman of the Naval Affairs Committee, Mallory had kept a close eye on the academy and was impressed with its results. Now as Secretary of the Confederate navy, he was determined to train the South's midshipmen with the same standards, or better, as that of the United States. Even though the war had yet to begin, the foundations of the Confederate States Naval Academy were already taking shape in the creative mind of Stephen R. Mallory.

1

The 42nd Tennessee
Infantry Regiment

The state of Tennessee contributed approximately 115,000 men to the Southern armies during the War Between the States. One of the many infantry regiments formed at the beginning of the war was designated the 42nd Tennessee Infantry Regiment. It was organized on November 28, 1861, at Camp Cheatham, near Cedar Hill, Alabama. Camp Cheatham, was named for Benjamin Franklin Cheatham its first commander, who in 1861 was appointed brigadier general in the Provisional Army, Independent State of Tennessee. The training camp was established in this area in June of 1861, and was used by numerous Confederate units, including the 3rd Tennessee Infantry, 11th Tennessee Infantry, and 42nd Tennessee Infantry.

The 42nd Tennessee would be the unit in which Hubbard T. Minor would first experience Confederate military life. Although Minor eventually left the army to join the navy, his comrades in the 42nd Tennessee struggled on, and by the war's end only a small percentage of them remained, forming the 4th Consolidated Tennessee Infantry Regiment, which was paroled at Greensboro, North Carolina. During the time of Minor's service the 42nd was commanded by Colonel William A. Quarles, who later was promoted to brigadier general and commanded the brigade which included the 42nd. When Quarles moved to brigade command, Colonel Isaac N. Hulme became commander of the 42nd Tennessee Regiment.[1]

William A. Quarles was born near Jamestown, Virginia, on July 4, 1825. Quarles studied law at the University of Virginia and was admitted to the Tennessee bar in 1848. Opening a law office in Clarksville,

Tennessee, Quarles practiced law, and was appointed a judge on the Tennessee circuit court. In addition to his law practice and judgeship, Quarles was appointed supervisor of banks for the state of Tennessee, and president of the Memphis, Clarksville, & Louisville Railroad. He served as a delegate from Tennessee at the Democratic convention in 1860. When Tennessee seceded and the 42nd Tennessee Infantry Regiment was formed, he was elected the regiment's colonel.[2]

Soon after its organization the 42nd Tennessee Regiment was moved to Camp Duncan, near Clarksville, Tennessee. Later the regiment was moved to Fort Sevier, at New Providence, near Clarksville, and on January 21, 1862, according to official records, the 42nd and 48th Regiments were reported at Clarksville.

On January 31, 1862, the Central Army of Kentucky, which was commanded by Major General William J. Hardee, reported that Brigadier General Charles Clark's Brigade of Brigadier General Simon B. Buckner's Division was composed of the 8th Kentucky Regiment, 1st, 3rd Mississippi Regiments, 42nd Tennessee Regiment, 7th Texas Infantry Regiment and General Nathan Bedford Forrest's cavalry command.

On February 12, 1862, the 42nd Tennessee was ordered to Fort Donelson, on the Cumberland River. Transported down the river by steamboat, the regiment arrived on February 13, in time to participate in the initial defense of the fort.

Marching directly from the boats, the 42nd Tennessee was ordered to support the 30th Tennessee, which was being hard pressed by the Federal attack. Later causality reports indicated that the 42nd had 498 engaged, and sustained 15 casualties. When the fort was surrendered, a few members of the regiment escaped, but the majority were taken prisoner and transported to Camp Douglas, Illinois. The officers were sent to Johnson's Island.

After spending more than six months as prisoners of war, most members of the regiment were paroled at Vicksburg, Mississippi, in September of 1862. After an

Brigadier General William A. Quarles (National Archives).

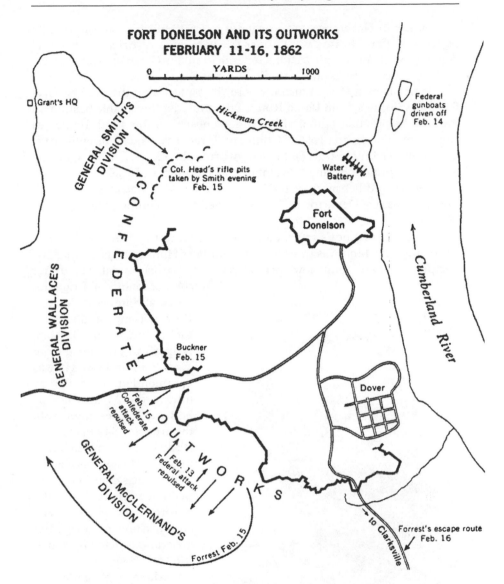

FORT DONELSON AND ITS OUTWORKS
FEBRUARY 11-16, 1862

YARDS

0   1000

☐ Grant's HQ

GENERAL SMITH'S DIVISION

Hickman Creek

Federal gunboats driven off Feb. 14

Col. Head's rifle pits taken by Smith evening Feb. 15

Water Battery

C O N F E D E R A T E

Fort Donelson

Cumberland River

GENERAL WALLACE'S DIVISION

Buckner Feb. 15

Dover

O U T W O R K S

Feb. 15 Confederate attack repulsed

Feb. 13 Federal attack repulsed

GENERAL McCLERNAND'S DIVISION

to Clarksville

Forrest's escape route Feb. 16

Forrest Feb. 15

Map of the area around Fort Donelson (*Official Records of the Union and Confederate Armies in the War of the Rebellion*).

exchange of a like number of Union prisoners, the 42nd was declared exchanged on November 10. After reorganization and camping for a short time at Clinton, Mississippi, the regiment moved to Holly Springs, Mississippi, on October 9. During the remaining portion of October 1862, the 42nd Tennessee was shuffled among various brigades and divisions until at last in November it was ordered to Port Hudson, Louisiana. The batteries at Port Hudson were under the command of Brigadier General William N. R. Beall, but Major General Franklin Gardner would arrive by December 27 to assume overall command.

It was here at Port Hudson, where the batteries on the bluff twenty-five miles up river from Baton Rouge constituted a formidable bastion on the Mississippi, that Hubbard T. Minor enlisted in the 42nd Tennessee Regiment. The muster role of Company E records his date of enlistment as November 15, 1862, when he was sworn in by Colonel W. A. Quarles. Minor was present during November and December of 1862, but returns for January and February of 1863 record him as "on detached duty with the Commissary Department." He returned to his company on April 16, 1863.[3]

Soon after Minor's return, and in reaction to the growing threat to Vicksburg, the 42nd was transported from Port Hudson to Jackson, Mississippi. The regiment now formed part of a brigade that was under the command of Brigadier General Samuel B. Maxey. Born at Tompkinsville, Kentucky, on March 30, 1825, Maxey was graduated from West Point in 1846. He was commended for gallantry during the Mexican War; however, he resigned from the army in 1849 in order to study law. Moving to Texas in 1857, Maxey was elected to the state senate and practiced law there until the outbreak of the war. His commission as brigadier general was dated March 4, 1862.[4]

Maxey's Brigade was attached temporarily to Major General W. W. Loring's Division, but on June 21, 1863, his brigade was transferred to the division of Major General Samuel G. French. Prior to this organization, however, the

Major General Franklin Gardner (National Archives).

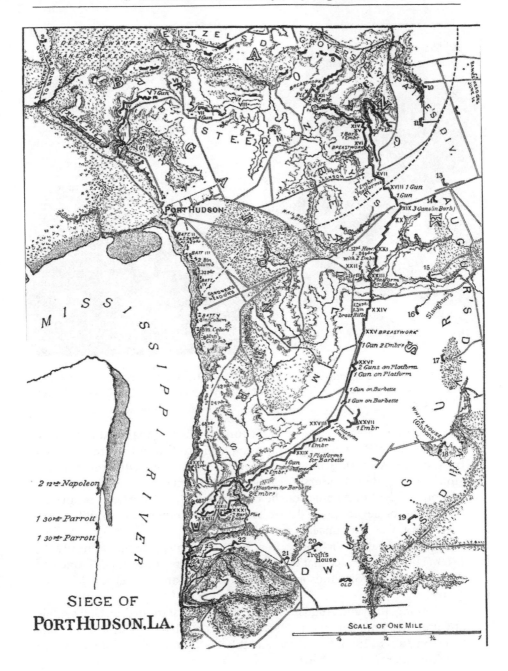

Map of the fortifications at Port Hudson (*Official Records of the Union and Confederate Armies in the War of the Rebellion*).

Left: **Brigadier General Samuel B. Maxey (National Archives).** *Right*: **General Joseph E. Johnston, who led an army for the relief of Vicksburg (Library of Congress).**

42nd Tennessee had left Jackson on June 1, where it marched to Canton and then on to Benton before returning again to Canton where it arrived on June 23. As part of the force assembled by General Joseph E. Johnston for the relief of Vicksburg, the 42nd Tennessee, including Private Minor, was within 20 miles of the city on July 4, 1863, when the surrender of the besieged Confederate army of Lieutenant General John C. Pemberton was announced.

With the fall of Vicksburg, Port Hudson also surrendered on July 10, 1863. There is evidence that certain small elements of the 42nd Tennessee were present at Port Hudson, for they are listed on Federal parole documents.

During July and August, the regiment was stationed at Hall's Mills at Camp Memminger, and at Harrell's Mills, Alabama. It was during this time, on July 6, 1863, that Private Hubbard T. Minor was transferred to the Confederate States Navy.

While Minor and a number of his comrades were on their way to the navy, the 42nd Tennessee soldiered on. Although Minor had no more official relationship with the 42nd Tennessee, it is only fitting that we briefly continue the story of his former army unit.

On September 30, 1863, the brigade, now under the command of Brigadier General Charles A. Quarles (his commission to brigadier general was dated August 25, 1863) was transferred to the Department of the Gulf. This district, with headquarters at Mobile, Alabama, was under the command of Major General Dabney H. Maury. From this point forward, the 42nd Tennessee would remain as a part of Quarles' Brigade until the end of the war. The brigade now constituted, in addition to the 42nd Tennessee, the 48th, 49th, 53rd, and 55th Tennessee Regiments as well as the 1st Texas Sharpshooters, Hutchinson's Engineers, and Gallimard's Sappers and Miners.

During October of 1863 the regiment was reported at Camp

Lieutenant General John C. Pemberton (National Archives).

Cummings, Mobile, Alabama, but it is not until May and June of 1864 that the regiment is again mentioned in official reports. Prior to this report, Quarles' Brigade, on the last day of December, 1863, had joined the Army of Tennessee which was encamped at Dalton, Georgia. There the brigade was placed in Major General John C. Breckinridge's Division that was part of Major General T. C. Hindman's Corps.

Returns indicate that when joining the Army of Tennessee, Quarles' Brigade included the 4th and 30th Louisiana and the 42nd, 46th/55th, 48th, 49th, and 53rd Tennessee Infantry Regiments. Due to the increased Federal navy and army pressure on Mobile, Alabama, Quarles' Brigade was sent back sometime during the early spring to the Department of Alabama, Mississippi, and East Louisiana. It was during this time, April 2, 1864, that General Maury in a report of his department listed the 42nd Tennessee as having only 169 men present for duty out of a total of 242.

By the end of July 1864, Quarles' Brigade had returned to the Army of Tennessee where it joined Major General Edward C. Walthall's Division, which was part of Lieutenant General A. P. Stewart's Corps. The brigade would remain in this organizational position from this time until the end of the war.

The 42nd Tennessee was engaged in fierce fighting during the battles around Atlanta in the summer of 1864. While individual regimental accounts are lacking, Thomas A. Turner of Company G reported the battles of the regiment in his *Lindsley's Annuals*. In that publication he states

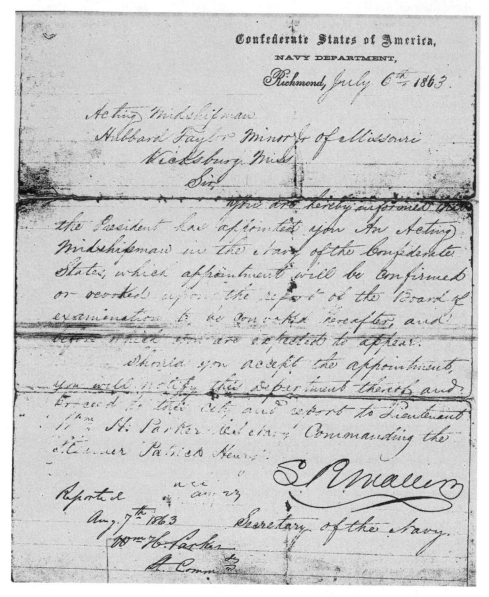

Copy of original orders from Secretary Mallory appointing Minor to the Naval Academy (Minor Papers, U.S. Army Institute).

Top: Map of the approaches to Vicksburg (*Official Records of the Union and Confederate Armies in the War of the Rebellion*). *Bottom:* Federal naval bombardment of Port Hudson on March 13, 1863 (*Battles & Leaders of the Civil War*).

that the 42nd Tennessee fought at New Hope Church, May 1864; at Pine Mountain and Kennesaw Mountain, June 1864; at Smyrna Depot, Peach Tree Creek, Atlanta, and at Lickskillet Road in July of 1864.

Operations of Walthall's Division were recounted in the general's report from Tuscumbia, Alabama, dated January 14, 1865. In that report he states that from July 18, 1864, until January of 1865, Quarles' Brigade was in position in the lines at Atlanta during July 1864; on July 22 the 42nd Tennessee was in reserve at Ezra Church; on August 18 it was in the trenches around Atlanta; on August 19 it moved to East Point, Georgia. The next reference reveals that the brigade crossed the Chattahoochee River on August 27 and then marched up through Georgia, destroying the railroads as far as Tuscumbia, Alabama.

The brigade was part of General John B. Hood's invasion of Tennessee and crossed the Tennessee River November 20, 1864. Passing through Spring Hill, Tennessee, November 29, the brigade was thrown into the firestorm that was the Battle of Franklin on November 30.

In his report, General Walthall wrote: "Brigadier-General Quarles was severely wounded at the head of his brigade within a short distance of the enemy's inner line, and all his staff officers with him on the field were killed; and so heavy were the losses in his command that when the battle ended its officer highest in rank was a captain." During the battle Colonel Hulme was wounded, and the regiment lost its colors with all of its color bearers killed.[5]

Hood pushed on and attacked Nashville but suffered a shattering defeat on December 16, 1864. When the retreat began, 100 men from Quarles' Brigade stood fast in the redoubts on the Hillsboro Road and

Left: General John B. Hood. *Right:* Major General Edward C. Walthall (both photographs from Library of Congress).

formed part of the rear guard to protect what was left of Hood's Army as it withdrew toward Tupelo, Mississippi.

Gathering together the remnants of the Army of Tennessee, now under the command of General Joseph E. Johnston, the Confederates made an attempt to stop the northward advance of General Sherman in North Carolina. On March 19, 1865, what was left of Quarles' Brigade fought the Federals at the Battle of Bentonville. When Johnston finally surrendered the Army of Tennessee on April 26, near Durham Station, North Carolina, only a few members of the 42nd Tennessee remained. Parole records indicate that on May 1, 1865, men of the 42nd Regiment were paroled at Greensboro, North Carolina as part of the 4th Consolidated Tennessee Infantry Regiment.

Thus ended the illustrious record of Hubbard T. Minor's old infantry regiment. It was perhaps fortunate for him that he was transferred to the navy, for only a pitiful handful of the 42nd Tennessee were able to answer their last bugle call.[6]

2

The Confederate Naval Academy

Any reading of Minor's diary requires a brief study of the Confederate Naval Academy—which in turn must begin with the United States Naval Academy, for it is within that august institution that we find the framework for the Southern school.

Prior to the establishment of the U.S. school at Annapolis, Maryland in 1845, the training of all American junior naval officers (known, while in training, as midshipmen) was sporadic and haphazard at best. The appointment of these young men to the U. S. Naval Academy was the prerogative of the president of the United States, the secretary of the navy, and influential ship's captains.

Before the academy at Annapolis was established, appointed midshipmen, who were normally between the ages of fourteen and eighteen, were sent directly to the fleet where they were little more than captain's errand boys. (This fact reflects the origins of the term "midshipman," which dates from the seventeenth century, when British commanders would station a junior officer amidships to relay messages.) After performing the many and disagreeable duties thrust upon them by sometimes wretched and bellicose senior officers, midshipmen found that precious little time was left for the study of seamanship, navigation, mathematics and science. Even if they found the time, there were usually no officers willing or able to render instruction.[1]

Family connections and political influence were the principal factors which secured appointments. Matthew Fontaine Maury, destined to become renowned as the Pathfinder of the Seas for his scientific study of the ocean currents, and later a commander in the Confederate Navy,

The U.S. Naval Academy at Annapolis, Maryland, on the eve of war (U.S. Naval Institute).

received his appointment after enlisting the support of certain influential congressmen. Samuel F. DuPont, who would obtain the rank of rear admiral in Union service during the War Between the States, secured an appointment after his grandfather wrote a letter of introduction to President Jefferson. David Farragut, the conqueror of New Orleans and Mobile, received his appointment at the tender age of nine from a ship's captain. It was not until 1831 that midshipman appointees were required to be able to read and write and to understand the basics of mathematics, grammar, and geography.

During the 1820s and 1830s, as America expanded, a growing number of naval secretaries from the south filled the ranks with boys from the states below the Mason Dixon Line. This caused a shift away from New England, which had dominated the junior officer corps, and by 1842, 44 percent of midshipmen on duty were from Maryland and Virginia. An early historian of naval education, Charles O. Paullin, wrote:

> The most important factor in the selection of midshipmen was political and personal influence; and many statesmen of the older times left memorials of their families in the navy list by making midshipmen of sundry sons, grandsons, nephews, and cousins.[2]

The competition for appointments was intense, and a boy with no influence stood little possibility of nomination. Various reasons motivated young men to seek a position in the navy, but chief among these were the romance and lure of the sea, an opportunity for excitement, prestige, and a longing perhaps for security. Some were appointed, however, because they were misfits or trouble makers, and it was thought that a good dose of naval discipline would straighten them out. Abel P. Upshur, secretary of the navy under President Tyler from 1841 to 1843, wrote:

> ... wayward and incorrigible boys, whom even parental authority cannot control, are often sent to the navy as a mere school of discipline, or to save them from the reproach to which their conduct exposes them on shore. It is not often that skillful officers or valuable men are made out of such material. The belief, heretofore prevailing, that an officer of any standing in the navy could not be driven out of it, or at least that he could not be kept out of it, has a strong influence in ruining its discipline and corrupting its morals and manners.[3]

Intelligent senior executives and administrators realized that the naval education system was flawed, and some efforts at formal education were attempted, but these were frequently opposed by the older, more traditional navy officers. As early as 1807, a naval school of sorts was begun at the Washington Navy Yard, and others followed in 1825 at Boston, New York, and Norfolk. Attendance, however, was voluntary, and the schools were all disbanded by 1839. Still, many reformers continued to push for a distinct naval academy, however, one that would not only prepare a young man for his duties as a naval officer, but also polish him into a gentleman, a fit representative of his country in a foreign port.

By 1839, one important event had brought the navy to the realization that something finally had to be done regarding the education of its junior officers. That event was the introduction of steam powered vessels into the naval arsenal. Even the most conservative senior officer realized that it would require a whole new breed of well educated engineer officers to operate the noisy, smoke-belching engines that would propel their ships of the future.

Abel P. Upshur, secretary of the U.S. Navy, 1841–1843 (U.S. Naval Institute).

In 1842, a naval school was established at the old Naval Asylum in Philadelphia, a former home for retired naval officers, but this venture was short-lived, and by 1845 it, too, was disbanded. On June 6, 1845, Secretary of the Navy George Bancroft wrote a letter to Secretary of War William L. Marcy requesting the transfer of Fort Severn at Annapolis to the care and custody of the Navy Department. The old fort had outlived its usefulness, and the army was only too glad to transfer it to the naval service. On August 7, Bancroft charged Franklin Buchanan with the task of establishing the school, and on September 3, 1845, he assumed the position as commandant. On October 10, at precisely 11:00 A.M., the first of many classes of midshipmen gathered in one of the old fort's classrooms to hear the forty-five-year-old Buchanan's opening remarks. The United States Naval Academy had been born.[4]

Over the next fifteen years the naval school on the Severn River in Annapolis, Maryland, grew and flourished. Additional property was purchased, recitation halls were built, and quarters were constructed for the midshipmen.

Within a few years the number of "middies" attending the Academy had quadrupled. It was during this period that a freshman senator from Florida arrived to take his seat in the United States Congress. As chairman of the powerful Naval Affairs Committee, Stephen R. Mallory had ample opportunity to observe the spectacular growth of the naval school and was greatly impressed by its accomplishments. In early 1861, Mallory, now secretary of the Confederate navy, was convinced that the South would profit by having its own naval school. But with the immediate challenge of purchasing and constructing warships, and with the Southern states now subjected to a naval blockade and an invasion by powerful Federal armies, Mallory's plans for establishing an academy had to be delayed.

The first tenuous step toward the founding of a Southern naval school

Top: Captain Franklin Buchanan, first commandant of the U.S. Naval Academy (Naval Historical Center). *Bottom:* Stephen R. Mallory, Secretary of the Confederate States Navy (Library of Congress).

occurred on March 16, 1861, when the Confederate Congress authorized that the existing naval laws of the United States be applied to the navy of the Confederate States, and "that some form of education be established for midshipmen."[5] In his report to Congress on February 27, 1862, Secretary Mallory recommended that such a school be instituted. Shortly thereafter, precise action was taken by the Confederate lawmakers when they enacted legislation to provide for the establishment of a naval academy, and in addition, stipulated that 106 acting midshipmen could be appointed to the school by members of Congress from their respective districts and by the president at large.[6] Although the Confederacy, even at this early date, was waging a war for survival, farsighted Southern legislators—and Secretary Mallory—firmly believed that the future of the country could well depend on the young, properly trained junior officers of the Confederate Navy.

A few scholars have been critical of Mallory and the Confederacy for even establishing a naval academy. They argue that the Southern nation, with its meager resources and limited manpower reserves, should have expended its energy in other fields more directly related to the defense of the invaded country. One must realize, however, that there was absolutely no doubt in the minds of most Southern leaders that their struggle would eventually lead to Southern independence. It was necessary, therefore, to look beyond the current conflict, and to prepare the young men of the navy to take their place in the world as skilled officers and exemplary representatives of their country once the war was concluded. The fact that the Confederacy was eventually defeated by overwhelming Federal forces in no way diminishes the South's effort to train its leaders of the future.

That Secretary Mallory understood this pressing need is evident when, writing to President Davis, he said:

> The instruction of midshipmen is a subject of the greatest importance to the Navy. The naval powers of the earth are bestowing peculiar care upon the education of their officers, now more than ever demanded by the changes introduced in all the elements of naval warfare. Appointed from civil life and possessing generally but little knowledge of the duties of an officer and rarely even the vocabulary of their profession they have heretofore been sent to vessels or batteries where it is impossible for them to obtain a knowledge of its most important branches, which can be best, if not only, acquired by methodical study.[7]

Throughout the war Mallory continued to remain adamant in his belief that naval schooling was of supreme importance. He wrote:

> Naval education and training lie at the foundation of naval success; and the power that neglects this essential element of strength will, when the battle is

fought, find that its ships, however formidable, are but built for a more thoroughly trained and educated enemy.[8]

Mallory originally intended to utilize the old ship-of-the-line *United States*, which had been discarded by Federal forces at Norfolk upon its evacuation on April 20, 1861, as a school ship. The *United States* had been commissioned on July 11, 1798, and along with the *Constellation* and the *Constitution* (both of which are still in existence today) became one of the first of three warships to be constructed for the U. S. Navy. By 1861, the Union considered that old frigate surplus, and rather than attempt to destroy her, they simply abandoned her and left her to fate. Virginia forces quickly appropriated the undamaged warship when they took over the Gosport Navy Yard, and upon the transfer of personnel and vessels to the Confederate Navy, she was designated a receiving ship. Placed under command of First Lieutenant Van Rensselaer Morgan, the old frigate was now referred to as the CSRS *Confederate States*.

While the *Constitution* became a training ship at the United States Naval Academy, serving from 1860 until 1882, such would not be the case for Mallory's projected school ship. In April of 1862, Union General McClellan launched his ponderous but powerful Peninsular Campaign, and with the loss of the North Carolina sounds posing a threat from the rear, the Confederate authorities were forced to abandon Norfolk on May 10. With the navy yard in flames, the *Confederate States* was towed into the middle of the Elizabeth River and sunk as an obstruction to the passage of Federal ships. With the loss of the old warship, another vessel to train the eager midshipmen of the Confederate navy would have to be found.[9]

Mallory's choice of a replacement for the *Confederate States* would prove to be an excellent one. On May 15, 1862, at the conclusion of the Battle of Drewry's Bluff, the side-wheel steamer CSS *Patrick Henry* was designated to become a military college—the Confederate States Naval Academy.

In August of that year, the steamer's commander, John R. Tucker, was reassigned to Charleston, where he took command of the Confederate ironclad CSS *Chicora*. Following Tucker's departure, the *Patrick Henry* was withdrawn from active duty with the James River Squadron, and taken up the river to Rocketts landing at Richmond where alterations were begun to convert her into a school ship. It would be a long gestation period, for it took almost a year to complete the modifications necessary to accommodate the first class of midshipmen.[10]

The Confederate Navy, like to the U. S. Navy, was administered by several departments or "offices." The naval school fell under the Office of Ordnance and Hydrography which was responsible for the collection,

The CSS *Patrick Henry,* school ship of the Confederate Naval Academy
(Naval Historical Center).

presentation, and distribution of navigational information and equipment.
In March of 1863, Commander John M. Brooke was assigned as the officer
in charge, and was given as a high priority the task of implementing the
navy's school for midshipmen. Brooke had gained renown within the Confederacy, and respect from his enemies, as the designer of the powerful
Brooke rifle, acknowledged by friend and foe alike to be one of the finest
naval guns of the war. The inventive commander would bring the same
drive and ingenuity to the formation of the Naval Academy.[11]

While Commander Brooke's department had assumed the responsibility for establishing and overseeing the school, and the decision regarding the school ship had been settled, there was still a great deal to be
accomplished before the academy would become a reality. First and fore-
most was the assignment of the chief administrator of the institution,
including his staff, and the appointment of the requisite number of professors. Secretary Mallory again displayed his intelligence and foresight
when in May of 1863, he appointed First Lieutenant William Harwar
Parker to the position of superintendent and commandant of the Naval
Academy. Parker, who was serving as executive officer on the ironclad
CSS *Palmetto State* at Charleston, had just returned from an attempted
attack on Union warships in the Stono River when he learned of his reas-
signment. In his book *Recollections of a Naval Officer,* Parker wrote:

Upon my return to Charleston, I received a letter from Mr. Mallory, our Secretary of the Navy, directing me to make out an estimate for books, apparatus, etc., necessary for the establishment of a naval school. I accordingly did so, and sent it as instructed to the house of Frazer, Trenholm & Company who were to direct their agent to purchase the articles required in England. Soon after this I received orders to report in person at the Navy Department in Richmond.[12]

In the same month, Mallory appointed First Lieutenant Benjamin P. Loyall to the post of Commandant of Midshipmen. The Virginia born lieutenant was serving on the ironclad CSS *Richmond,* which operated with the James River Squadron, when Mallory tapped him for the important position at the naval school. Loyall would serve only until October of 1863, however, at which time he was detailed upon a secret mission to free the starving Confederate prisoners who were incarcerated on Johnson's Island in Lake Erie. In the same month, the position of Commandant of Midshipmen was filled by First Lieutenant Wilburn B. Hall, who served until Loyall's return near the end of the year. In late February, 1864, after helping lead the successful attack on the USS *Underwriter,* Loyall was once again detached from the academy, this time to command the CSS *Neuse* in North Carolina, and Hall again assumed the role of Commandant of Midshipmen. In the summer of 1864, he was replaced

Top: **Commander John M. Brooke, director of the Office of Ordnance and Hydrography.** *Bottom:* **1st Lt. Wm. H. Parker superintendent of the Confederate Naval Academy (Both photographs from Naval Historical Center).**

by First Lieutenant Oscar F. Johnston, which enabled Hall to devote more attention to the instruction of cadets. In November, Hall, at his own request, was transferred to the CSS *Chicora* at Charleston. Lieutenant Loyall returned for a short period in November, but in the early days of 1865, First Lieutenant James H. Rochelle assumed the duties of Commandant of Midshipman and held that position until the school was disbanded.[13]

Additional staff members were appointed, while during the war-torn summer of 1863, members of the Confederate Congress bestowed appointments upon boys from their respective districts. Prospective cadets had to be between fourteen and eighteen years of age and had to pass an entrance examination based on the criteria of good moral character, the ability to read and write, and an elementary knowledge of mathematics. A physical examination was also administered, and any boy who did not measure up to the standards was rejected.

The Navy Department drew up regulations, printed in a circular, which spelled out in detail the entrance requirements that a prospective candidate had to meet in order to be accepted into the Naval Academy. Among these was the stipulation that:

> No candidate will be admitted on board the School Ship unless he is found, in the opinion of the medical board, to be composed of the surgeon of the school-ship, and two other medical officers to be designated by the Secretary of the Navy, qualified to discharge the arduous duties of an officer of the navy, both at the time of his examination, and probably, during the rest of his life, until age shall disable him; and shall have passed a satisfactory examination before the Academic Board.

First Lieutenant James H. Rochelle (Scharf: *History of the Confederate States Navy***).**

The circular then listed numerous physical deficiencies that would be grounds for rejecting a prospective candidate. The document concludes by stipulating:

> Mess mates will jointly procure for their common use, and will keep their rooms at all times supplied with one looking glass, one wash-basin, one water-pail, and one slop-bucket.[14]

Other requirements specified:

A candidate who has passed the required examinations will receive the appointment of an acting midshipman.... A candidate who has once presented himself for examination, under the authority of the Navy Department, and been rejected, cannot be allowed to present himself for examination a second time.... No one who may be admitted on board the School-Ship under these regulations shall receive a warrant as a midshipman in the navy, unless he graduates thereat.[15]

By late summer the alterations to the *Patrick Henry* had been completed, and she was taken down the James River on Saturday, October 10, and anchored at Drewry's Bluff. Although the school on board the *Patrick Henry* had actually begun operations in August of 1863, it was not until October that all fifty-two midshipmen had reported for duty as ordered to the Academy.[16] The remaining fifty-four of the original 106 acting midshipmen awaited their turn to attend the school by serving at their assigned stations, aboard ships, at shore installations, or abroad. The fifty-two midshipmen would soon be augmented by eight late arrivals, one of which would be Hubbard T. Minor, and the dream of Secretary Mallory was now a reality. The Confederate States Naval Academy was in business.[17]

Parker did not waste any time in drawing up and publishing the regulations of the Academy and interior police of the school ship. The subjects addressing the regulations of the *Patrick Henry* included:

Organization of the Crew; Daily routines which affected roll call, meals, studies, and recitations; Police of the student's quarters; Superintendent of steerage; Officer of the deck; Section formations; Instructors; Indulgence of leave; Dress; Reports and excuses; Offices; Suspension from duty; Boats; Officer in charge; Executive officer; Mess arrangements; Examination of the candidate for admission.[18]

Parker even produced a textbook on the regulations of the naval academy which was entitled *Regulations of the Confederate States School-Ship Patrick Henry* (see Appendix A). It contained fifteen chapters:

I. Organization
II. Academic Board
III. Rules of Admission
IV. Uniform
V. Course of Instruction
VI. Academic Examinations
VII. Merit Rolls
VIII. Final Examination of Midshipmen
IX. Conduct Roll
X. Discipline
XI. Leaves of Absence

XII. Hospital
XIII. Secretary
XIV. Pay Master
XV. Miscellaneous[19]

Just prior to the opening of the school, Parker published another text-book titled *Questions on Practical Seamanship; Together with Harbor Routine and Evolutions*. In the preface of this intriguing book, dated September 28, 1863, Parker notes that the work was prepared from notes he had made while he was an instructor in Naval Tactics and Seamanship at the United States Naval Academy in Annapolis. He clarifies that the greater portion of his notes were left behind there, and that consequently this work is incomplete, but he advises that "at some future day I hope to issue it in a more creditable manner."[20]

With all that had finally been accomplished, it was with unmitigated pride that Commander Brooke was able to report to Secretary Mallory on November 25, 1863:

The CSS *Patrick Henry* fitted out as a school ship (*Official Records of the Union and Confederate Navies in the War of the Rebellion*).

The steamer *Patrick Henry*, without alteration diminishing her efficiency as a vessel of war, has been fitted up as a school-ship for midshipmen, of whom 52 are now on board receiving instruction in the various branches of education essential to the naval officer. The organization of the school has been perfected by Lieutenant W. H. Parker, and it is now only necessary to complete the number of officers contemplated in the plan of organization to ensure the most satisfactory results. Lieutenant Parker states that the behavior of the young gentleman generally has been all that he could have expected; those just appointed are generally much further advanced and a better class than those received at the United States Naval Academy during his stay there. Lieutenant Parker, who, from his high professional and scientific acquirements, is particularly well qualified for the position of commander and superintendent of the school-ship, has surmounted many obstacles in carrying out the views of the department.[21]

Parker did indeed deserve the praise of Commander Brooke, but it took more than just the superintendent to make the school a success. Mallory was keenly aware of the necessity of putting together a first-class staff of professors, and, acting upon the suggestions of Parker and Brooke, he accordingly appointed some of the best minds in the South. The departments that concerned naval exercises and knowledge, astronomy, navigation, seamanship, gunnery, etc., were consigned to the direction of professional naval officers, most of whom, like Superintendent Parker, had served and taught in the United States Navy prior to the war. Mathematics, physics, English literature, French, Spanish, etc., were taught by former instructors from the Confederate Army who were transferred to the navy and given the rank of acting master. The staff was paid according to their military rank: lieutenants received $1,500 annually; acting masters, $1,000. The midshipmen, prior to their being graduated as passed midshipmen, were paid $550.[22]

Every effort was made to outfit the students in the regulation Confederate uniform required for their respective rank. As the war dragged on, and the shortages of material became more acute, this became increasingly difficult. The officers and men of the home squadrons, including the school ship *Patrick Henry*, were reasonably well attired, however, and to the best of their abilities conformed to the correct navy dress. The naval uniform differed from the army in that gray trousers were prescribed instead of blue, and the frock coat, or jacket, had a rolled collar with shoulder straps to indicate the wearer's rank. For midshipmen, rank was designated by a strip of gold lace four inches long and one-half inch wide on each shoulder, and three medium-sized navy buttons around the upper edge of the jacket's cuffs. In the summer, at the discretion of a local commander, navy whites could be worn in place of the steel gray. The naval uniform for both staff and students was to be strictly adhered to.

Confederate naval records are notoriously incomplete when com-

pared to the voluminous documentation available on the Union navy during the war. Not that the Confederacy did not keep meticulous records— they did; however, in the navy's case, much of their documentation was burned when Richmond was evacuated in April of 1865. The Navy Department shared officers with the War Department in Mechanic's Hall, a stately office building on 9th Street, which was consumed in the inferno that engulfed parts of the city as the last Confederate troops streamed across Mayo's Bridge to begin their painful trek to Appomattox. A small number of the records were hurriedly packed in boxes by navy clerks and shipped by rail to Charlotte, North Carolina, but unfortunately, most of these, too, were destroyed on the approach of Northern troops.

Fortunately, in spite of this scarcity of records, both Parker and J. Thomas Scharf, a midshipman assigned to the school, left accounts listing the staff of the academy. Parker acknowledges in his *Recollections of a Naval Officer,* published in 1883, that he had no notes, but was recounting the names of the faculty members strictly from memory. Scharf, on the other hand, kept many notes, and corresponded with numerous former officers prior to writing his *History of the Confederate States Navy* in 1877. Scharf, therefore, would seem to be the more creditable source. Accordingly to his records, the faculty on duty at the Academy in October of 1863 included:[23]

First Lieutenant William H. Parker, Superintendent.
First Lieutenant Wilburn B. Hall, Commandant of Midshipmen.
First Lieutenant Oscar F. Johnston, Professor of Astronomy,
    Navigation, and Surveying.
First Lieutenant Thomas W. W. Davies, Assistant Professor of
    Astronomy, Navigation, and Surveying.
First Lieutenant Charles J. Graves, Instructor in Seamanship.
Second Lieutenant G. W. Billups, Assistant Instructor in
    Seamanship.
Second Lieutenant William V. Comstock, Instructor in Gunnery.
Acting Master George M. Peek, Professor of Mathematics.
Acting Master George W. Armistead, Professor of Physics.
Acting Master Lewis N. Huck, Professor of English Literature.
Acting Master George A. Peple, Professor of French and Spanish.
Acting Master Richard S. Sanxey, Professor of Infantry Tactics and
    Sword Exercise.
Acting Master William B. Cox, Professor of Drawing and Painting.
Assistant Surgeon W. J. Addison.

Opposite: Mechanic's Hall in Richmond, site of the War and Navy departments (*Richmond Dispatch*).

Assistant Surgeon James G. Bigley.
Assistant Paymaster William M. Ladd.
Second Assistant Engineer Elias G. Hall.
Boatswain Andrew Blackie.
Gunner E. R. Johnson.
Sailmaker William Bennett.

The academic program, although rather rigid for boys between the ages of fourteen and eighteen, was extremely practical and was patterned after the course of instruction at the U.S. Naval Academy. The regulations formulated by Parker and submitted by Brooke to Secretary Mallory for his approval on July 23, 1863, were very specific. The midshipmen entering the Academy embarked upon a program that was divided into six departments and twenty-two branches. There were four courses annually, and the midshipmen were arranged into four classes, each class pursuing one of these courses, as follows:

Fourth Class
Practical Seamanship, Gunnery, Artillery, and Infantry Tactics; Arithmetic and Algebra to Equations of the First Degree; English Grammar; and Descriptive Geography.

Third Class
Practical Seamanship, Gunnery, Artillery, and Infantry Tactics; Algebra, Geometry, Plane and Spherical Trigonometry; Physical Geography and History; and French.

Second Class
Seamanship and Steam, Gunnery and Field Artillery, Astronomy, and Navigation; Application of Algebra and Trigonometry to the Mensuration of Planes and Solids; Political Science; and French.

First Class
Seamanship and Naval Tactics; Gunnery and Infantry Tactics; Navigation and Surveying; French and Spanish.[24]
With the refurbished *Patrick Henry* anchored at Rocketts Landing, the regulations published, the curriculum established, the administrative and teaching staff in place, and the fifty-two midshipmen on board, including Hubbard T. Minor, the South's Naval Academy was off to an excellent start.

3

The Academic Staff

Minor's diary has little to say about the instructors on the *Patrick Henry*. All were extremely qualified as teachers, and many had served in combat situations prior to and during the Civil War. To better understand the men who shaped Minor's navy life, their accomplishments, up to the time they joined the academy's staff, are presented here.

William Harwar Parker, Superintendent and Commandant

First Lieutenant William H. Parker was no stranger to the subjects to be taught at a navy school. Not only had he graduated first in his class at the U.S. Naval Academy in 1847, but he had taught at the academy from 1853 to 1857, and again in 1860 to 1861.

Parker was born in New York City on October 8, 1826. His northern birth, however, belied an aristocratic Virginia lineage. The Parker family could trace their ancestry back to 1650 when George Parker, along with his family, had settled in the tidewater area of Virginia.[1]

Midshipman Scharf in his *History of the Confederate States Navy* (1877), included a short biography of Parker:

> Lieut. Parker was a son of Com. Foxhall Parker, U. S. N., and brother of Com. Foxhall A. Parker U. S. N. While one brother went with the South, the other remained in the Federal navy during the war, and attained distinction. Wm. H. Parker entered the U. S. Navy in 1841, when he was 15 years old, and graduated at the head of a class at the Naval Academy that gave to the United States and Confederate States service more distinguished officers than any other single class. Previous to the War Between the States, he had attained high reputation as an officer and instructor, and held the position of assistant professor of mathematics at the Annapolis Institution. In the Confederate Navy he had taken part in the battles in the North Carolina Sounds; had commanded the gunboat *Beaufort* at the battle of Hampton Roads, and was executive officer

31

of the iron-clad *Palmetto State*, at Charleston, in the breaking of the blockade....
After the war he commanded vessels of the Pacific Mail Steamship Company,
was subsequently President of the Maryland Agricultural College, and is now
(1887) U.S. consul at Bahia.[2]

William's father, Foxhall A. Parker, whom Scharf mentions, was a
career naval officer who had served more than forty years in the U. S. Navy
and had retired as a captain. The older brother to whom Scharf refers,
Foxhall A. Parker, entered the navy in 1839, as a midshipman at the age
of seventeen. The young Foxhall would also serve forty years in the navy,
rising to the rank of commodore and serving for a time as superintendent of the U.S. Naval Academy. William's eldest brother, Richard B.
Parker, graduated from West Point, but died in Philadelphia on September 13, 1842, less than a year after joining his regiment.[3]

With a family heritage so closely entwined with the military, it seemed
only natural that William would one day follow in their footsteps. On
October 19, 1841, fifteen-year-old William entered the United States Navy
as a midshipman. Assigned to the 74-gun ship of the line *North Carolina*
commanded by the famous Matthew C. Perry, he was taken on board by
his father, and William related amusingly how he thought the old commodore was referring to his father when he addressed him as "Mister
Parker."

Parker's first tour as a midshipman rook him to the blue waters of
the Mediterranean where, in between his duties afloat, he spent many
delightful hours in various ports of call. His second year involved a tour
of duty with the South Atlantic Squadron then stationed off the coast of
Brazil. Argentina and Brazil were being torn by bloody civil upheavals
instigated by one political faction or another, and American and Euro-
pean warships constantly cruised the coasts to safeguard the interest of
their respective citizens ashore. Parker's one complaint was that there were
no exotic ports of call to visit such as he had experienced in the delightful Mediterranean.[4]

Parker's third cruise found him assigned to the USS *Potomac*, a frigate
and flagship of Commodore David Conner. As the Commodore's aide,
Parker was thrust into the swirling vortex of the Mexican war that lasted
from 1846 to 1848. During the battles for Palo Alto and Resaca de la
Palma, the young midshipman participated in the seizure of Port Isabel,
just north of the Rio Grande. In addition, Parker was witness to the
amphibious landings at Vera Cruz and was assigned to a naval battery
ashore which had been designed by a young army captain on General
Winfield Scott's staff by the name of Robert E. Lee.

Returning from the dusty battlefields of Mexico a seasoned combat
veteran, Parker was ordered in September of 1847 to the new naval school
at Annapolis, Maryland. After a short session there, Parker appeared

before a board of examiners in June of 1848, and on July 1, he became a Passed Midshipman and was assigned to the frigate *Constitution,* which was bound for the Mediterranean. William petitioned for a change in his orders, however, and was instead transferred to the sloop *Yorktown* whose destination was the lonely coast of Africa. Cruising off the dark continent, the *Yorktown's* mission was to intercept the slave traders who were still doing a profitable business in human flesh.[5]

After this African cruise, Parker returned to Annapolis and the Naval Academy, this time as an instructor. He taught from 1853 to 1857, the first two years of which he was an instructor of mathematics; the second two years were spent teaching navigation and astronomy. Parker produced numerous manuals that were used as textbooks, not only at the Confederate Naval Academy, but also at the U. S. Naval Academy for many years thereafter. Among these were: *Elements of Seamanship, Harbor Routine and Evolution, Naval Tactics, Naval Light Artillery Afloat and Ashore,* and *Remarks on the Navigation of the Coast Between San Francisco and Panama.*[6]

In 1853, after only a few months of teaching at the academy, Parker courted and married a Virginia girl from Norfolk by the name of Margaret Griffin. He wrote little concerning his married life, but it is known that he and Margaret remained married until his death in 1896, some 43 years, and that they had no children.

In 1857, he was ordered to the USS *Merrimack* that was fitting out at Boston and was bound for the Pacific. Parker served two years on the *Merrimack,* but in the summer of 1860, he was back at the naval academy as an instructor of seamanship and naval tactics.

An ominous cloud now hung over the school, and in December the news reached the midshipmen and staff that South Carolina had withdrawn from the Union. Soon Mississippi, Alabama, Florida, Georgia, Louisiana and Texas also seceded, and it was almost certain that a dreadful war would soon spill over the land. Parker wrote:

> It may well be imagined that the constant state of excitement in which we were kept was not conducive to hard study; yet so good was the discipline that everything went on as usual, and the midshipmen were kept closely to their duties. As the states seceded, the students appointed from them generally resigned with the consent of their parents; but their departures were very quietly taken, and the friendships they had contracted at the school remained unimpaired. Affairs remained in this state until the bombardment of Fort Sumter, April 11–13 (1861); but after that, as war was now certain, the scholastic duties were discontinued and the place assumed more the appearance of a garrison.[7]

Parker resigned his commission in the United States Navy shortly after the secession of Virginia on April 17, 1861. According to one source, William and his brother Foxhall were together in Washington just prior to Virginia's action, and discussed what each would do if it came to a fight. At that time, Foxhall stressed the importance of their strong ties with Virginia and their family's southern heritage, while William argued the importance of loyalty to the Union. So convincingly did each present his own case that when the time came to decide, each followed the other's advice. Whatever the truth of this tale, it is a fact that Foxhall remained in the Union navy while William resigned and subsequently accepted a commission in the Confederate navy. The two brothers faced each other indirectly only once during the war. During the siege of Charleston, South Carolina, in 1863, William was executive officer of the CSS *Palmetto State,* and Foxhall commanded the USS *Wabash.* Many years after the war, the story is told, William pointed out his brother to a friend and told him: "There goes Foxhall, the disloyal unionist, on full pay, and here stands William, the loyal secessionist, down on his uppers."[8]

Upon his resignation, Parker traveled to Richmond to offer his services to his native state. In his "Recollections," he paints an interesting picture of the state of affairs in the Virginia capital at this time:

> Upon my arrival in Richmond I reported to Governor [John] Letcher, and was immediately commissioned a lieutenant in the Virginia State Navy; and I may as well say here that as soon as the State was regularly entered into the Confederacy I was commissioned a Lieutenant in the Confederate Navy. Richmond at this time was in a state difficult to describe. The hotels were thronged, troops were coming in, messengers were riding to and fro, and everybody was in motion. I particularly noticed this fact: even at the hotels the seats were not occupied; no one could sit still. I suppose the great excitement accounted for this. The dispatches coming in hourly, the reports spread from mouth to mouth, the news contained in the daily papers even, were enough to drive a reasonable man crazy. We heard the most wonderful rumors; nothing was too absurd or ridiculous for belief, and men's time seemed to be taken up in spreading stories that would have put Gulliver to shame, and made Munchausen hide his diminished head. The emanations from the brain of a maniac were logical in comparison![9]

Parker was commissioned a first lieutenant in the fledgling Confederate States Navy on October 21, 1861, to rank from October 2. His first assignment was to organize a battery of six 12-pounder howitzers that were to be manned by a company of sailors, for duty with the army. This kept him busy for several months and required his constant presence in Richmond. There were, however, no guns or carriages available in the city; consequently, Parker forged an agreement with several local carpenters to build the carriages, and the Tredegar Iron works agreed to cast the guns.[10]

While Parker was organizing his battery, he discovered that the *Yorktown,* a 1,300-ton side-wheel passenger and freight steamer which only recently had been plying the waters between Richmond and New York, was being fitted out as a warship. The Old Dominion Line's side-wheeler had been seized by Virginia authorities upon the secession of the state, and soon she would be re-commissioned as the CSS *Patrick Henry*. Parker was much impressed by the conversion work being done on the big steamer, little realizing that in a few short years she would become the school ship for the Confederate Naval Academy, and he her commander. While the formation of the battery and the fitting out of the *Patrick Henry* were important to the defenses of Richmond, it was not long before the Parker's services were urgently needed elsewhere.

Parker's howitzer company was finally organized, but instead of operating with the army, they were ordered to form the nucleus of the crew for the newly commissioned *Patrick Henry*. Parker, instead of accompanying his men, however, was ordered to take command of the tiny CSS *Beaufort* that was operating in the waters of eastern North Carolina. Hatteras Inlet had fallen to Federal forces on August 29, 1861, and all Confederate defenses were now being concentrated on Roanoke Island. If it fell, Albemarle Sound and the greater portion of eastern North Carolina would be open to enemy incursions. In orders dated September 2, Parker was urged to hasten by rail to New Bern, North Carolina, and take charge of the *Beaufort*. By September 9, Parker had reached the North Carolina town. He later wrote:

> Upon my arrival there I found the *Beaufort* at the wharf with a few of her officers on board, but no crew. She had been commanded by Captain Duval while in the State service, and he and his officers and men had left. The *Beaufort* was a small iron propeller, built for service on the canal. She was 94 feet long and 17 feet broad; her iron was one-fourth of an inch in thickness. Her deck had been strengthened and shored up, and forward she carried a long 32 pounder which was soon afterwards exchanged for a banded and rifled 57 cwt. 32 pounder. Her magazine was just forward of the boiler, and both magazine and boiler were above the water line and exposed to shot. She carried 35 officers and men.[11]

Parker and the *Beaufort* became part of Captain William F. Lynch's "Mosquito Fleet," eight small steamers which mustered only nine guns among them. With this small flotilla the Confederate commander was expected, in conjunction with the forts on Roanoke Island, to halt the anticipated Federal advance. The Union force, termed the "Burnside Expedition," was a combined army and navy contingent which had, by February 4, 1862, crossed into Pamlico Sound through Hatteras Inlet. The Burnside Expedition consisted of 20 warships of Rear Admiral Louis M. Goldsborough's fleet mounting 62 guns, with 15 of these being the new and deadly nine-inch rifle. General Burnside, in addition to the numerous army transports carrying his soldiers, had assembled his own fleet of gunboats, with an additional 108 pieces which could be brought to bear. Early on the morning of February 5, this grand armada of 170 guns and 13,000 troops headed north up Pamlico Sound. Awaiting their arrival were fewer than 1,500 untrained and dispirited Confederate troops.[12]

On the morning of February 7, 1862, the battle for Roanoke Island began. The enemy's main assault was against Fort Bartow, situated on the western shore of the island. Lynch positioned his Mosquito Fleet, which included Parker's *Beaufort*, seven other small steamers, and one schooner, behind a row of obstructions in the main channel. From there the Confederate vessels delivered effective fire against the numerous Federal warships, but by 4:00 P.M. their guns fell silent. They were out of ammunition. Later that night, with one gunboat sunk and another in tow, Lynch pulled his battered little flotilla out and headed for Elizabeth City. Roanoke Island fell to the smothering Union attack the following day.[13]

Two days later, on February 10, Lynch's Mosquito Fleet fought its last when it was virtually destroyed in a brief but fierce battle at Elizabeth City. Parker and his crew were ordered to man the guns of a nearby fort, while the *Beaufort*, now minus her crew except the pilot, sped to safety up the Dismal Swamp Canal that led to Norfolk. After a sharp and bitter resistance, Parker and his men, along with Captain Lynch, avoided capture and made their way through the swamps and over the country roads to Norfolk. It was a stinging defeat, one that the Confederate government, and in particular the infant Southern navy, would not soon forget.[14]

Upon reaching Norfolk, Parker resumed command of the *Beaufort*, which had arrived safely and had been incorporated into the naval forces at Norfolk commanded by Captain Franklin Buchanan. The newly commissioned ironclad CSS *Virginia*, built upon the hull of the burned and scuttled USS *Merrimack*, was nearing completion, and Buchanan was eager to attack the Federal fleet then stationed in Hampton Roads.

On March 8, "Old Buck," as his sailors styled him, eased the big ironclad out into the Elizabeth River and turned her head downstream toward Hampton Roads. While most on board, including the numerous workmen who were putting the finishing touches to her, believed she was making only a trial run, Buchanan had other ideas. He was determined to steam directly for the Federal vessels blockading the mouth of the James River, attack, and destroy them. The *Raleigh* and the *Beaufort* kept station with her as she steamed past the numerous onlookers on shore. Parker later wrote of this emotional moment:

> As we steamed down the harbor we were saluted by the waving of caps and handkerchiefs; but no voice broke the silence of the scene; all hearts were too full for utterance; an attempt at cheering would have ended in tears, for all realized the fact that here was to be tried the great experiment of the ram and ironclad in naval warfare.[15]

Buchanan had notified John R. Tucker, commander of the James River Squadron, of his intentions to attack the Federals on March 8. Tucker was instructed to bring the *Jamestown*, the *Teaser*, and the *Patrick Henry* down the river and be ready to cooperate in the assault. The three vessels now lay in the James just above Newport News, and the destined Confederate school ship was about to receive her baptism of fire.

Arriving in Hampton Roads, the *Virginia* took in a tow line from the *Beaufort*, and she and her two companions headed straight for the nearest Union warships, the *Congress* and the *Cumberland*. Lessons about to be learned in the coming action would serve Parker well he became an instructor of midshipmen like Hubbard Minor. The actions of the smaller vessels in the two days of fighting at Hampton Roads have long been overshadowed in history by the accounts of the struggles between the *Virginia*, the *Cumberland*, the *Congress*, and the *Monitor*. The smaller vessels, in particular the *Beaufort*, the *Raleigh*, and the *Patrick Henry*, however, were in the thick of the fighting on that first day and contributed greatly to the havoc and devastation suffered by the Union vessels.

While the *Virginia* delivered her devastating blows against the *Cumberland*, the *Beaufort* and the *Raleigh* fiercely engaged the *Congress* which had been purposely run aground. The effect of Parker's fire, and that of the *Raleigh*, was attested to by Lieutenant Pendergrast, executive officer of the Union vessel, when he reported that while the *Virginia* dealt with the *Cumberland*, "the smaller vessels then attacked us, killing and wounding many of our crew."[16] Shortly, however, the mighty guns of the Confederate ironclad were added to those of the *Beaufort* and the *Raleigh*. The *Patrick Henry*, the *Jamestown*, and the *Teaser*, all from the James River Squadron, joined in, and soon the *Congress* was a shattered and blazing inferno. After an hour of this slaughter, the Union frigate raised a large white flag and the firing ceased. Later that evening a thunderous explosion shook the surrounding Virginia countryside as the Federal Warship was blown to pieces.

The following day, the *Virginia*, along with the smaller vessels, returned to deal with the USS *Minnesota*, which was also hard aground. The USS *Monitor*, however, had arrived during the night, and thus the stage was set for the famous first-ever battle between two ironclad warships. During the battle, the smaller vessels continued to engage the *Minnesota*, while throwing an occasional shot at the *Monitor*. By day's end, the battle between the two armored vessels had culminated in neither side gaining an advantage, but in the two days, the Union fleet had suffered an enormous and staggering defeat at the hands of the Confederate Navy.[17]

The domination of Hampton Roads by the Southern warships was not to last, however. Federal General George B. McClellan's Peninsula campaign, coupled with the loss of the North Carolina sounds to the south, forced the Confederates to abandon Norfolk. On May 10, 1862, the Gosport Navy Yard was set on fire for a second time, this time by retreating Confederate forces. Because of the *Virginia's* deep draft (22 feet), she could not be taken up the James River to safety, and she had to be destroyed. The smaller vessels, including the *Patrick Henry* and the *Beaufort*, steamed up the James and anchored near Drewry's Bluff, where fortifications were hurriedly being constructed.

Parker was not in command of the *Beaufort*, however, when Norfolk was evacuated. On April 12 he had been detached from her and assigned to a new gunboat, the CSS *Dixie*, which was nearing completion at Graves Shipyard in Norfolk. When the evacuation orders arrived, the *Dixie* was still not finished, and Parker sadly had to apply the torch. Catching one of the last trains out of Norfolk, he traveled to Richmond via Weldon, North Carolina, arriving in the Confederate capital on May 15, just as the Federal warships were being beaten back on the James River in their attempt to pass the batteries at Drewry's Bluff.[18]

Parker was given command of the gunboat CSS *Drewry*, a small 166-ton wooden steamer mounting two Brooke rifles, a 6.4 inch and a 7 inch. He commanded this vessel until the fall of 1862, at which time he was ordered to report to Flag Officer Duncan L. Ingraham, commander of the Charleston Squadron. There Parker, much to his liking, was assigned to the new CSS *Palmetto State* as executive officer, reporting to the ironclad's commander, First Lieutenant John Rutledge. While serving as the *Palmetto State's* executive officer, Parker participated in the attack upon the Federal blockading squadron which was stationed outside of Charleston harbor.

Before dawn on January 31, 1863, the *Palmetto State* in consort with her sister ironclad, the CSS *Chicora*, steamed across the bar and opened fire on the startled Union vessels. By daylight not one Federal warship was in sight, and General Beauregard, Confederate army commander at Charleston, declared the Federal blockade broken. United States authorities, however, ignored the proclamation, and the next day the blockaders cautiously returned, although at a more respectful distance.

Parker enjoyed his position on the *Palmetto State* and was impressed with the quality of the vessels and the personnel that constituted the Charleston Squadron. His expertise as an instructor and an administrator, however, was more important to the Navy Department, and in May he received his instructions from Secretary Mallory to report to Richmond and to begin the formation of the Confederate Naval Academy. His combat experience in the waters of North Carolina, at Hampton Roads, and at Charleston, would serve him well as commandant of the new naval school.[19]

Benjamin Pollard Loyall, Commandant of Midshipmen and Executive Officer

Benjamin P. Loyall was an excellent choice to be Commandant of Midshipmen. Unfortunately, he would be called away to other duties just as the school was beginning its operation, but he had much to do with its initial organization, and still more involvement with its students later on. The Virginia-born naval officer was also an alumnus of the United States Naval Academy, having graduated at the head of his class on June 12, 1855. Loyall entered the U. S. Navy on March 5, 1849, and was assigned as an acting midshipman to the frigate USS *Raritan,* which that was part of the home squadron. He later saw service on the sloop USS *St. Mary* in the Pacific, and then back in home waters he was stationed aboard the frigate USS *Columbia,* from which he was ordered to the Naval Academy at Annapolis. After his graduation, he served from 1856 through 1858 in the Mediterranean on board the USS *Congress,* the same vessel that would later be sunk by the CSS *Virginia* at the Battle of Hampton Roads. His last tour of duty in the "old navy" was aboard the sloop USS *Constellation* off the coast of Africa.[20] With the coming of war, he made his decision on October 5, 1861, to resign—a decision that was made well after his home state had passed its Ordinance of Secession. By this time the Navy Department in Washington no longer accepted resignations, and Loyall was summarily dismissed, an act intended to impart a sense of shame and disgrace on the officer's actions. After spending thirteen years in the service of the United States, Loyall held the rank of lieutenant at the time of his dismissal. On November 26, he was commissioned a first lieutenant in the Confederate States Navy, but before he could physically offer his services to the government in Richmond, he was arrested and imprisoned at Fort Warren in Boston harbor. This was the fate of many Southern officers, particularly those who resigned after the firing on Fort Sumter. Transferred to Hampton Roads, Loyall was held for a short time onboard the USS *Cumberland.* Fortunately, he was soon released and by the end of the year the new Confederate lieutenant was serving at the Gosport Navy Yard in Norfolk.[21]

On January 9, 1862, Loyall received orders to report to Major-General Benjamin Hugar, commander of the land defenses on Roanoke Island. Because he would be instructing and commanding land forces, Loyall was also given the rank of an army captain. On Roanoke Island he was placed in command of Fort Bartow, and upon the fall of that island to the Federal forces on February 8, Loyall was taken prisoner. Shortly thereafter, on February 21, he was given his parole and exchanged at Elizabeth City, North Carolina.[22]

Loyall's next assignment was to the ironclad CSS *Richmond,* which was nearing completion at the Virginia city of the same name. Construction had begun on the *Richmond* at Norfolk, whence she was launched in an unfinished state on May 8, 1862. Towed to Richmond when Norfolk was abandoned by the Confederates, she was completed at the navy yard at Rocketts and commissioned in July of 1862. The *Richmond* was the first of three ironclads constructed at the Confederate capital that would eventually serve with the James River Squadron.[23]

Loyall was stationed on the *Richmond* when, in May of 1863, he was designated to be the Commandant of Midshipmen at the Confederate Naval Academy. Because the *Patrick Henry* was not yet ready to receive the midshipmen, Loyall continued to serve on the ironclad while preparing for his important role at the naval school. By August the school was fairly underway, but in October, just as the first middies were settling into their shipboard routines, Loyall was reassigned to a very special mission. That mission was a secret expedition to capture the USS *Michigan*—the only armed Federal vessel on Lake Erie—and to release the Confederate prisoners being held on Johnson's Island.

A commando group consisting of approximately fifteen officers and sailors was formed under the command of Midshipman Minor's uncle, Lieutenant Robert D. Minor. At Wilmington, North Carolina, on the dark night of October 10, 1863, Loyall along with his fellow commandos filed aboard the blockade runner *R. E. Lee* which was commanded by Lieutenant John Wilkinson. After a harrowing run through the Federal blockaders offshore, in which the *Lee* was struck and momentarily set on fire, the group reached Halifax, Nova Scotia, on October 16. Dividing into separate parties, the men set out overland through Canada with instructions to rendezvous later in Montreal. Just when it seemed that their plan was assured of success, an informant betrayed them to U. S. Secretary of War Stanton, who immediately contacted the governor-general of Canada. Not wishing to incur the wrath of their neighbor to the south, Canadian officials broadcast a warning to all their military outposts to be on the lookout for the commandos. With the plan now revealed there was little possibility for its success, and the enterprise was called off. One by one the Confederate officers and men made their way back home, or to Europe for further assignments. Loyall returned to the Confederacy and to his former position as Commandant of Midshipmen, but he was not to remain idle for very long.[24]

In January of 1864, a naval expedition was organized to assist the army in the attempted recapture of New Bern, North Carolina. Men and officers were detailed from various stations, including the James River Squadron, and Loyall was appointed second in command of the venture under John Taylor Wood. On the night of February 2, 1864, Wood's commando group captured the USS *Underwriter* off New Bern. Unable to raise steam, and under fire from Union land batteries nearby, the *Under-*

writer had to be destroyed; however, the mission was still deemed successful.

Loyall returned to the James River Squadron after the mission, and after a tour of duty as the commander of the ironclad CSS *Neuse* in North Carolina. It was in November of 1864 that he again reported aboard the *Patrick Henry*, this time relieving Lieutenant Johnston as Commandant of Midshipmen. Loyall served in this capacity until relieved by Lieutenant James H. Rochelle in March of 1865. He was still with the school, however, when the bitter end came, and was finally paroled at Greensboro, North Carolina, on April 28, 1865.[25]

Wilburn Briggs Hall, Commandant of Midshipmen and Executive Officer

Born and reared in South Carolina, Hall graduated from the United States Naval Academy at the top of his class in 1859. He served one year on the sloop USS *Constellation* before the outbreak of war. Scharf, in his *History of the Confederate States Navy*, included a short biography of Hall:

> Lieutenant Wilburn B. Hall was appointed to the U. S. Naval Academy from Louisiana in 1855 and graduated at the head of his class. In 1861 he was attached as acting flag-lieutenant to Commander Inman, commanding the squadron on the African coast, and at the outbreak of the war returned to the United States in a captured slave ship with 700 Negroes on board. Lieutenant Hall was ordered to take them back to Africa and deliver them to the Liberian government. He then entered the Confederate service, for which he purchased and carried South from New York the steamer *Huntress*. He took this vessel into Charleston, March 18th, 1861, with the flag of Georgia flying from her masthead. During the war Lieutenant Hall served on and commanded various vessels and at various stations. He was with Commander Tattnall at the fall of Port Royal, in all the actions around Richmond, Charleston, and during its siege, as well as in those around Savannah and its adjacent waters. He aided Tattnall to provision Port Pulaski when the fort was cut off by the United States ships-of-war and batteries, running in under a terrific fire from Federal guns in broad daylight and through a line of thirteen vessels. He marched the crew of the *Harriet Lane* across the State of Texas to man the iron-clad *Louisiana* [*Missouri*] on the Red River, and subsequently commanded the *Webb*, *Savannah*, *Drewry*, *Resolute* and other vessels. He married the daughter of Commander Ingraham, the great granddaughter of Henry Laurens, president of the Revolutionary Congress, as well as of John Rutledge, Governor, with power of dictator, of South Carolina, in the Revolution, and later Justice of the U. S. Supreme Court. He was detached from the Naval Academy at his own request November 1864, and ordered to the iron-clad *Chicora*, at Charleston, South Carolina. Since the war Lieutenant Hall has served as major of engineers on the staff of the Khedive of Egypt, being selected for that position by General W. T. Sherman. He is now (1887) a leading instructor in Baltimore.[26]

Having only recently been graduated from the academy at Annapolis, Hall was still a midshipman when he resigned from the U. S. service on March 7, 1861. His first appointment, July 24, 1861, was that of a master, but he quickly proved his worth and was commissioned a lieutenant on September 19, 1861. As Scharf points out, Hall served on the Confederate steamers CSS *Resolute* and CSS *Savannah* with the Savannah Squadron during the latter part of 1861 and into 1862. Next Hall went to Charleston where he was assigned for a short time to the CSS *Huntress*. He also saw duty on the CSS *Tuscaloosa* at Mobile and at the naval station in Selma, Alabama, during 1862. From there, Hall was transferred west of the Mississippi River to Galveston, Texas, where he joined the officers on the CSS *Harriet Lane*. At this time the Red River Squadron at Shreveport, Louisiana was desperately short of officers and men, and on April 21, 1863, Hall led a contingent of forty men to Shreveport to reinforce the depleted squadron. By October he was on the *Patrick Henry*, where he relieved Lieutenant Loyall as Commandant of Midshipmen. Hall served at the academy for more than twelve months, being in charge of the students as bitter fighting swirled around Richmond and Petersburg during the summer and fall of that year. Later, in November of 1864, he requested a transfer to the CSS *Chicora* of the Charleston Squadron. Within a few months Hall returned, and ended the war serving with the James River Squadron in defense of the Confederate capital.[27]

James Henry Rochelle, Commandant of Midshipmen and Executive officer

     Rochelle came to the academy late in its existence, arriving in Richmond as part of the naval contingent that had evacuated Wilmington, North Carolina. He had seen more than his share of the war when he reported to Parker in March of 1865. Reporting aboard the *Patrick Henry*, he replaced Lieutenant Loyall as Commandant of Midshipmen and Executive Officer. Scharf wrote a succinct biography of Rochelle—one that needs no elaboration:

     James Henry Rochelle was appointed an acting midshipman in the U.S. Navy September 9th, 1841, and after six months' service at sea received a warrant as midshipman, bearing the same date as his acting appointment. During the war with Mexico he served on the sloops-of-war *Falmouth* and *Decatur* in the Gulf, and took part in the capture of Tuxpan and Tabasco. He reported to the Naval Academy November 13th, 1847, and graduated on July 10th, 1848, his warrant as passed midshipman assigning him that rank from August 10th, 1847. After duty in the Mediterranean squadron on the frigate *Constitution*, steamer *Allegheny*, steamer *Princeton* and frigate *Independence*, he was ordered to the storeship *Southampton*, which formed part of Commodore Perry's expedition to Japan in 1853. On his return to the United States, he was assigned to the coast survey, and on the steamer *Corwin* and schooner *Madison*, the latter of which was for some time in his charge, assisted in the survey of the New York Harbor, Casco Bay, and Florida Reef. On September 14th, 1855, he was promoted to master, and on the next day was commissioned lieutenant. He was assigned to the steamer *Southern Star* in the Paraguay expedition, commanded by Flag-officer W. B. Shubrick, and was on the steam-frigate *Fulton* when she was wrecked on the coast of Florida. His final service in the U. S. navy was on the sloop-of-war *Cumberland* in the home squadron, and he resigned his commission April 17th, 1861, while his ship was at the Norfolk navy-yard. While awaiting the action of the department upon his resignation he was placed in a very painful position by the false alarm of an attack on the navy-yard by the Virginia forces. "I had resolved," Capt. Rochelle writes, "that I was bound to obey the command of the Virginia Convention and leave the navy of the United States, and here was the probability of my having to do the very thing I had resigned my commission to escape from doing. I cannot say, however, that the situation caused any hesitation on my part. As long as I was on duty as a lieutenant in the U. S. navy I was fully determined to do that duty, and in case of necessity would have stood to my guns." To be relieved from this embarrassing position, he obtained permission from Flag officer Pendergast to leave the *Cumberland*, and on May 2nd., was appointed lieutenant in the Virginia navy, and on the 29th was ordered to command the gunboat *Teaser*. His commission as lieutenant in the C. S. navy was issued June 6th, and until June 27th he commanded the gunboat *Jackson* at Memphis, when he was ordered to the *Patrick Henry*, then fitting out at Richmond, as executive officer. He participated in the subsequent operations of the James River Squadron, including the battle of Hampton Roads and the repulse of the Federal vessels at Drewry's Bluff, shortly after which he was transferred to the command of the gunboat *Nansemond*, and thence to the steamer *Stono*, which was preparing to run the blockade at Charleston. The *Stono* was discovered by the Federals in the bay and in attempting to regain the city was wrecked on the rocks near Fort Moultrie, June 5th, 1863. Resuming command of the *Nansemond*, Capt. Rochelle continued on the James River until September 6th, when he was sent to Charleston to organize the flotilla of guard-boats. On April 2d, 1864, he was ordered to the command of the iron-clad *Palmetto State*, remaining on that duty until the evacuation of Charleston, when he was dispatched to Wilmington to command of a detachment of about 300 officers and men of the Charleston squadron, and cooperated with the army in the defense of that city. From Wilmington he was ordered to report at Richmond as commandant of the midshipmen of the C. S. naval school, and after the evacuation, guarded the specie and bullion of the treasury to its transfer to the army at Abbeville, S.C.[28]

Oscar F. Johnston, Professor of Astronomy, Navigation, and Surveying

Johnston also was a graduate of the United States Naval Academy, passing his examinations in 1852. He was born in Virginia, but at the secession of the Southern states, was a resident of Tennessee. Resigning his lieutenant's commission upon the withdrawal of Tennessee from the Union, Johnston was commissioned a lieutenant in Confederate service on May 16, 1861. His first assignment was to the Savannah station, where he served on the CSS *Resolute* during the remainder of 1861 and into the following year.[29]

The *Resolute* was a small side-wheel steam tug that had been constructed at Savannah in 1858. During most of her service she operated as a tow boat, transport, receiving ship, and tender to the armed side-wheeler gunboat CSS *Savannah*. On November 7, 1861, a large Union force attacked and captured Port Royal Sound, and the small Confederate flotilla, which included Johnston and the *Resolute,* could offer only token resistance.

Lieutenant Johnston later served on the ironclad floating battery CSS *Georgia,* but was soon transferred to the newly built ironclad-ram, CSS *Savannah,* which was captained by Commander Robert F. Pinkney. The *Savannah* was arguably one of the most serviceable ironclads constructed within the borders of the Confederacy, and Johnston filled the position of third lieutenant on her. The *Savannah* continued to bar the way against Federal naval forces seeking to capture the Georgia city until December of 1864, when she was purposely destroyed by the evacuating Confederates upon the approach of General Sherman's forces from the land side.

Johnston was not on board the *Savannah* when the end came, for in the summer of 1863, Secretary Mallory had selected him for the important position of instructor of Astronomy, Navigation, and Surveying at the Confederate Naval School. Johnston continued his teaching duties until the early summer of 1864, when he relieved Lieutenant Hall as Commandant of Midshipmen so that the latter might devote more time to the instruction of the students. In August of 1864, Johnston was ordered to the CSS *Virginia II* of the James River Squadron as her executive officer. With the vessel's captain absent, Johnston was in command when on August 17, at the request of General Robert E. Lee, the *Virginia* and the *Richmond* steamed down the river and engaged the enemy batteries at Signal Hill several miles below Drewry's Bluff. After an afternoon and an all-night heavy bombardment, the Federal forces abandoned the works and the Confederate lines below Richmond were secured.[30]

After this action, Johnston was transferred to South Carolina and given command of the wooden gunboat, CSS *Peedee*. It was here on the Great Peedee River, near Marion Court House, that his wartime service ceased. Upon the evacuation of Charleston on February 18, 1865, the *Peedee's* commander set her on fire and began the long, painful retreat toward North Carolina.[31]

With no ships to man, and no fleets to join, the officers and men of the Charleston, Savannah, and Wilmington squadrons congregated in Richmond to await the end. When the Confederate capital was abandoned, Lieutenant Johnston found himself at Danville, Virginia, in command of an infantry "regiment" of sailors who were now serving as part of the Semmes Naval Brigade. When word reached Danville of Lee's surrender, Raphael Semmes was ordered to take his naval brigade to North Carolina and join Joseph E. Johnston's Army of Tennessee. Upon their

arrival, General Johnston, too, had surrendered. Oscar Johnston continued south, but records indicate that he was captured by Union forces near
Athens, Georgia, at which place he was later paroled.[32]

Thomas W. W. Davies, Assistant Professor of Astronomy, Navigation
and Surveying
 Prior to the war, Thomas Davies had attended the U. S. Naval Academy at Annapolis, where he was a member of the class of 1858; however,
there is no record of his having graduated from that school.[33] Listed as a
teacher who hailed from Wetumpka, Alabama, he enlisted in Company B,
8th Alabama Infantry Regiment, on May 13, 1861, at the beginning of the
war. Rising to the rank of captain, Davies resigned from the army on
March 18, 1862, in order to enter the Confederate Navy, where he was
appointed a lieutenant with his commission dated the same day as his resignation from the army.[34] Upon his acceptance into naval service, he was
assigned to the Charleston station and served there continuously until
being designated as an instructor at the Confederate Naval Academy in
the summer of 1863. Returning to Richmond, he assumed the responsi-
bilities of an assistant professor of astronomy, navigation, and surveying.
In May of 1864, he was temporarily ordered to the CSS *Virginia II* of the
James River Squadron. While serving on that ironclad, Davies was made
accountable to the commanding officer of the James River Squadron,
Captain John K. Mitchell, for all torpedoes received and expended on the
river.[35] By the end of the summer Davies was relieved of his teaching
duties at the academy and was transferred to the naval squadron at Mobile,
Alabama. The end of the war found him at the naval station in Selma,
Alabama.[36]

Charles Iverson Graves, Instructor in Seamanship
 Confusion abounds concerning Lieutenant Graves. According to the
Register of Officers of the Confederate States Navy, 1861–1865, compiled by
the United States Navy Department in 1898, Graves' first and middle
names were "Charles Iverson." Several references in the navy *Official
Records* refer to him as "C. J." Graves. In addition, the *Register* states that
during 1863 and 1864, Graves saw service abroad, yet both Scharf and
Parker list Lieutenant Graves as a member of the academy staff at the
beginning of the school in August of 1863. There is no record of a Lieutenant Graves having served in Europe. After exhaustive research, it is
this author's opinion that there was only one Lieutenant Charles Graves,
and that his middle name was Iverson.
 With that said: Charles I. Graves was born on July 28, 1838, in Newton County, Georgia.[37] Graduating fourth in his class at Annapolis in
1857, Graves attained the rank of lieutenant in the United States Navy.

He is not listed, however, as being among the 373 naval officers who submitted their resignations to the Navy Department in Washington at the outbreak of the war. It is likely that, for whatever reason, Graves had already resigned his commission in the navy prior to the crises which caused Georgia, following South Carolina's lead, to secede from the Union. It was not until December 27, 1861, therefore, that Graves was given a commission as a first lieutenant in the Confederate Navy.

His first assignment was to the naval batteries that had been erected along the Aquia Creek just north of Fredericksburg, Virginia. With the advance of the Federal Army on Manassas, these fortifications were soon abandoned. On January 23, 1862, Secretary Mallory penned a letter to Judah P. Benjamin, Confederate Secretary of War, requesting that Graves and several other naval officers be released from their duties at the batteries. As a result of this request, Graves, on February 3, received orders to report to the Navy Department in Richmond.[38]

From there he was dispatched to Mobile, Alabama, where Graves joined the complement of officers on the newly converted gunboat CSS *Morgan*. The *Morgan* was a side-wheel steamer armed with six guns, and was one of the mainstays of the Mobile Squadron until the completion of the ironclad CSS *Tennessee*. Graves served on the *Morgan* until the late summer of 1863, after which he was ordered to return to Richmond to become the instructor of seamanship at the Naval Academy.[39]

Graves continued his teaching duties from the opening of the school in the fall of 1863 through the summer and fall of 1864. The winter of 1864–65 was unusually cold, with periods of heavy snow and rain falling throughout the Richmond and Petersburg area. In early January, severe rainstorms, coupled with melting snow, created freshets and high water in the James. Secretary Mallory repeatedly urged Mitchell to take his ironclads through the breech in the Federal obstructions at Trent's Reach, which had been washed away by the raging waters, and to attack the enemy forces in the lower part of the river.[40]

On January 21, in preparation to make the attack, Lieutenant Graves was detached from the navy school and assigned to the CSS *Virginia II* on temporary duty as flag lieutenant of the squadron on Mitchell's staff. On January 23, the big ironclads made the attempt, but two of them ran aground, while only one—the *Fredericksburg*—succeeded in passing the obstructions. The following day, the two grounded ironclads, the *Virginia II* and the *Richmond,* endured a terrific pounding at the hands of the Federal guns before they were able to free themselves with the rising water. By the twenty-fifth, they were back at their anchorage, and Graves, who was commended by Mitchell for his service, was ordered to resume his duties on the school ship.[41]

When Richmond was finally evacuated in April of 1865, Lieutenant

Graves, along with Parker and the midshipmen, acted as an escort to Mrs. Jefferson Davis and a guard for the Confederate treasure as they retreated southward.[42]

William Van Comstock, Instructor in Gunnery

Comstock was from Louisiana and had resigned as an acting midshipman from the United States Navy on January 30, 1861. It was not until after the firing on Fort Sumter, however, that he was appointed an acting midshipman in the Confederate Navy on April 25. At the time of his assignment to the Naval Academy, he had risen to the rank of second lieutenant and would attain the grade of first lieutenant in 1864. (The rank of "lieutenant" was changed to "first" and "second" lieutenant by act of the Confederate Congress in 1862. A first lieutenant was equivalent to a major in the army, and a second lieutenant to that of a captain.)[43] Comstock's initial assignment was as commander of the receiving ship CSRS *St. Philip* at New Orleans. The *St. Philip* had been employed as the noted passenger steamer *Star of the West* that operated between New York and the California coast prior to the war. In January 1861, she was chartered by the Federal government to carry reinforcements to Fort Sumter in Charleston harbor. When within sight of the fort, she was greeted by fire from harbor defense guns manned by cadets from the Citadel Military Academy and was compelled to return to New York without accomplishing her mission. Three months later, the Federal Government again chartered her to carry troops from the coast of Texas to New York, but on 17 April she was captured by the Confederates and sent to New Orleans. There the Confederate Navy employed her as a receiving ship and renamed her *St. Philip.*[44]

Later Comstock was transferred to the CSS *Slidell,* a wooden gunboat which had been constructed at New Orleans in 1862, where he served for a short time. Transferred briefly to the Jackson station, he was next assigned to the Savannah Squadron, where he received his orders to report to the Naval Academy on the James. There he filled the position of gunnery instructor, but in the late fall of 1864, Comstock left the Academy and was again stationed at Savannah. He was serving there when the war ended.[45]

G. W. Billups, Assistant Instructor in Seamanship

Other than the information which was recorded in the *Register of Officers of the Confederate States Navy, 1861–1865,* little else is known concerning the remaining staff at the Confederate Academy. Second Lieutenant G. W. Billups was commissioned on June 2, 1864, and began teaching at the academy, according to Parker, when the school moved to Drewry's Bluff in October of 1863.

Upon the evacuation of Richmond in April of 1865, Billups had the unenviable task of destroying the school ship. He then made his way to the Semmes Naval Brigade, and made the long trek to North Carolina where he was paroled along with the rest of the brigade near Greensboro on April 28.[46]

George M. Peek, Professor of Mathematics

The remaining instructors were transferees from the army and were given the rank of acting master in the Confederate Navy. Peek was appointed from Virginia and eventually was nominated to the rank of lieutenant but it is unclear whether he was ever commissioned. He stayed with the school until the end, being paroled on May 15, 1865, at Charlotte, North Carolina.[47]

George W. Armistead, Professor of Physics

Like Peek, Armistead also hailed from Virginia and was appointed an acting master on November 14, 1863. He too made the long retreat to North Carolina where he was paroled on May 15, 1865.[48]

Lewis N. Huck, Professor of English Literature

Another Virginian, Huck was appointed to acting master on the same day as Armistead. He was finally paroled on May 15, at Charlotte, North Carolina.[49]

George A. Peple, Professor of French and Spanish

Peple was of French birth, but resided in Virginia when he was ordered to the academy. His appointment as acting master was made on July 20, 1863, but the records are silent as to his disposition at the end of the war.[50]

Richard S. Sanxey, Professor of Infantry Tactics and Sword Exercise

Professor Sanxey is not included in the *Register of Officers of the Confederate States Navy, 1861–1865* published by the U. S. Navy Department. However, both Parker and Scharf list him as the instructor of Infantry Tactics and Sword Exercises.[51]

William B. Cox, Professor of Drawing and Painting

Cox's home state is unknown, and his date of appointment to acting master is also unknown. He, as well as all of the other acting masters on the instructional staff, was promoted to the rank of "master not in line of promotion" on June 2, 1864, when the "provisional" navy ranks were created. The provisional navy allowed younger officers to be advanced without damaging the ego of the more senior officers in the regular navy. Cox was paroled, along with most of the other instructors, at Charlotte on May 15, 1865.[52]

Other officers were assigned to the school in supporting roles. they included: assistant surgeons W. J. Addison and James G. Bigley; assistant paymaster William M. Ladd; second assistant engineer Elias G. Hall; boatswain Andrew Blackie; gunners E. R. Johnson and William F. Brittingham; and sailmaker William Bennett. In addition, the *Patrick Henry* was kept manned by an enlisted crew because she was still part of the defensive force employed by the James River Squadron.

4

The Diary

Although the Confederate Naval Academy's "official" opening has most often been recounted as occurring in October with the move to Drewry's Bluff, in reality midshipmen were onboard and working diligently on their studies as early as July of 1863. At this time the school ship was still moored at Rocketts Landing on the Richmond waterfront while the finishing touches were being applied to her living quarters and recitation rooms.

These government facilities on the James River had, by the summer of 1863, turned the Confederate capital of Richmond into a bustling and strategic naval center. The navy yard referred to as Rocketts was situated around a landing on the city side of the river and housed several wharves, dock equipment, storage sheds, and numerous warehouses. Here, while the finishing touches were being applied to the *Patrick Henry*, the ironclad CSS *Fredericksburg* had been completed and was now awaiting only her armament prior to being commissioned. In addition, sprawled across the river was the navy facility known locally as the "yard opposite Rockett's." Another ironclad, the CSS *Virginia II*, was nearing completion there, and a fourth, the CSS *Texas* (the *Richmond* was already in service), was in the beginning stages. It was here among this thriving center of naval activity that Acting Midshipman Hubbard T. Minor found the school ship *Patrick Henry*.[1]

Report to the Academy

Richmond, Virginia
Friday, August 7, 1863

Reported for duty & got permission to remain on shore until Wednesday when I will go to hard study. Today has been quite a warm one & I have suffered a good deal from the heat & oppressiveness of the atmosphere today. I was fortunate enough to meet with Hack Wilkensen from Mo. & spent quite a pleasant time with him. Now good-night.

Saturday, August 8

All of this day I have spent in looking for the articles I was to send Henry [Henry Minor, Hubbard's brother] with some I was successful with others not. I am now very much fatigued after my walk & will lay down & take a nap. So goodbye.

Sunday, August 9

Went to Hollywood [Cemetery] before church & then went to [Saint James] Church & sat in the old place & heard one of the best sermons I ever listened to. Shook hands with Mrs. [Joshua] Peterkin & saw & spoke to Judge Meridith & his wife. Late this evening called to see Mrs. Marshall & spent quite a pleasant time with her & Miss Ellen who is beautiful but I do not intend to fall in love with her. Now Good Night.

Tuesday, August 11

Not quite as warm a day as yesterday tho' quite disagreeable. Have spent it quite lazily most all of the evening asleep. Saw about the making of my uniform and furnished buttons for same. The whole suit will cost $100.00. It will be made at Mr. Spece's. Late in the evening called on Judge Meridith & family. Miss Ella was out & I did not enjoy her music as I had anticipated. Spent altogether quite a pleasant evening.

Wednesday, August 12

Succeeded in getting Hen's [Henry's] Articles off By the express Co. & whilst there was seized with a fainting fit & did actually faint & became utterly senseless. Wrote to Aunt Betts in Lexington, Va. Finished my letter to my brother & will mail it at the first opportunity. Reported for duty & left shore as I had no right to remain longer in enjoyment of idleness. Also wrote a letter to my friend S. A. Cowley. When I got on board of the [schoolship] *Patrick Henry* it was quite late & I now am a little disappointed, but I hope [everything] will be all right soon. I sleep tonight in a hammock.

Thursday, August 13

My sleep was a little interrupted last night for the boys tied ropes to my hammock & swung me all night nearly. In the evening of this day I went up to my assigned watch for four hours with sad thoughts.

Friday, August 14

Last night my thoughts were quite sad & if I had been allowed I should [have] written some thing to while away the weary four hours [in] which I had to watch a bad man in prison who no doubt will be shot or hung ... [His crime] is that of attempting to strike an Officer. This day I have been busy studying & will if possible catch up to the first class [a number of cadets had begun their studies in 1862 prior to the establishment of the Academy]. I was on duty again today & will be on every other four hours until 8 o'clock Sunday morning.

St. James Episcopal Church, which Minor attended on August 9, 1863 (Library of Congress).

Saturday, August 15

Was relieved from watch for four hours from 12 to 4 [P.M.] & spent them in town & got my uniform which was quite well made & impresses me much. I got on this day $50.00 from Uncle Will Hart & am in his debt now for the amount of $100.00. Just after 3 o'clock took a nice bath & had a good row in our fastest boat.

Sunday, August 16

Went on watch at 4 o'clock & came off at 8 for about a week. Went to church at about 20 minutes past ten but failed to hear Mr. [Joshua] Peterkin. Saw his son Guy at church also Mr. Claiburne who invited me to come & see him & told me he would think [it] strange of me if I did not do so. Returned from church & took Dinner with Uncle Will. Exchanged some little tales in the Southern literary class & at 5 o'clock [ran] into a fellow Middy & had a pleasant walk. Went [past] the President's house & saw my old school & house [&] returned by the Baptist college. Also, I called to see Cousin Rob Minor [Lieutenant Robert D. Minor, CSN] but he was absent. Saw at his [house] the poet [James Barron] Hope who is staying with him. Had a warm walk down to the vessel & soon went to supper & then smoked my Powhattan pipe that Uncle Will gave me.

> Robert D. Minor, Hubbard's cousin, was born in Virginia, and was formerly a lieutenant in the United States Navy. He resigned his commission, however, upon the secession of Virginia, and served briefly in the Virginia Navy during April of 1861. He was commissioned a first lieutenant in the Confederate States Navy on June 10, 1861, and promoted to first lieutenant on October 23, 1862, to rank from October 2, 1862. During 1861–1862, Minor served as director of the Bureau of Ordnance and Hydrography, and participated in the capture of the United States steamer *St. Nicholas* on June 29, 1861. He also served on the ironclad CSS *Virginia* where he acted as flag lieutenant to Admiral Buchanan. He was severely wounded during the battle of Hampton Roads, Virginia, on March 8, 1862, and after his recovery, served on ordnance duty at Richmond during 1862 and 1863. Here he was in charge of the Naval Ordnance Works at Richmond through most of 1864. Robert D. Minor was paroled at the end of the war on May 3, 1865, at Richmond, Va.[2]
>
> James Barron Hope was a prestigious Virginia poet who in 1857 published, in Philadelphia, his first volume, *Leoni di Monota, and Other Poems*. In this appeared his spirited "Charge at Balaklava," which was widely admired. The same year, acting as the poet at the two hundred and fiftieth anniversary of the settlement at Jamestown, he began to deliver those memorial poems which gained him the sobriquet of "Virginia's laureate." Hope was the nephew of Captain Samuel Barren, CSN, and served as a captain in the Confederate army during the war.[3]

Monday, August 17

Studied hard all day long and will in a day or two catch up with the class for which I am now studying. This morning went in & had a nice swim & also got a single drawer cut large enough to [fit] the few clothes I have & put most of them in it together with [my] smoking tobacco which I find it quite difficult to keep under lock & key. We have it a great deal worse on board that I expected & sometimes I wish I were still in the army, but then when I think that here I am getting a good education & at the same time serving my country I am content.

Lieutenant Robert D. Minor, cousin of Hubbard Minor (Naval Historical Center).

Minor's class was seven months ahead of him, and during the next week he worked hard in order to catch up with them. Studying did not seem to interest him, however, for according to his diary, he applied the next week for a leave of absence in order to visit his relatives and friends. He finally returned to the *Patrick Henry* on August 30, 1863.

Sunday, August 30

Went to St. Paul's [Episcopal] Church with Miss Savage & had quite a good sermon from Mr. Menegerrode [Reverend Charles Minnigerode] & late in the evening called to see Cousin Bob Minor & his wife & he promised to get me orders for sea if I could skimp one year. After tea returned to the vessel & reported for duty.

> Founded in 1845 by members of Monumental Church, St. Paul's was at the center of Confederate Richmond, counting numerous soldiers and leaders among those in attendance, including General Robert E. Lee and President Jefferson Davis. The Rev. Dr. Charles Minnigerode stood out among nineteenth-century rectors because of his leadership of the church during the war.

Monday, August 31

Have been studying all day & have written as I said some distance behind from the 18th up to the present time. Went down just a moment ago to see how much pay was due me & found that I was in debt but not as much as I expected. I succeeded today in catching up with the class in everything except algebra. Now good night.

Wednesday, September 2, 1863

Succeeded in having my teeth fixed & returned to the ship & went steadily to work. I have still one tooth to plug for which will cost me 12 dollars & this will make 37 dollars in all for fixing my teeth. Tomorrow I will go up by ten o'clock & have the above job done.

Friday, September 4

Went uptown in the morning & in the evening took a delightful sail in one of our large boats. Jams. Minnegerode

James Barron Hope (National Archives).

Top: Wartime photograph of St. Paul's Episcopal Church, Richmond, Virginia (Library of Congress). *Below left:* The Rev. Dr. Charles Minnigerode (St. Paul's Episcopal Church, Richmond, Va). *Below right:* Midshipman James G. Minnigerode (Author's Collection).

[Midshipman James G. Minnigerode who most probably was the son of the Episcopal bishop] & another young man was with me.

Saturday, September 5

Went uptown & saw as much as possible of Aunt Vinnie & all before the leave which will be over Monday. In the evening called to see Miss Mary Savage & spent quite a nice time with her, then carne back to my boat & rolled into my hammock.

Sunday, September 6

Again went up town & went to Centenary Church to hear Mr. Duncan one of the finest preachers in the city, then met with Theodore Martin who was wounded at Gettysburg, also with William Maben & with Miss Savage with whom I walked home. Took dinner with Edgar Hill & in the evening came back to my boat.

Monday, September 7

Studied hard & did very well & in the evening read some few pages in Bulwer's "What will he do with it" & became intensely interested though I had read some portion of it before.

Tuesday, September 8

After study hours took another good sail in the glorious James & enjoyed myself very much for I had a good wind for the most of the time & besides was with two agreeable companions.

Wednesday, September 9

Studied hard all day & feel quite tired on this day. I also heard from Stephen A Cowley who writes in a very despondent mood of the Army of which I was a member. With his letter was enclosed one to me from my brother which was written before he saw me at Chattanooga. Mr. Cowley informed me that my transfer had arrived all safe & approved & now I perhaps might have occupied a good position & among troops less noble than none in the field. He speaks of the enemy's having reached the door of the Confederacy, Chattanooga, & says that he thinks that they are unable to force an entrance.

Friday, September 11

Don't recollect what I did on this day so you must excuse me if I do not interest you. I recollect that being on watch at midnight & thinking of my first boyish love & its object my love returned with full force, & I resolved to write Rosalie & ascertain my fate, but recollecting that Bulwer who I have been reading all along says that when we see the object of our affection after an absence of many years that we love no longer & wonder that we could ever have loved such a personage, but in Darrel that was false for he looked at the object of his earliest love & felt that he could love no other but his whom he first loved for he never loved his wife. At any rate I resolved to await until I had again seen Rosalie before I in any way committed myself, but how long that resolve will last I do not know.

Saturday, September 12

All of this day I spent on board ship & wrote a long letter to Edward Rives & in the evening was put in charge of a boat to convey the secretary of the navy, Mr. Mallory [Stephen R. Mallory] & his wife, across the river to the gunboat. After that I copied in my little book of original poetry a piece I had written in Cousin Lou Scott's album.

Another image of Secretary of the Navy Stephen R. Mallory (Scharf: *History of the Confederate States Navy*).

Stephen R. Mallory was born at Port of Spain in 1811 or 1812 (records are unclear). In 1820 his family moved to Key West, Florida. There he grew to manhood, and in 1850, he was elected to Congress as a United States Senator. During much of the next ten years, as the nation slipped down the slope toward civil war, Mallory served as Chairman of the Naval Affairs Committee. After Florida's secession from the Union, young Mallory resigned his senate seat, and on February 25, 1861, President Jefferson Davis appointed him Secretary of the Confederate States Navy.

Tuesday, September 15

After study hours took another sail with same boat & same companions as the last time. The wind was fairer this time than either of the others & our only fault was in getting too far down the river & the wind dying away with the sun we were forced to pull back to our quarters.

Wednesday, September 16

On this day studied hard & have been at the head of my class for some days.

Thursday, September 17

I will skip from this day to the 28th of this month which is today Monday. On Thursday, 24th I learned that Cousin Robert Minor was going to sea & went up in the evening of the following day to see him, but he was absent from town so I wrote to him & have not yet received an answer to my letter. I asked him to take me to sea with him & I am in hopes that he will be able to do so. Today is a beautiful one & I have just come out of a lecture room.

*****

On Board Steamer *Patrick Henry*
Richmond, Va., *Sept. 24th, 1863*

Lieutenant Robt. Minor, C. S. N.
Dear Cousin:

Having learned that you were going to sea, I am anxious to go with you, & went, last night, to Capt. Parker, & asked permission to go up town & see you. He told me that you were not in town, that he had written to you; & that his letter, would be delivered, to you as soon as you returned; when he thought you would come on board, but that I might go up in the morning, & inquire when you would return. I went up town this evening, & found that John, & yourself also, were out of town, & not likely to return until the day of starting from this point. I therefore obtained your address, & have taken this mode of communicating writing. You told me some time ago that you could arrange to get me orders to sea & if you could manage to take me with you, I shall be much obliged to you. I had rather establish a reputation under you, than anybody I know of; for should I do so, it would surly be deserved; & then, too if I do not first enjoy the good opinion of one who takes more than a common interest in me, how can I hope to enjoy that of others who do not. Besides, I prefer you, as do many others, with whom to serve. Should Mr. Mallory object to my going to sea, because I am in the fourth class, I am willing, at any time, to stand an examination for the third, without the fear of the results. I asked Capt. Parker if it would not be of advantage to me, to go to sea now, if possible, & he said that it would be, & I think he will approve any application for orders you think it necessary to make. Mr. Brittingham, the gunner, made application to be sent with your party, and his application was approved by Capt. Parker. Mr. B. thinks that he will be able to go if you ask for him. Remember me to Mrs. Minor whom I suppose you are with. I hoped to have the pleasure of hearing her sing before she left Richmond, but could not get off ship for a single day she was here. I am very tired of staying here, & would like very much to go with you, & promise to do my duty as well as I am able, & to study hard all the while. Now good-by.

Very respectfully,
Your Obt. Servant,
Midn. H. T. Minor, Jr., Steamer *Patrick H.*
Richmond, Va.

*****

Tuesday, September 29

All of this day have been spent in hard study & onerous duty. Nothing of any importance has occurred, so I will close until tomorrow. At night had a fight with midshipman [unintelligible, probably Lewis Levy] & got the best of it. Was suspended & so was he.

Wednesday, September 30

This is the day in which Cousin Robert Minor was to return & having been released from suspension I obtained permission to go uptown & see him. He had not received my letter for which circumstances I was sorry, for he was very busy & would have paid more attention to it than to myself, & besides I wished him to see it. He said that there would be no chance for me [to go to sea] until I had graduated, so I have made up my mind to get through as soon as possible, then come what will I am prepared for it.

Thursday, October 1, 1863

Spent like the most of my days here in hard study & duty on this day. While reading over the [Richmond] Inquirer, I saw the death of Cousin Joe Pannell announced & quite a beautiful tribute attached to it. I have the tribute with the announcement of his death now & will preserve it. It is signed "W." I intended to have gone over to Petersburg tomorrow & had asked for permission to do so which was refused, & when I saw the notice of Cousin Joe's death, which took place on Monday, I was reconciled to the refusal.

Friday, October 2

Went on watch at midnight & stood until four in the morning. On this day we had quite a hard lesson in algebra, in which I stood quite a good examination.

> The cadets at the Academy were required to be enrolled in one of four classes. Minor studied, besides algebra practical seamanship, gunnery, artillery, infantry tactics, geometry, plane and spherical trigonometry, physical geography, history, and French.

Saturday, October 3

Will go on watch again today from 12 to 4 & then shall go up town. Was paid off also on this day & the amount I received is not sufficient to pay my mess bill. I hope this evening to get some letters from uncle Will & to have a good game of billiards.

Sunday, October 4

Went up to church & heard quite a good sermon from Mr. Peterkin then went round to church to see whom I knew, & as I expected, met Miss Mary Savage & walked home with her, then called on Miss Anna Dean & Frank who arrived here from the army 2 days ago. After that, took dinner at the American Hotel & then returned to the ship. As I was coming down Main Street I overtook the funeral procession of a soldier & the band was playing one of the sweetest tunes I ever heard. 'Twas soft, sad, &

sweet. It forcibly reminded me of the first funeral tune I heard since I left home to join the army & which I mentioned sometime ago at the time I heard it.

Monday, October 5

Came off duty this morning & have been demerited for smoking during study hours. Saw this evening Miss Mary Savage, her sister & several other ladies & expect to see them again tonight. They have gone down to Drury's [Drewry's] Bluff & will return by dusk.

> Drewry's Bluff was the principal fortification on the James River seven miles south of Richmond. It was here on May 15, 1862, that Union warships were repulsed, and it would later become the anchorage of the *Patrick Henry* and the living quarters for the midshipmen attending the Academy.

Tuesday, October 6

All of this day has been spent in hard study & nothing of importance has occurred. The days all slip swiftly by here in the same monotonous way.

Friday, October 9

Was informed that we would go to this Bluff [Drewry's] tomorrow evening & that in the meantime, all who were not on duty were at liberty to go to town, so I went up & told all of my friends good-by & also wrote a letter to Cousin Ellen Jackson by flag of truce she was to forward it to Pa. Left the letter with Uncle Will & returned to the ship.

An artist's sketch of Drewry's Bluff as seen by one coming up the James River (*Battles & Leaders of the Civil War*).

Top: A 10-inch Columbiad currently mounted at Drewry's Bluff (photograph by R. Thomas Campbell). *Bottom:* The CSS *Patrick Henry* (*Official Records of the Union and Confederate Navies in the War of the Rebellion*).

Saturday, October 10
   Again went uptown & returned by twelve o'clock. left at 2 o'clock &
with our huge craft started for the Bluff where we arrived safely.

Drewry's Bluff

   Drewry's Bluff, named for local landowner Captain Augustus H. Drewry,
rose 90 feet above the water and commanded a sharp bend in the James
River, making it a logical site for defensive fortifications. On March 17, 1862,
the men of Captain Drewry's Southside Artillery arrived at the bluff and
began fortifying the area. They constructed earthworks, erected barracks, dug
artillery emplacements, and mounted three large seacoast guns (one 10-inch
Columbiad and two 8-inch Columbiads) in the fort.
   On May 9, 1862, Norfolk fell to Union forces. The crew of the CSS *Virginia*, forced to scuttle their vessel to prevent her capture, joined the Southside Artillery at Drewry's Bluff. Commander Ebeneezer Farrand supervised
the defenses of the fort. He ordered numerous steamers, schooners, and
sloops to be sunk as obstructions in the river beneath the bluff. Six more large
guns occupied pits just upriver from the fort. Men worked around the clock
to ensure a full state of readiness when the Union fleet arrived.
   The Federal squadron steamed around the bend in the river below
Drewry's Bluff early on the morning of May 15. The force, under Commander John Rodgers, consisted of five ships. The ironclad *Galena* and gunboats
Port Royal, *Aroostook*, and *Naugatuck* joined the famous *Monitor* to comprise
Rodgers' force. At 7:15 A.M. the *Galena* opened fire on the fort, sending three
giant projectiles toward the Confederate position.
   The five Union ships anchored in the river below the fort. When Confederate batteries in the fort replied, the whole vicinity shook with the concus-
sion of the big guns. Confederate Marines and infantry lined the banks of
the river to harass the sailors. On the *Monitor*, the rifle balls of the sharpshooters "pattered upon the decks like rain."
   On the bluff the defenders encountered several problems. The 10-inch
Columbiad recoiled so violently on its first shot that it broke its carriage and
remained out of the fight until near the end. A casemate protecting one of
the guns outside the fort collapsed, rendering that piece useless.
   After four long hours of exchanging fire, the "perfect tornado of shot and
shell" ended. With his ammunition nearly depleted, Commander Rodgers
gave the signal to discontinue the action at 11:30. His sailors suffered at least
14 dead and 13 wounded, while the Confederates admitted to 7 killed and 8
wounded. A visitor wrote that the *Galena* "looked like a slaughterhouse" after
the battle. The massive fort on Drewry's Bluff had blunted the Union advance
just seven miles short of the Confederate capital. Richmond remained safe.
   Following the repulse of the Union flotilla in May 1862, Drewry's Bluff
saw no battle action for two years. Captain Sydney Smith Lee (General
Robert E. Lee's brother) took command of the site and supervised its expan-
sion and strengthening into a permanent fort. While some workers constructed an outer line of entrenchments to protect the land approach to

The *Galena* firing on Drewry's Bluff (Naval Historical Center).

Richmond, others built improvements for the fort, including a chapel, barracks, and quarters for the officers.

During this time, Drewry's Bluff became an important training ground for the Confederate Naval Academy and the Confederate Marine Corps Camp of Instruction. It was also during this time that Midshipman Minor arrived.[4]

Drewry's Bluff, Virginia
Sunday, October 11, 1863

Obtained permission to go on shore & look around & was charmed with the place, & only wish that I was in command of a piece of heavy ordnance & stationed here on the bluff. There is quite a little village here now & two churches in one of them. Bishop Johns preached today but as it was a very small one, I did not get in but stood on the outside of the door for some time & at length went away. I walked around the fortifications & was charmed with their appearance also. Took dinner on the Bluff with some midshipmen who are stationed there & in the evening walked down with them to the shore & hailed the *Patrick Henry* which is lying out in the river opposite the Bluff. A boat was sent for us & we all went on board, & later in the evening I was sent in charge of a boat to bring Mrs. [William H.] Parker aboard who had remained on shore after church.

Monday, October 12

On this day while at the black board there was one of the strangest things happened to me I ever saw. I was unable to do anything at all & I could not reason one bit.

Wednesday, October 14

Studied here all day & will try to take a sail this evening with some members of the [CSS] *Nansemond.*

> The CSS *Nansemond* was a small wooden steamer built at Norfolk, Virginia, in 1862. The 166-ton gunboat was armed with two 8-inch guns and was assigned to duty with the James River Squadron under Flag Officer Samuel Barron, CSN. With Lieutenant John Rutledge, CSN, in command, she sailed from Norfolk with the other vessels of the squadron on May 4, 1862, just prior to the evacuation of the Gosport Navy Yard. The *Nansemond* continued on active duty in the James River until the end of the war. Her commander in November of 1863 was Lieutenant James H. Rochelle, CSN.[5]

Thursday, October 15

Studied hard & got good marks. This evening will review all I have been over lately & perfect myself for the coming examination.

Friday, October 16

Read today a letter from Grand Pa Minor forwarded by Uncle Will stating that he would be in Richmond on the 15th which was yesterday & that I must come up & see him. I applied for permission to do so but cannot go until tomorrow. I then have permission to stay until Monday morning until 9 o'clock.

Saturday, October 17

Awoke by 4 o'clock & then walked two miles, after being put on shore, to the Petersburg railroad when I took the cars for Richmond.... I arrived at 7 o'clock took a good Breakfast at a restaurant & then sat about finding my grand father, but did not succeed until dinner time. Spent the evening with him & then we both went to Mrs. Hills & took supper where he stayed all night. A little while after supper we called upon Mrs. Herndon & family & then separated to meet in the morning.

Sunday, October 18

Today Grand Pa left. He came around to uncle Wills soon, with whom I staid, & fixed up his bundle of purchases & told us good by. Sometime latter I dressed myself & went down to the Spottswood Hotel & got breakfast. I then went to St. James Grammar School & saw Miss Savage, Miss Meridith, & Mr. Christian, & several others. Then to St. Paul's & heard Mr. Minnigerode & after church went home with James Dunlop & took dinner with him & was invited to come up at any time & make myself at home there. After dinner lit my segar & walked out to Camp Lee & then

Wartime photograph of a Confederate Columbiad at Drewry's Bluff (Naval Historical Center).

returned by way of Grace St. & called on the Miss Savage but they were out. I then left word that I would call that night & take them to church. Took supper at the American & then proceeded to fulfill my promise. I spent quite a pleasant time with Miss Mary, Miss Parker being too unwell to accompany us. After I had sat a little while when I had returned from church told her good-by & went to uncle Wills soon & stayed all night with him.

Monday, October 19
    Awoke early & walked to Rocketts [Rocketts Landing] to be in time for the boat which ought to have left at eight o'clock but did not do so

The Spottswood Hotel at 8th and Main Streets where Minor took Sunday breakfast. Photograph was taken after the fire and evacuation of Richmond (Library of Congress).

until after 9 some time & in consequence I was too late for the morning duties but was excused as I had done all I could to get here.

Tuesday, October 20

Studied hard all day & have done pretty well. Today has been a sad one with me. Late this evening I was ordered to hold myself in readiness to take charge of the boys for Richmond & am now ready & must bid you good-by until the morrow when I will tell you of my trip to the city.

Wednesday, October 21

Last evening I had a crew of six men & the Capt. & Mrs. Parker went with me to the city. We went up on the *Nansemond,* a screw steamer, & got to Richmond at about 20 minutes to seven & the Capt. then told me that he would be there at 9 o'clock. I then allowed all of my crew to go on shore well knowing that they would all be quite intoxicated but determined never the less to gratify them knowing I could easily control them no matter in what state they were. I remained on board not caring to go

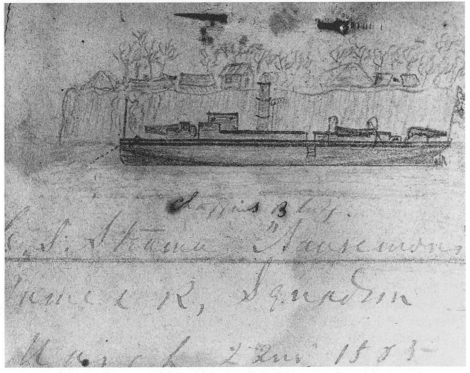

Top: Rocketts Landing and the Confederate Navy Yard on the far side of the James River. The school ship *Patrick Henry* was usually docked at the landing to the left (Library of Congress). *Bottom:* Pencil sketch by Lieutenant Walter R. Butt, CSN, depicts the CSS *Nansemond* off Chaffin's Bluff on the James River, Virginia, 22 March, 1865 (Naval Historical Center).

uptown for so short a time of [on] the steamer along side of which I had ordered the barge to be lashed. At five minutes to 9 o'clock the Capt. came on board & asked if I was there & I immediately advanced & recd him & informed him that all was ready my crew having returned as I had ordered some minutes before nine & assisting the Capt. & his wife in the boat gave the orders to shove off & pulled rapidly down the river beneath the silvery light of the moon. Along the way I conversed with Mrs. Parker for some time. I found that she knew both my father & mother. I pulled that night against a flood tide 7½ miles in an hour & 25 minutes & then went to rest. All of this day I have spent in hard study.

> As recounted earlier, Lieutenant William H. Parker, superintendent of the Naval Academy, was a son of Commodore Foxhall Parker, USN, and brother of Commander Foxhall A. Parker, USN. While one brother went with the South, the other remained in the Federal navy during the war and attained distinction. William H. Parker entered the US navy in 1841, when he was only 14 years old, and was graduated at the head of a class at the Naval Academy that gave to the United States and Confederate States service more distinguished officers than any other single class. Previous to the War Between the States, he had attained a high reputation as an officer and instructor, and held the position of assistant professor of mathematics at the Annapolis Institution. In the Confederate Navy he had taken part in the battles in the North Carolina Sounds; had commanded the gunboat *Beaufort* at the battle of Hampton Roads; and was executive officer of the ironclad *Palmetto State* at Charleston in the breaking of the blockade. His professional writings were used as textbooks at Annapolis and in the Confederate Naval Academy. They were *Elements of Seamanship, Harbor Routine and Evolutions, Naval Tactics, Naval Light Artillery Afloat and Ashore,* and *Remarks on the Navigation of the Coasts between San Francisco and Panama.*[3]

Thursday, October 22

Today I have been looking over my last volume of memorandum & have been making out there from an account against the government which I will collect if possible on Saturday coming. On this day I wrote to Miss Rosalie Rives & hope that she will answer my letter.

Friday, October 23

Spent the morning in study & in the evening took a walk of three miles over to Stark's [Major Alexander W.] Battalion of Artillery & inquired for Mr. Rives & William Harrison, but they had left his battalion & I understand are now with Col. Lightfoot [Lieutenant Colonel Charles E.]on the other side of Richmond. I expect to go up to tomorrow & will call & see them.

Saturday, October 24

Got permission to go up in town to collect my account against the government & return the following morning, so I arose early & started in

Present-day view down the James River from the ramparts of Drewry's Bluff (photograph by R. Thomas Campbell).

the rain for the cars & got to Richmond & stopped at the Spotswood House & it being raining I played billiards nearly all day & not being able to collect my account without my orders, which I had forgotten to bring, had to get the proprietor of the hotel to credit me which he readily did knowing me well. Mrs. Betts & Uncle Will, being out of town, I could do nothing but go to him.

Sunday, October 25
Went to St. James grammar school & was asked to teach a class of young ladies but not feeling my self capable of doing so declined. I borrowed from Mr. Dashids a book on confirmation by Bishop McIlwaine & intend to prepare myself for confirmation at the earliest opportunity. At 20 minutes to eleven o'clock left for the wharf to come down on the *Schultz* [CSS *Schultz*], but the boat starting as I believe before her schedule time ½ past eleven, I was left & had to remain until the following morning. [I] then went to St Paul's church & after dinner went out to see Mrs. Rives & Wm. H. & was surprised to find Edward Harrison a lieutenant of the battery. William was out but came before I left & walked

Present-day view of the interior of Drewry's Bluff (photograph by R. Thomas Campbell).

into town with me. We then called to take the Miss Savage to church but they had already gone so we went ourselves to St Paul's & then I told him good-by, promising to meet him at the Spotswood Hotel next Saturday. I also [saw] Mr. Rives who is now married.

> The CSS *Schultz*, also known as *A. H. Schultz*, was built at New York, N.Y. She served the Confederates in the James River, as a flag-of-truce boat, and was probably armed. *Schultz* was accidentally blown up in the James River by a Confederate torpedo that may have drifted from its original position.

Monday, October 26

As I said above I was forced to remain in the city until this morning & when I got on board I was quarantined for two weeks & cannot now leave the vessel for any purposes whatsoever & though I have promised to meet William Harrison at the Spotswood House on the coming Saturday I fear I shall disappoint him, but not if I can help it for I shall ask permission to go up on Saturday.

Tuesday, October 27

This day, like many, has passed swiftly away & I do not know anything of importance that has occurred except that I have all the day that I could call my own been reading the Scottish Chiefs & have been intensely delighted.

Wednesday, October 28

Again I have passed those hours which my duty allowed me in perusing Mrs. [Jane] Porter's matchless production of the Scottish Chiefs. I read of the noble deeds of Wm. Wallace, [and] I feel myself elevated to something beyond my finer self & think that it is one of the most beneficial works to inoculate the principals of virtue, but one ought not read it until he is able to appreciate it in its true spirit. Most persons read this volume too soon.

Thursday, October 29

Was put on duty for a little while but I was relieved & again, when opportunity afforded, have followed Miss Porter as she forcibly attracts me with a heaving bosom & attentive interest.

Friday, October 30

On this day I have felt quite gloomy & have walked the deck for my hours in communing with myself. Ah! how I long to be once more at home among those who love me so well & who now mourn over my wearisome stay. I feared I cannot get off to see my friend but intend to ask the Capt.'s permission to do so to night. Now farewell.

Saturday, October 31

Nearly all of this day it has been raining & I have been unable to go uptown on account of the rain, but intend doing so this evening, rain, hail, or shine. As I intended I go uptown this evening & it has cleared off beautifully & I shall enjoy myself much. I have permission to remain in town until Monday morning & then I must again betake myself to my duty here. On this day I was released from my quarantine & feel in quite a good humor.

Tuesday, November 3, 1863

All of this day I have been studying & also finished the Scottish Chiefs & was quarantined for ten days again, & I think quite unjustly, by the Capt. as there were many committing the same offense at the time with myself & not one of them in any way was punished. I fear that I will have to be at eternal war with Lt. Hall [Lieutenant Wilburn B. Hall, Commandant of Midshipmen] the executive officer as long as he or I remain aboard, for I was bound by duty to report him one day & he has taken outrage at my having done so & now looks for every opportunity in his power to get me into trouble. He has a contemptible disposition & no chivalric feeling or he would not use such petty revenge. I feel almost at times like it would do me good to humble his mean spirit.

The USS *Harriet Lane* (Naval Historical Center).

Born and reared in South Carolina, Wilburn B. Hall was also graduated from the United States Naval Academy at the top of his class in 1859. He served one year on the sloop USS *Constellation* before the outbreak of war. Having only recently been graduated from the academy at Annapolis, Hall was still a midshipman when he resigned from the U. S. service on March 7, 1861. His first appointment, July 24, 1861, was that of a master, but he quickly proved his worth and was commissioned a lieutenant on September 19, 1861. Hall served on the Confederate steamers CSS *Resolute* and CSS *Savannah* with the Savannah Squadron during the latter part of 1861 and into 1862. Next Hall went to Charleston where he was assigned for a short time to the CSS *Huntress*. He also saw duty on the CSS *Tuscaloosa* at Mobile and at the naval station in Selma, Alabama, during 1862. From there, Hall was transferred west of the Mississippi River to Galveston, Texas, where he joined the officers on the CSS *Harriet Lane*. At this time the Red River Squadron at Shreveport, Louisiana, was desperately short of officers and men, and on April 21, 1863, Hall led a contingent of forty men to Shreveport to reinforce the depleted squadron. By October he was on the *Patrick Henry* where he assumed the duties of Commandant of Midshipmen.[4]

Wednesday, November 4

On this day we were drilled in the launch with a boat howitzer & I was one of the stroke oarsmen & was not like a good many obliged to jump overboard when we landed the howitzer. On this day I was again reported & very unjustly. I am getting into a snare with everybody, but know not why. I look every day for an answer to my letter from Miss Rosalie Rives, but have begun to despair of ever hearing from her. Now good-by.

Thursday, November 5

Drilled in small arms & I fear that I will be reported for being late at drill, but did not know that it was time or I would have been there. Today has been a beautiful one, & there was a party of young men & I was invited to be one of them who chartered the steamer *Schultz* & brought a nice party of young ladies, most of whom I knew down to the Bluff. I should like to have been with them but owing to my quarantine could not.

Friday, November 6

All of this day has been a beautiful one & in the evening we were drilled in the launch with the howitzer & I was one of the stroke oarsmen a place given to good oarsmen. I no longer expect to hear from Miss Rives nor will I again trouble her with my correspondence. I am not allowed to leave the ship except on duty being still under quarantine.

Saturday, November 7

Today all on board was quiet for almost all of the midshipmen have gone away on liberty & those who have not are with the boardroom offices or in the cutter sailing. I stood some time & watched the noble little vessel plough the white cap waves & not able to bear my disappointment at not being one of those who [rode] in her came below & and now writing my disappointment down.

Sunday, November 8

This is another beautiful day & again some are out & enjoying it but I, besides being debarred pleasure of even liberty, am on duty on board.

Monday, November 9

Again all is bustle on board for all are now present & ready for the duties of the day & I too am relieved of duty & ready to do my part in what takes place on every week day. Today we drilled at the great guns & I was first sponger of the gun to which I was attached.

Tuesday, November 10

Hard study is the order of the day & I have struggled hard to do my part in carrying it out. We had today a hard lessen in algebra & I think that I got through it quite well. Nothing of much importance has occurred. I think it quite strange that uncle Will Pannell has not answered my letter & must write & find if possible a list of Pa's Law Book's which was among Cousin Jos Pannell's papers. Must also write to Grand Pa, & all.

Wednesday, November 11

Again have gone through my daily routine of duty & study & am now at leisure not knowing what to do. On this day we again drilled in launch & I had my old place of stroke oarsman. We fired blank cartridges & they made quite a noise & a great many were unable to keep the stroke for jumping when she fired, but I have gotten used to them & had as soon hear them as not. But don't like them with balls.

Monday, November 15

Awoke early from a comfortable sleep & walked down to the cars & got off to the Bluff & have gone through my duties with a heavy heart. In the evening I asked permission to go to Petersburg on business but was not allowed to do so. Today we drilled at great guns & shot some rounds at a target & most of the shots struck.

Tuesday, November 16

Drilled in launch & fired some shrapnel & shell but only burst one or two of the former.

Wednesday, November 17

All of this [day] have been studying & this evening drilled with small arms.

Thursday, November 18

Drilled in launch & fired shell & shrapnel again & bursted most of them all.

Friday, November 19

Been hard at study & will drill again in the launch this evening.

Saturday, November 20

I do not know what occurred on this day nor on any of the succeeding ones of this month so I shall skip up to the period on which I do recollect. Today is the 7th of December, 1863, Sunday, & I shall commence on the 1st of December, Tuesday, 1863.

Tuesday, December 1, 1863

On this day I was challenged to a duel which I accepted knowing that nothing would come of it & such was the case.

Wednesday, December 2

On this day I asked permission to go to Petersburg but did not get it.

Thursday, December 3

On this day went to Richmond & there met Willie Harrison & promised to come & see him before I was ordered off from the state & he told me that he had something nice to tell me. I spoke to him of going up in Albemarle Co. [County] before I left the state.

Midshipmen who had passed their examinations would most likely be ordered to active duty with the various squadrons within the Confederacy.

Tuesday, December 8

On this day they examined my class in mathematics & I passed in a class of 50 or more No 2 or 3. I will now prepare for the examination on grammar tomorrow.

Wednesday, December 9

Today I passed the examination on grammar & think that I am entirely through & still retain the same study as on my mathematical examination. On this day a great many of the graduates left for their respective stations & we are expecting our orders everyday as it is determined not to give us the above mentioned leave of absence but to assign us immediately to duty.

Thursday, December 10

On this day some of my class received their orders but they were all ordered to Mobile Ala. & we still await ours. I went up town today & saw uncle Will & got from him the sum of 40 dollars which makes 310 dollars in all that I have gotten from him.

Friday, December 11, 1863

I returned onboard of the ship in time to get my orders to Savannah Ga. & immediately set to work to pack up my things in order that I might go up to Richmond for I had no idea of going directly off but intended to apply for a two weeks leave of absence which I did but only got three days leave to visit my Grand Pa in Caroline Co. This was on Saturday that I applied for the leave & I intended to go up on Sunday Dec. 13th 1863, & this I did, but did not see my Grand Father but spent the few days I stayed there quite pleasantly.

> Although Minor had passed his initial exams, he was not considered a "passed" midshipman, but still a student of the Academy. His next course of training involved assignment to an operational unit, and he was now directed to report to the Savannah Squadron at Savannah, Georgia.

Assigned to the CSS Savannah

> Minor returned to Richmond after his stay in Caroline County, and from there he began his journey to Savannah. This part of midshipman training was extremely important, for it provided realistic applications of the seamanship and gunnery courses just completed. Because of the press of war, however, many midshipmen, including Minor, were thrown into combat command situations that in more normal times would have been reserved for commissioned officers.
>
> Arriving in Savannah on December 21, 1863, Minor was posted to the ironclad CSS *Savannah* which was commanded by Captain Robert F. Pinkney. The Savannah Squadron at this time consisted of, in addition to the *Savannah* which was armed with four guns, the CSS *Georgia*, an ironclad steam-

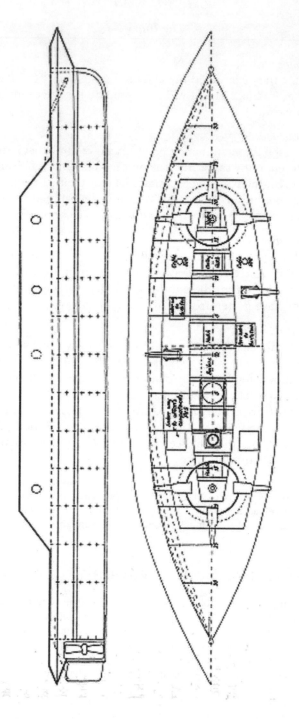

Plan drawing of the ironclad CSS *Savannah* (Courtesy of Robert Holcombe).

powered floating battery with nine guns under First Lieutenant Washington Gwathmey; the CSS *Isondiga,* a steam gunboat mounting three guns commanded by First Lieutenant Joel S. Kennard; and the CSS *Sampson,* a small steamer with one gun under First Lieutenant Thomas B. Mills.[8]

Minor settled into the daily routine of life onboard a Confederate ironclad, but was still required to continue his studies. He found time to socialize, however, and soon became captivated with one Miss Annie Lamar, "one of the wealthiest [ladies] of Savannah." His romantic thoughts would soon be interrupted, however, for at the end of May, 1864, he was assigned to accompany the mission that would attempt the capture of the USS *Water Witch.*

Minor was not particularly happy with his assignment to the Savannah Squadron. He had become bored with the squadron's doldrums and felt that more should be done to harass the enemy. Before the expedition to capture the *Water Witch,* he was writing to his cousin, Robert D. Minor, explaining his standing in his class, bemoaning the squadron's inactivity, and requesting that his cousin have him assigned to his command.

Savannah Georgia,
Saturday, December 26, 1863

... On this day & played some fun games of billiards in most of which I was successful.

Sunday, December 27

I wanted to go up to church but could not do so, so I went writing letters & wrote a very long one to Harvey and another to William Harrison & intend writing one to Uncle Will Hart, & Pa., tomorrow or next day & one to Edward Rives & his sister & one to Cousin Lou Scott & one to Miss Mary Savage.

Monday, December 28

Wrote a long letter to Uncle Will Hart & then went up town. Tomorrow will try to finish writing my letters on this day. Got a letter from Midshipman J. T. Scharf & must answer it soon.

Tuesday, December 29

Wrote a long letter to Miss Mary Savage & also one to Uncle Will Pannell & requested Cousin Bettie to find out for me if it was not Miss Rowlett that I saw on the C_____ on the eighteenth of this month. On this day all of the prisoners were taken off from the ship, having been sentenced by the courts martial & some of the poor fellows will still wait the miserable ornaments that clapped their limbs here in the prison to which they were sent. By sending them away I have but three good men from my crew.

Wednesday, December 30

On this day wrote a long letter to Edward Rives. Spent all of the morning on duty & in the evening took a nice sail as there was a good breeze blowing directly up the river, but before I had finished my sail my

St. John's Church, Savannah (Library of Congress).

mast carried away & I was forced to give it up & pull on another sail with what's called an _____ breeze back to my vessel.

Thursday, December 31

Went up town & had quite a pleasant time there, met Mr. [First Lieutenant William Van] Comstock who told that my standing was very high. Also met Midshipmen [William S.] Hogue who has just returned from home to duty. While at home he was married to a very wealthy young lady by name of Miss Ward. He is from Florida & so was the young lady. Mr. Hogue is only 19 years of age & I think married entirely too soon. He & I are not very good friends nor likely to become so. All of this day has been quite windy & I spent most of my time in the billiard saloon play-ing with the executive officer of our ship, Mr. [First Lieutenant William R.] Dalton who is one of the finest men I ever expect to see.

Friday, January 1, 1864

On this day wrote a letter to Cousin Maria Lou Scott & I then spent the rest of the morning on duty. All of this day has been quite a stormy one & the waves have been breaking all over our vessel. One of the men lost his cap over board & got into one of the other boats to get it but when he got our from the vessel he was unable with the assistance of his com-panion to get back to the vessel again, & was cast by the violence of the waves ashore some distance below the station of our vessel. This evening with a stout crew I was ordered to man a boat belonging to a vessel lay-ing opposite ours, but along side of the shore & to leave the boat at the vessel to which it belonged & to then proceed on shore to where the boat was laying & bring back it up to the vessel when I got to the boat. She was lying stranded about thirty feet from the edge of the water for the tide had fallen, besides there were no arms in the boat. The man who had been cast ashore in her having taken them up to the ship. I had just left ____ along side the shore. So I sent one of our four men after my oars & ____ about to launch my boat it was very cold & the waves raging at the same height as they had been all the morning. It was dark when, after work-ing in mud up to my knees, & I got my boat once more in her element & the men sent for the oars having in the meantime returned with them, I had nothing to do but to ship my rudder & give way but the shipping of the rudder was a very difficult job for the boat was pitching so that it was almost an impossibility, but I determined to see what I could do at it myself. The sailor who I had ordered to do it having given it up in despair, as I expected [him] to do, I succeeded in doing so & there with my leak-ing boat pulled away for our vessel where I arrived after a hard buffeting of the mad waves, wet through and though, very cold, my wetting all came from the waves which dashed against my little boat & then threatened every moment to swamp her, but I headed her just so she would rise on the waves and would not give them a chance to break over her, for it would in that case have been certainly swamped for I had nothing to bail with in the boat. It was delicious to see her ride the waves as majestically as she did & I fell in love with her right off. She will continue against the same waves tonight as she goes down the river as the guard boat, but I thank heaven that I'm not to be her commander. Poor little craft, she is so hard used for she is leaking badly and yet they give her no rest. She would not have gone down tonight though, if it had been possible to lower any one of our other boats, but should they attempt to lower any of them they would be knocked all to pieces before they reached the water for the waves would knock them against the vessel's side until they would not hold water. Smoked a nice cigar tonight & enjoyed it much.

Saturday, January 2

Awoke early & I was supposed to see the cook of my brother's mess inquiring for us. He had arrived in the city and promised my brother to see me if possible & so he succeeded in doing, he goes back tomorrow & as I have lately written from this place to my brother I shall not write by him. He persuaded me to go up town with him & see his little daughter that I might let him know when I wrote to my brother how she was getting along here. I have taken an interest in his little girl & shall inquire concerning her whenever I have an opportunity of doing so. I had quite a pleasant time in town & came down late in the evening & got a mattress from the purser's clerk & shall sleep comfortably on it tonight.

Sunday, January 3

I wished very much to go up to church today but it was inconvenient for me to do so & I was compelled to remain on board & had the *Wrinkles* [Minor was reading a book entitled "*Wrinkles*"] with which I was very much amused. Today has been quite a disagreeable one & it is quite gloomy to be sitting here in the dark with no bright faces to cheer me up.

View of Savannah from the Cupola of the Exchange, looking east toward Fort Jackson (*Frank Leslie's Illustrated Newpaper*).

I shall go hard to work at study. As soon as the *Wrinkles* have been finished by myself, which will be some time tomorrow, & then the next day which will be Tuesday will find me being _____.

Monday, January 4

All of this day I have been being rather employed at reading the *Wrinkles* and will finish it, too, as I expected to do. I was interrupted once or twice to guard duty but soon accomplished whatever was given me to do & returned to enjoy my book. I have four messmates: Messrs. Hogue, Trimble, Long, & Doak. The latter is now sick & Mr. Long on watch, but Mr. Trimble is with me and is reading all about I know not what. Today was laid by Mr. Long, Mr. Trimble, & myself to take a trip to the point from which we can see the movements of the Yanks as we meditate a little this distance from them, but a owing to the rain of yesterday we did not go, but the latter part of the day was quite a beautiful one, but as it will take a whole day to accomplish, we couldn't take advantage of the beauty of the shore & proceeded on our way. But on tomorrow we will.

> Midshipman William S. Hogue was from Florida and had served on the ironclad CSS *North Carolina* at Wilmington, North Carolina. Midshipman John D. Trimble was from Maryland and had been a classmate of Minor's on the *Patrick Henry*. Midshipman James C. Long was from Tennessee and had served on board the CSS *Virginia* during the Battle of Hampton Roads, March 8 and 9, 1862. He too attended the Naval Academy on the *Patrick Henry*. Midshipman A. Sidney Doak was also from Tennessee and had attended the Academy on the *Patrick Henry*. It was proper navy protocol that officers of the same rank would mess together.

Tuesday, January 5

Again we have been disappointed by the gloomy weather for we have been unable to take our trip. All of this I have spent wither on duty or in studying but also found time to write two short letters. One to Scharf, and one to W. A. Lee. I was ordered to go on board of the *Resolute* & take on cords of wood & then to return when I was signaled so to do. The signal came before I had got on quite four cords, but I shoved off and landed along side of the *Savannah* in good stride & unloaded. Today the Dr. decided that Mr. Doak, who has not eaten a mouthful for 5 days, has got the typhoid fever & he will be transferred to the hospital tomorrow.

> The CSS *Resolute* was a side-wheel steamer of 322 tons and acted as a tender to the ironclad CSS *Savannah*.

Wednesday January 6—8
[Illegible]

Saturday, January 9

On this day the sun for the first time shone forth & Mr. Trimble and

Mr. Long were able to take the trip we had so long contemplated doing together, but I being on duty was compelled to remain behind & wait for what they may tell me about the enemy. As I said above, I have been on duty all day & it has been very erroneous duty, too.

Sunday, January 10

Went up to church today & heard a very fine sermon from Bishop Elliot. He argues in favor of a sober ____ life & showed that such a life brought the most happiness to the creature who thus lived it. Tonight I go in charge of the guard boat again with the same congenial companions, but tonight I will have the last half & Mr. Trimble who has already gone in charge of the finest boat will have the first part of this disagreeable night. This ought to have been a mild & pleasant night for we have had such a day & always all together we enjoyed it very much. I am looking every day for an answer to each one of my many letters, but do not think that I shall soon be rewarded. I have not yet become acquainted with anyone here & am almost determined not to be, for the Capt. of my vessel [Commander Thomas W. Brent] does not allow us to go up to town to any of the parties we may be invited to, & then if I do not become acquainted I shall pursue the studies which I have already commenced with the greater vigor. I must now turn in & get some sleep, for you know that I have got the guard boat duty & of course you will excuse me of describing the pretty faces I saw today to you, but rest assured that none of them were so pretty as to make me forget one, that struggle as I may to do so, I cannot. Her name is Annie & she lives in the far off west where there is much oppression and wrong & I shall ever cherish her memory although I believe her forever lost to me. I sometimes think that affection as pure & true as mine ought to be requited & that I may yet be happy, but, alas, such thoughts banish as suddenly as they come, for I am awakened by the many proofs that [she is] affianced to another. The letter I got the other day from my brother was written before he had received mine, written him while in Caroline County, & since I have written to him since I have been here. I shall not write again until I hear from him & then, too, I may hear from my sweet little Cousin Lou & my fair friend Miss Mary Savage & now good night for I must go & dream of my little Sister Ellen & all the rest as I have often done. Good night.

Monday, January 11

Turned in last night at about 9 1/2, but did not get to sleep for at least an hour, so I only got about 1/2 hour sleep up to 12 o'clock the time I had to turn out & take charge of the guard boat. I soon reached my post of duty for the tide was ebbing at the rate of 8 knots per hour & I went with it. I revived my mess mate Mr. Trimble who decided to wait until morning when the flood tide would commence running in, so we all put up together by a nice line on shore, for it would have been impossible for my boat coming up the river to make any headway—at least until the tide was slack. After daylight I found no difficulty at all in getting up to the station of our vessel & arrived here soon after Mr. Trimble who had at least 2 hours the start of me. I did not attempt to go to sleep for it was very near breakfast. So I determined to wash myself & get ready to go up to the city on business. I spent the day quite pleasantly in the city & returned in time for evening quarters & found a great many ladies on board but did not get acquainted with any of them. I have long looked for someone to answer my letters, but it seems that I am to look in vain.

Tuesday, January 12
All this day I have spent quietly on board of the vessel & it has passed duty for I was ordered to take charge of the barge & go up to the city & wait for Lieut. [Thomas K.] Porter who would return to the vessel with me & while I waited on shore to look for him he came down to the boat and none of the crew telling him that I was in the city. He shoved off and left me to walk down to the vessel which I did, but I had to wad through a good deal of mud. On my way down I passed through a beautiful rice plantation. There was no rice growing on it, but it was beautiful. When I got tired I climbed up a hill and sat myself down on the most beautiful lawn I ever saw. It was surrounded by the most beautiful & singular circle of live oaks weeping with moss. Fronting the lawn was the country residence of Mr. Robt. Haberswham on whose place I was. Oh how nice it was. It made me wish that my mother could enjoy it & then, too, it would be sweet [to] sit there and talk to a certain fair one that I know & love. Now, goodnight.

Wednesday, January 13
Went up to the city & called on Miss Grace Mercer who was delighted with me & shall call often as she invited me to do. Got my boots on this day & spent all together a pleasant time, but being a rainy, foggy, evening, the boat did not go down as usual & I had to stay all the night. I did not go to the theatre as I wished to do. _____ if one missed seeing the play of "Hunchback" by Miss Ella Wren.

Thursday, January 14
Came down by the morning boat & went on duty where I continued all day long. All who were not on my duty went up to the city & I have spent the day all by myself, for Mr. Long was on duty. I had some very pleasant conversations with a Lieut. Harnes from near Memphis, Miss. On this day recd, an answer to my letter written some time ago from Edward Rives. He told me that he had had quite a pleasant time at a good many of the parties given by Cousin Lucy Tunior who was married to a

Mr. Abbott. They expected me at his father's ____, but I could not go for reasons above mentioned. It is quite early this morning & I am writing by candle light & as duty calls me & I have ____ all that happened on ____.

Friday, January 15
All of this day I have spent quietly on board with the exception of having the ship twice on duty for I was ordered to board two sloops that were going to attempt to run the blockade & see that they had on board nothing more than their pass allowed them. This evening I wished to take a nice sail but could not make it convenient to do so. I need an answer to my letter from my brother who had had a pleasant mass & also an answer from Miss Savage who likewise had a gay time. I must answer all of the letters soon so that they too will write to me again. My brother tells me nothing of my friends, but says that all who are very dear to us are well & that from all accounts Uncle Dan is a Brigadier Genl. I know that Wm. B. Richmond was killed at Chickamauga.

Saturday, January 16
All this day has been a beautiful one. I have been compelled to spend the most of it on board with the rest of my messmates except Mr. Long who is in the city. On this day another has been added to our mess by name ... a Mr. [Acting Master's Mate A. A. E. W.] Barclay. I have known him some time. I like him very much. His father was the British Consul at New York for many years & has now retired on a pension from his country. Our Mr. Barclay is a Georgian by birth & his father an English-man. On this day we also shifted the station of our vessel to one about a mile below our former one & are now lying within 130 yards of the shore.

Sunday, January 17
Another beautiful day & I got permission to go up to the city to church. I was on the last watch in the guard boat last night & feel a little the worse for wear, but went up to church, but as the boat did not get there until just before church broke up I did not go but walked out to the park. I wanted to go to church, but as I said above, the boat was too late for it & when I had got just a little way up the street it was lined with those coming from church. Most of these walked first to the park & after enjoy-ing the beauty of the day after a while, turned their happy feet homeward perhaps to meet their little children or brothers & sisters & to prepare them for a nice walk, under the charge of (a) nurse, out in the park to enjoy likewise the beauty of the day. I lingered in the park in order that I might watch the gambits of these little ones, of whom many were all ready for ____ perhaps had assumed the responsibility of taking them to walk & I do not think that their Mama's can be at all displeased at such procedures when they discover it. I then, having stayed too late & played myself with

the happy children, went to see my sick messmate, Mr. Doak, who was found better than when I last saw him, although he was unable to stand without assistance from someone. I recd. On this day two more letters, one form Midshipman Scharf and one from Midshipman W. A. Lee at Wilmington & will answer these soon. I wish to call upon Miss Marion today but did not find an opportunity of doing so. I must now tell you good-by.

Midshipman J. Thomas Scharf (Naval Historical Center).

Monday, January 18

I spent all of this day on board & on duty. I had intended writing some letters but did not do so, for I found no opportunity. I shall do so tomorrow if I can make it convenient. I stated sometime back that I intended to write once more at least to Miss Rosalie Rives but have not changed my mind upon the subject, for I think that I have no right to write again as she did not answer my first letter.

Tuesday, January 19

All of this day has passed by in quiet. I wrote or rather answered Uncle Will T. Hart's letter & promised to write to Annie again before I should expect her to answer mine written while on the *P. Henry*. I'm surprised that Cousin Lou does not write to me. I also answered Edward Rives' letter this evening & I expect a speedy return from him. I must write & write to Miss Emma Ferguson.

Wednesday, January 20

Expected to enjoy this day quietly in writing letters, as I would have been the only one of my messmates on board & had not been ordered off on duty up to the city. I was ordered to take eight men & go on board of our tender the *Sampson* & go up to the city & put on board with the assistance of the *Sampsons* crew 20 cords of wood & to be back & anchored off by sunset. It was a heavy piece of wood for we were not able to go at it until late, so I did not get on board quite twenty cords, but all of the other little articles I went for & among these was two lbs of salt horse, or what they give us here for salt beef, but as the bones are round and beef bones are always flat, we are all of the opinion, as such is often the case, that this must be salt horse. On this day I was very much surprised for I recd. an answer to my letter written to Rosalie Rives & she told me that she would not again answer any I might write, but I must write to thank her for what she did.

Thursday, January 21
    On this day I went up to the city and called on Miss Mercer hoping to meet Miss Mollie Herndau of whose beauty I have so often heard. I found them both out and determined to take a walk out to the park to enjoy, as a great many were doing, enjoying the beauty of the day, but I did not get to the park for on passing through one of the little squares that one has to pass through before one gets to the park, I saw a group of ladies sitting on one of the benches eating ground nuts & when one of them walked up to me, I stopped & recognized Miss Mercer & with her walked back to the bench to where Miss Mollie and two Miss Andersons were sitting & had quite a gay time and lively conversation with the whole party. We visited together the soldiers' wayside house & were very much interested in what we saw. I then walked home with Miss Molly, the other ladies having some calls to make, & told her good-by at the door & she told me that she had sent around to the hotel at which I was stopping in Augusta to see if I were there & avail herself of my escort from ____ hers & I told her that I should have been too happy to have escorted her all the way from Richmond.

On Flag Ship Savannah
at Savannah, Ga. Feb. 3rd 1864

Lieut. Minor,
    Dear Sir,
    I know that you were disappointed in your expectations of me, but I did all I could, except to study as much as I should have done, to equip myself creditably, and believe I succeeded in gaining the respect of all of the officers on board of the *P. Henry*. I know that you are aware, that I was found deficient in conduct, for I feel that you took the interest to inquire concerning me. I struggled to do my duty, & the greater portion of my demerits were for offenses committed through inexperience. As regards my standing in the class to which I belong, I, with the most of the class, thought that it was certainly not lower than number four, for at the examination I answered every question that was put to me, but one, & that one, I am still unable to answer, for I cannot find the proof that Capt. Parker desired. My standing thro' the session was not as high as I deserved, for I did, with the exception of two members of the class, the most difficult

of the examples. Why I did not get the standing I deserve, could not have been that I was wanting in my explanations, for I have the power of explaining what I know with clearness. Thro' my thoughtlessness I made some egregious mistakes, but do not think that they ought to have stood against me at the examination. I do not complain, but I wish you to see Capt. Parker & ask him if I did not stand a satisfactory examination. My being rated lower than I think I deserve to be, will cause me to redouble my efforts to take a higher one. I am not able to do much studying here, for I have neither time, nor place for it. I do not like this station for many reasons, & would like to change it for a more desirable one. If you have got a command, I wish you would try & get me with you, for I know where you are, there will be something going on. Here we have ample opportunity for distinction, if we had any officers of energy. Myself and two of my mess mates, made application to Com. Hunter for two torpedo boats to make some little fuss with, but were refused though our plan was a good one. I have miserable quarters, but have seen much worse in my life. Mr. Bradford is on this vessel, & I asked him of you, but he is unable to tell me where you now are, so I shall send this thro' Uncle Wm. T. Hart, who can forward it to you. I am told by Grand Pa that you heard from Papa, while in Halifax, & wish you would let me know the news from him. I intended corresponding with John, but have not had time to do so as yet. Please remember me to him & also to your wife. Miss Mollie Herndon is in this fair city, & I see her whenever opportunity affords me the pleasure. I like the appearance of this city very much, & have seen nearly all of the sights of interest it affords. The Pulaski monument is a very fine construction & I think that the representation of the count on horseback, is recognizable, as such, if I may be allowed to pass an opinion, from a portrait I once saw of the same. I hope that you will excuse me for talking of myself as much as I have done, but I feel that you take much interest in me, & I had rather first deserve your good opinion than any other man I know, for if I do not deserve yours first, how can I ever expect to deserve that of others. My brother when last heard from was well. I must now bid you goodby.

I am very respectfully,
Your Obt. Svt.
Midn. H. T. Minor, Jr.

★★★★★

Savannah, Georgia,
Thursday, February 25, 1864

Spent this day quietly on board of the vessel & finished Percival Keene & like it very much. Today another master's mate came in, a Mr. [J. D.]

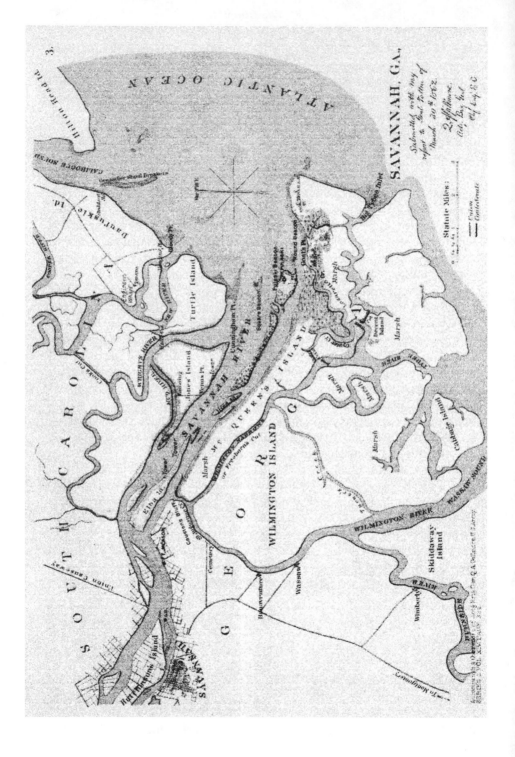

Graves, Midshp Doak has gotten almost well & has gone with his father somewhere in the country to recruit his strength, all of which he has lost by his illness. Mr. Graves is a master's mate & brother to our Lieut. of marines of this vessel. I must answer some of my letters soon.

Friday, February 26

Commenced to study in my algebra & intend to keep it up. This morning some pretty ladies came on board & I was introduced to Miss Maggie Dillard who was one of them & should liked to have become acquainted with a Miss Caruthers who is quite gay. There was another one along whose name I do not know nor care to know.

Savannah, Georgia,
Wednesday, March 9, 1864

Today the vessel weighed anchor & went up to the city for the purpose of putting on board the gun which has arrived to replace the one which was bursted some time ago. We were very busy after getting to the wharf in securing the ship. After the ship was secured, I went up to the post office for the mail but got no letters for myself. After supper I attend to lectures by Lieut. Howell Cobb on the state of the country for the benefit of the soldiers' wayside house of which institution I have spoken before. Lieut. Cobb spoke for two hours & I shall never forget his eloquence. Speculations & extortions found lustly at his hands. His speech was very impressive & I trust may produce good results for the future. He said that the new acts passed by Congress would, soon as the news of the acts became apparent, be looked upon as the wisest legislation that it would be possible for wise men to make.

Savannah, Georgia,
Sunday, May 29, 1864

Went up to the city to church in the sailboat. Heard quite a fine sermon from [Episcopal] Bishop [Stephen] Elliott then returned in sailboat to ship & ate dinner when I again sailed up to the city with Mr. [Lieutenant Henry L.] Graves & a crew of the men who wished to stay up to church. In the evening I intended going to hear vespers at the catholic church but we did not get up in time to do so, & seeing Miss Annie Lamar I overtook & joined her. I found her bent upon a charitable errand for she had coffee & sugar for a poor old woman. I went with her to the poor woman's house & waited at the door listening to the singing of the colored people whose church was just opposite. When she came out we went to walk & I asked her to go to church with me that night which she did.

Opposite: **The area surrounding Savannah, Georgia (*Official Records of the Union and Confederate Navies in the War of the Rebellion*).**

She gave over the cravat I alluded to above & we have promised to be good friends all of our life.

Monday, May 30

Spent the day on board & nothing of importance has occurred. I regret very much a little difficulty that occurred tonight between Mr. [Lieutenant W. W.] Carnes & myself, for I do not know a man who I had rather would consider me his friend than him, but all will come well soon. I hope but if it does not I am not to blame.

Attack on the USS Water Witch

For some time Confederate authorities at Savannah had observed a handsome seagoing side-wheel steamer used by the Federals as one of their blockading vessels. She was the USS *Water Witch*, a 378-ton gunboat mounting four cannon, engaged in patrolling the many sounds and marshes that surrounded Savannah. At the start of the Civil War, the *Water Witch* was assigned to the Gulf Blockading Squadron and operated between Pensacola, Florida, and the Mississippi River. Transferred to the South Atlantic Blockading Squadron, she operated mostly around Ossabaw Island off the Georgia coast.

Lately it was observed that she consistently anchored every night in Ossabaw Sound. The expedition to capture the USS *Water Witch* was planned by Flag Officer William W. Hunter, commander of the Savannah Squadron. To lead the expedition, Hunter selected First Lieutenant Thomas P. Pelot, commander of the floating battery *Georgia*, with First Lieutenant Joseph Price as second in command.

Savannah, Georgia
Tuesday, May 31, 1864

Started to write to Cousin Lou Scott but was interrupted soon after beginning as it was my watch on deck. While on deck an order came allowing me to be one of the officers who were to go on [an] expedition to start immediately, so I got ready right off & with my boat's crew of 20 well armed & good seamen, pulled over to the *Georgia* from which vessel the expedition was to start under Command of Lieut. Thomas P. Pelot. Mr. [John D.] Trimble, midshipman, had another boat from the *Savannah* with some arms & number of men that I had, & when we reached the *Georgia* & Mr. Pelot said that it was the finest body of men he ever saw. I think that it was the small steamer *Firefly* [that] was in readiness to tow us down to the Isles of Hope through St. Augustine Creek, so we soon went onboard of her & strung out our boats behind her & then steamed down the river through St. Augustine Creek to Isle of Hope where our boats were manned. [We] formed into two columns, & then pulled towards the Battery Beaulieu in Vernon River where we arrived safely, but learned that the vessel we were in search of lying in Ossabaw Sound had gone out that evening, but as she remained in the neighborhood all the time we determined to wait until the next day on which, when it came, Mr. Pelot with Mr. [Lieutenant Joseph] Price, Dr. [C. Wesley] Thomas of Richmond, Va., & a boat's crew went out on a reconnoitering expedition leaving me in charge of the camp.

> Pelot was from South Carolina and had resigned from the U.S. Navy on January 11, 1861. He was appointed a first lieutenant in the Confederate Navy on March 26, 1861. Pelot had commanded the C. S. privateer *Lady Davis* at the capture of the Northern merchant ship *A. B. Thompson* on May 21, 1861, but since then had been assigned to the Savannah Squadron commanding the steamers *Oconee*, *Resolute*, and finally the floating battery *Georgia*. Lieutenant Price hailed from North Carolina and was the executive officer of the *Sampson*.[9]

At 12 o'clock Mr. Pelot returned with all of his boat's crew except one, & Mr. Price & Dr. Thomas whom he had left on the foot of Green Island to watch the vessel he had discovered & which he told us that would attack that night. So about 5 o'clock I was ordered to go to work & launch the boats which composed the expedition with that of Mr. Pelot's. & which had for fear of discovery by the enemy [had] been hauled up early in the morning. At 7:30 P.M., we manned our seven boats & pulled down the river & took Mr. Price & his party aboard & then sought the enemy but did not find him so we left Boatswain [L.] Seymour & a man on shore near Ossabaw Sound & then went back to Battery Beaulieu, where I was ordered to see all of the boats white washed. Again on Thursday, June 2nd at 8:30 P.M., we started for the enemy & after taking on board Mr. Seymour & the man left with them pulled towards the vessel which he had discovered & to which, from his description of her whereabouts, our

The ironclad floating battery CSS *Georgia* (Naval Historical Center).

pilot said he could take us. When near the vessel we awaited in silence for the hour of attack & at 2 A.M. of June 3rd 1864, boarded & took her after a severe "fight for the enemy" on deck(at one time outnumbered us. In the affair Mr. Pelot was killed, Mr. Price & myself wounded, but both remained on duty all the while 5 men were killed besides our pilot included, [Moses Dallas, an African American] & a great many wounded. After Mr. Pelot was killed, Mr. Price became commander & I 2nd executive officer. The loss of our pilot created considerable confusion for we did not know where we were exactly & the Yankee pilot was not to be found nor was it safe to remain where we were. Mr. Price had several cutlass cuts across his head & for a little time his brain was confused so I had to do the main part of the business of which I understood but little but was assisted by the boatswains mate [John] Perry who came with me from the *Savannah* & who was quite badly wounded. Two of our boats behaved very badly & did not get on board of the vessel at all but were found out at Isles of Hope & the other at Battery Beaulieu on June 3. Some of the men in both boats were wounded having been fired into as they came along side when they steamed off, & said that they thought us all cut down on the deck. Mr. Pelot's & my boats were the first that touched the vessel for we traveled cords of the same arcs that the other boats were compelled to describe in order to get to their stations. Have written a full account of the affair & intend to preserve it for private perusal. After we got under weigh we got aground three times & then on shore off Battery Beaulieu a place of comparative safety. This was on the evening of June 3rd 1864, & on Saturday June 4th 1864, we got under weigh early & with the flood tide traveled up the river as far as 8 miles to White Bluff where we went to work to unload the vessel. While at Battery Beaulieu Mr. Carnes came on board [to take command] & Mr. Price went up to the city. Mr. Carnes shook hands with me very heartily & I think that all is well again. I am still executive officer. While at Beaulieu a lady, Miss Ida Hanleiter sent me a card with a little mule skin tobacco pouch as a token of her esteem for my gallantry in the capture of the [USS] *Water Witch* which was the name of the vessel we took. Late in the evening of this day I received a large bouquet from a Mrs. Tucker.

> The Confederates suffered heavy causalities. Six, including Lieutenant Pelot, were killed and twelve, including Midshipman Minor, were wounded. The Federals lost two killed, twelve wounded, and 77 men taken prisoner. The *Water Witch* became the CSS *Water Witch*, and patrolled the numerous bays and rivers around Savannah until the city was evacuated upon the approach of Sherman's army in December 1864, at which time she was scuttled and burned.[10]

June 5, 1864

At White Bluff, went to work unloading the vessel & was occupied

The USS *Water Witch* before its capture (*Official Records of the Union and Confederate Navies in the War of the Rebellion*).

all day. On board were a great many good things. I feel that I could write a good deal of interesting matter concerning this capture, but forbear as I do not like to write.

> The following is Hubbard T. Minor's official report on the capture of the USS *Water Witch* which was included with his diary.

On the Morning of Tuesday May 31st 1864, an expedition, under the command of Lieutenant Thomas P. Pelot, left Fort Jackson in the Savannah River. The total number of men composing the expedition, officers & men included, was one hundred & thirty-one. Of those was a Negro man named Moses Dallas, the only pilot along. There were seven boats, all of which were taken in tow by the C. S. Steamer *FireFly*. The officers, with the exception of the coxswains, & men going on board of the steamer in this way it went through Augustine Creek into Thunderbolt, both as far as the Island of Hope where the steamer was left to return to the city. There the boats were formed into two columns, the officers according to their rank commanding the highest numbered boats. Boat No. 1, commanded by Mr. Pelot led the port column. Boat No. 2, commanded by Lieutenant Price led the starboard column. Boats No. 3, No. 5 & No. 7, commanded respectively by Midshipman Minor, Boatswain Seymour, & Master's Mate [John A.] Rosler, followed each other in the port column, & boats No. 4 & No. 6, respectively commanded by Midshipman Trimble & Master's Mate [Hamilton] Golder, followed in succession in the starboard column. In Lieutenant Pelot's boat No. 1 was Master's Mate [Thaddeus S.] Grey, Engineers [George W.] Caldwell & [James L.] Fabian, & the pilot by name [of] Moses [Dallas]. In Midshipman Minor's boat No. 3 was Master's Mate [Arthur C.] Freeman, in Boatswain Seymour's boat No. 5 was Master's Mate [A. H. E. W.] Barclay, in Master's Mate Golder's boat No. 6 was Assistant Surgeon [C. Wesley] Thomas, & in Master's Mate Rosler's boat No. 7 was Assistant Surgeon [William C.] Jones.

The columns being thus formed were kept so, as far as practicable, until the expedition had passed through the Skidaway Narrows & come to Battery Beaulieu in the Vernon River. Here Mr. Pelot learned that the vessel he had intended to attack, if possible at night, had only on this evening gotten up steam & gone out, but as one remained in the neighborhood all the time, he determined to remain until morning & then reconnoiter. Should he be unable to discover a vessel in Ossabaw Sound, it was his intention to go into St. Catherine's Sound where he was sure to find one. It was now about 8:30 P.M., & as the men needed not the boats, all headed for shore where Mr. Pelot had already gone & the men went into camp for the night after supper. All but the watches paid a visit to dreamland, & I trust sweet was the sleep of many.

When the morning of Wednesday June 1st came clear & bright, Lieutenant Pelot took his boat & a picked crew, & accompanied by Lieutenant Price & Assistant Surgeon Thomas, went out on a reconnaissance leaving Midshipman Minor in charge of the camp. During the whole of this day the men remained in camp & kept their good spirits, & these latter were added to by the good mess of turnip salad they enjoyed with their hard bread & salt beef for dinner. The salad was tendered to Midshipman Minor early in the morning by the courteous Captain [Cornelius R.] Hanleiter, commanding at Battery Beaulieu, & that officer had appreciation enough for the salad & the motive that promoted the offer to accept it on behalf of his officers & men. At about 7:30 Lieutenant Pelot returned having left Lieutenant Price, Assistant Surgeon Thomas, & one of his boat's crew on a point of land near the vessel he had discovered [in order] to watch her movements. After supper Midshipman Minor was ordered to have all hands called to muster & then after all were found present Mr. Pelot addressed them. In his short speech he said that they had discovered a vessel & would board her that night, that he expected every man to do his duty & felt confident that they would do so. He also called their attention to the low muttering of the thunder that could be plainly heard & told them that it was an indication that God was with them for the thunder indicated a dark night which could be nothing but favorable to their enterprise. When he was done speaking the men gave him three hearty cheers, & then Midshipman Minor was ordered to go to work & launch the boats, which for fear of discovery by the enemy, had been hauled up on shore & concealed.

Early in the morning at about 8:30 the boats were all launched & manned. When the officers stepped into their respective boats, & amid three cheers from the men & officers of the battery, were pulled down Vernon River towards, Ossabaw Sound where we came to the point where Mr. Price had been left. Mr. Pelot went ashore & brought Mr. Price, Dr. Thomas, & the man with them to their respective boats. It was now about 11:30 & too early to proceed for the enemy was not a great way off, as far as Mr. Pelot could judge, so we returned up the river a little way & the noses of all of the boats were stuck into the marsh, & all of the officers were acquainted with the portion of the vessel they were to board & men appointed in each boat to go to different portions of the vessel where they should have gotten on board. Mr. Pelot intended to board the furthest portion of the vessel on the left side going, & the remaining boats of the port column were to board just behind him & each other respectively. The order on the right side was to be the same, Mr. Price taking the furthest portion from him going on that side & the other boats boarding respectively just after him & each other.

Lieutenant Joseph Price (National Archives).

At 12:30 the boats once more put off & were pulled for a long time towards where the enemy was supposed to be. They pulled about but saw no vessel. At this the men became much annoyed & soon it was found that the sea was not far, for the surf could be plainly heard. It was now about 3:30 & necessary that all possible speed should be made to get back, for the enemy had been evidently passed during the night & must be re-passed before it was light. At about 4:30 it was found that the point of land upon which Mr. Price & party had been left was near us, so Mr. Pelot took Boatswain Seymour & a man named Osburn in his boat & put them ashore with some rations to watch the vessel during the day when it should arrive. Mr. Barclay now had charge of Mr. Seymour's boat & with the rest returned toward Battery Beaulieu where they

all arrived at about 8 A.M. of the morning, Thursday, June 2nd 1864, &
went ashore & into camp as before but it was deemed unnecessary to haul
the boats out of the water so they remained anchored out in the river. At
breakfast time it was discovered that the rations were exhausted so Mr.
Pelot ordered Midshipman Minor to go up & see Captain Hanleiter & ask
him to let him have 20 lbs. of bacon which he would return. The courteous captain sent the bacon & the men had a good meal having some meal
sent out in time for dinner from Savannah by wagon.

When supper again was over all were called to muster & Mr. Pelot
told the men that he did not think it necessary to say anything more to
them. The men responded with cheers & said that "they were in for it."
At about 8 P.M., the boats were again manned & put off down the river
but this time no cheers came from the men of the battery but they stood
and watched us in silence. That day the enemy's vessel had taken such a
position to be seen from the bomb proof with glasses of the battery &
when we put off this time some perhaps thought that many were doomed
to return no more as they went away. When near the point where Mr. Seymour had been left, Mr. Pelot again went ashore & brought him & Osburn
over to their boat. Mr. Seymour had discovered the vessel we had been
looking at during the day from the bomb proof & by picking out her position on the chart found her to be in 40 feet of water & Moses said that
he knew where she was that she was laying just in the spot he thought she
was during the day. Mr. Seymour being in his boat, we again put off &
went through Hell Gate & up to the east for a short distance when the
boats were again stuck in the marsh & silence preserved. This night the
order of attack was somewhat changed, it being decided best for Mr. Pelot
to board the nearest portion to him going on the left side, & Midshipman
Minor the furthest. The other two boats were to board one just forward
of the wheel & the other just aft. The order on the right side was the same,
Mr. Price boarding the portion on that side going & Midshipman Trimble the furthest. Mr. Golder was to board between the two anywhere he
could. It was now about 12:30, so the boats again put off & were pulled
in columns towards the west.

It was a favorable night for it was very dark & every now & then the
lightening lit up the waters all around us & there was not much fear of
our again passing the vessel without seeing her. Our boats were riding
silently on, apparently through a sea of fire, & at about 2 A.M., we discovered a light which we supposed to be that of a vessel, as nearer we came
by the lightning's flash we discovered the vessel we were in search of.
When discovered she bore about 2 points off our starboard bows distant
over a thousand yards. As closer we came the lightening discovered her
plainly to us while our boats being white washed were not so easily discovered. When with in three hundred yards all seemed to be asking God,

as I know I was, to prosper our undertaking, to shield us from harm, & to make us do our duty. When within 80 yards they hailed. When Moses answered, "Runaway Negros," but the chivalric Lieutenant Pelot shouted almost in the same voice, "We are Rebels, give way boys!" All of the boats except the two last in the port column were well up & gave way with a will. The two boats in advance on the port column touched the ship about the same time & the men were on board some seconds before those of the star board column as the starboard column had to describe arcs of circles while those of the port ran across the chords of same arcs. Mr. Pelot was said to be the first man on board & did not live long after getting there for he was shot directly through the heart. The fight lasted not more than ten or 15 minutes & in it we lost, besides Mr. Pelot, 5 brave & good men & among them our pilot. All of the boats but Nos. 5 & 7 boarded where they were ordered, & these two did not board at all. Mr. Price & Midshipman Minor were wounded early in the fight but both remained on duty. At the death of Mr. Pelot, Mr. Price became commander & Midshipman Minor executive officer. After much confusion, a great deal of it occasioned by the loss of our pilot, we got underway, & after getting aground three times anchored safely on Saturday evening June 3rd off Battery Beaulieu.

When we came up we had a boat pennant flying above the stars & stripes & we met with hearty cheers from all the assembled spectators. Were it my place to mention the gallant deeds of the members of this expedition I know of nothing that would give me more pleasure. I must say that all who boarded the vessel merit honor for so doing & none but gallant men dare do such things. Had we not lost our pilot we would have gotten up to Beaulieu without the loss of the provisions which were thrown overboard to lighten the vessel the last time we got aground. Our capture proved to be the U.S. Steamer *Water Witch*, [a] side wheel of [378] tons & a crew of 68 men & officers, Lieutenant [Austin] Pendergrast, commanding.

Signed:

One of the officers of the expedition

Following is the official report filed by Lieutenant Joseph Price on the capture of the USS *Water Witch*:

C.S.S. *Sampson, June 8, 1864.*

SIR: I have the honor to make the following report of the late expedition under the command of First Lieutenant Thomas P. Pelot, C. S. Navy, which resulted in the capture, by boarding, of the U. S. steam gunboat *Water Witch*, lying at anchor in Ossabaw Sound, on the night of the 3d June, 1864.

The expedition, consisting of 7 boats, 15 officers, and 117 men, detailed by your order from the vessels of the squadron, a correct list of whom you will find enclosed, left the C.S.S. *Georgia* at 1 o'clock P.M. on Tuesday, 31st of May, in tow of the steam tender *Firefly*, arriving at the Isle of Hope battery at 5 o'clock P.M. Cast off from the steamer and rowed to Beaulieu Battery, on Vernon River, where we camped for the. night. The next day our scouts discovered one of the enemy's vessels lying at anchor in the Little Ogeechee River, close under Raccoon Key.

At 8 o'clock P.M., the expedition got underway and formed in two columns. Boats Nos. 1, 3, 5, 7 composing the port column, Nos. 2, 4, and 6 the starboard column. Lieutenant Thomas P. Pelot, commanding with Second Assistant Engineer Caldwell, C. S. Navy; and Moses Dallas (colored), pilot, led in boat No. 1; Lieutenant Price with Master's Mate Gray and Second Assistant Engineer Fabian in No. 2; Midshipman Minor, with Master's Mate Freeman, in boat No. 3; Midshipman Trimble in boat No. 4; Boatswain Seymour, with Master's Mate Barclay, in boat No. 5; Master's Mate H. Golder, with Assistant Surgeon Thomas, in boat No. 6; Master's Mate Rosler, with Assistant Surgeon Jones, in boat No. 7, and proceeded with muffled oars to the spot where we supposed the enemy's vessel to be. On arriving we found that she had either drifted her anchorage, or that we had been mistaken as to her position. After searching in vain till nearly daylight, Lieutenant Pelot ordered Boatswain Seymour, with one man, to remain on Raccoon Key as scouts, and the expedition to return to camp at Beaulieu Battery. On the next day (June 3), at 9 o'clock P.M., we again got underway, proceeded to Raccoon Key where we took on board our scouts, who reported that one of the enemy's vessels was lying in Ossabaw Sound, about 3 miles from where we then were. After waiting there until midnight, we were ordered to get underway and pull cautiously. The night being dark, and raining, we got close aboard of her without being discovered. On being hailed Lieutenant Pelot answered we were "rebels," and gave the order to "board her." The vessel having steam up at the time, as soon as the alarm was given, commenced turning her wheels backward and forward rapidly, thus thwarting the earnest efforts of Boatswain Seymour and Master's Mate Rosler to get on board with their entire boats' crews.

The port column, led by Lieutenant Pelot, boarded on the port side; starboard column, led by Lieutenant Price, boarded on the starboard side. In coming alongside, the enemy's fire with small arms was quite severe; in fact it was during that time, and while the boarding netting, which was tied up, was being cut through, that most of our loss in killed and wounded was sustained. After a sharp hand-to-hand fight of some ten minutes the ship was taken. Lieutenant Pelot was the first to gain the deck, and while bravely fighting was shot and instantly killed. In his death the country has lost a brave and gallant officer, and society one of her highest ornaments.

The command then devolved upon me, and I proceeded forthwith to extricate the vessel from the position she was then in, to avoid recapture by the enemy. Our pilot having been killed before the boats reached the side of the ship, I sought for the enemy's pilot and found that he was too badly wounded to assist me, but finally procured one of the quartermasters, whom I compelled to pilot me to the upper end of Raccoon Key, where at the top of high water the ship grounded. I then found it necessary to lighten her, which I did by throwing overboard some barrels of beef and pork, a few coils of hemp rigging, the remainder of the chain which I had slipped as noon as we took the vessel, and lowering two of the guns in the boats. On getting ashore, I immediately landed the killed, wounded, and prisoners at Beaulieu Battery. At 4 o'clock P.M., having in the meantime obtained a pilot from the shore, I succeeded in getting off, and anchored her at 7 o'clock P.M., under the guns of Beaulieu Battery above the obstructions, when Lieutenant Carnes, C. S. Navy, by your order, arrived on board and assumed command.

In the darkness and confusion on board, it was impossible for me to observe each and every man, but I will state, with pride, every one, officers and men, did their duty most gallantly. I would state, however, that I owe my life to E. D. Davis, ordinary seaman, of the C.S.S. *Savannah*, he having cut down every opponent when I was sorely pressed by them. Boatswain's Mate J. Perry, of the steamer *Savannah*, and Boatswain's Mate W. S. Johnson of the steamer *Sampson*, rendered me most valuable assistance in lightening the vessel and general duties on board. The former, although severely wounded, remained on deck as long as he could.

The *Water Witch* is a side-wheel steamer, schooner-rigged, of 378 tons burden, carries four guns (one 30-pounder rifled gun forward, two broadside 12-pounder Dahlgren howitzers, and one 12-pounder rifled brass gun aft, and a crew of 15 commissioned and warrant officers and 85 men, commanded by Lieutenant-Commander Austin Pendergrast, U. S. Navy.

Enclosed you will find the surgeon's report of killed and wounded.

I am, very respectfully, your obedient servant,

Jos. Price,
Lieutenant, C. S. Navy,

Flag-Officer W. W. Hunter, C. S. Navy,
Commanding Afloat, Savannah.[11]

Sunday, June 6, 1864

Went up to the city & found two letters for me one from Henry & the other from Miss Mary Savage. Also found out that Mrs. George Mercer had been around to the hospital to see me & that many of my friends here were anxious concerning me. Among them Mr. Cohen & Bishop

Elliott had both prepared a room for my reception. My acquaintance with Mr. Cohen & family came from the letter I received from Edward Rives.... I walked in the park, or rather limped for I was shot in the leg, & returned quite stiff with Miss Annie Lamar & shall not soon forget the compliment she paid me. All of this month up to the 17th I was on the *Water Witch* & on that day was ordered back to the *Savannah*. Since then nothing of importance has occurred. On the *Water Witch* the grand man on board of her, Paymaster Billings, presented me with

Top: Lieutenant Joseph Price. *Bottom:* The wartime waterfront at Savannah, Georgia (both photographs are from National Archives).

his sword which I will preserve carefully all of my life. I skip all of the little events that have occurred up to this Sunday June 28th 1864, except that Dr. Quintain has been in the city & that I saw him & sent back by him to Uncles Dan & Paul & Henry each a fine tooth comb captured on the *Water Witch* as a trophy from her. Today I am compelled to remain away from church as I have a watch soon & in the meantime have employed myself in chronicling from the end of May up to this time at Savannah Ga.

★★★★★

C. S. Prize Str. *Water Witch,*
Off White Bluff in Vernon River
June 12th 1864

Dear Cousin Bob,

I suppose that you have seen an account of the capture of this vessel, & also know that I was one of the officers of the expedition. I was third officer in rank to Mr. Pelot, & when he was killed became 2nd & executive officer. The wound I recd. was a slight one, the ball lodging in the fleshy part of my thigh in the rear of the bone. Mr. Pelot's and my boat touched the ship about the same time, & we were on board some seconds before the other boats, which had to describe the arc of a circle while we traveled the cord to same arc. Mr. Pelot is said to be the first man on board from his boat, & I was the second from mine, the man forward who threw the grapnel being the first. I was shot soon after touching the deck by one of the lookouts, who after shooting me ran down the hatch which I was guarding. I shot the man going down the hatch, but only wounded him. I will not describe the vessel as you know all about her. The mode of our attack you know also, I suppose, therefore, I am silent in every particular except as regards myself, & am writing to you freely, knowing that you will be gratified at my conduct. The commodore complimented me upon it, & said that the dept should hear of it, as well as that of my brother officer Mr. Trimble. We are the only midshipmen on the station & have both tried to do our duty. Some speak of a chance of our being promoted, & should we be, I promise to fit myself either before, if necessary, or afterwards for whatever position I may occupy. If they will not promote us without our passing the examination for a passed midshipman, I wish you to obtain permission for me to be allowed to stand an examination as soon as I think myself ready for it. I should like very much to be able to have an opportunity for learning seamanship, & think that I will progress rapidly in it, as I already comprehend some of it quite clearly. I wrote to you requesting that you would have me ordered away from here, but I do not wish to be ordered away at present unless I am to be made useful. I have remained executive officer on this vessel ever since she was taken, but do not hope to retain the position much longer. We are lightening the vessel with the intention of getting her to Savannah. You are acquainted with the difficulties which attend such a move, therefore, I will not name them, but only state that in some way or other, [Lieutenant William W.] Mr. Carnes, who is now in command, expects to succeed in his attempt. I suffer but little inconvenience from my wound & have been on duty ever since receiving it, & intend to remain on duty as long as possible. The Dr. told me yesterday that there were some signs of inflammation, and that I must be more quite & I am following his advice & have but slight duty to perform. We are enjoying a great many good things on board & have a great many visitors. I must now tell you goodby. Give Uncle Will the news when you see him, for I will not be able to write to him for a day or two yet. I have a report written by myself of the whole affair which I wish you to inspect some of these days; it is designed only for private use & reference. At the time I last wrote you I did not know of this expedition's being on foot or would not have wished to get away so soon. I was selected by the brave Mr. Pelot without my knowledge to be one of the party, & he knew that Mr. Long & myself with Mr. Trimble were all anxious to be in some such affair. As I said above, I write you all this knowing that you will be gratified & I wish you to be & I want you to entertain a good opinion of me. Remember me to John & Capt. Pegram. Now Goodby.

Very Respectfully,
Midn. H. T. Minor, Jr.

★★★★★

Monday, June 27
Went up to the city & to see Miss Annie Lamar & enjoyed myself hugely. I forgot to state that the Rev. Dr. Quintain has been here & that I saw a good deal of him during his stay. I sent by him to my brother, Uncle Dan, & Paul, each a fine tooth comb captured on the *Water Witch*.

Tuesday, June 28
Spent this day onboard & on duty until about 5 o'clock of the evening, when I went up to see the Miss McDonald where I met Miss Annie Lamar & formed a solemn compact with her to be friends for ever. I have commenced a regular course of study & hope soon to be proficient enough for becoming a passed midshipman.

> After the capture of the *Water Witch*, Minor's good friend Midshipman James C. Long was transferred to the CSS *Albemarle* in North Carolina. On June 28, Minor received a letter from him:

C. S. Stm. *Albemarle*, Plymouth, NC,
June 28th 1864

Dear Minor,

Your letter of the 13th was received several days ago. I was very glad indeed to hear from you. I was beginning to fear that you were badly wounded. I was pleased very much to hear that you and Trimble were spoken of so highly by Com. Hunter. I hope you will get promoted soon.

Capt. Maffitt, formerly of the *Florida*, has taken the command of this vessel. We have finished repairing the ship, and I suppose will attack the enemy in a few days. I hope you will hear a good account of us. But Minor, you must not expect too much of the *Albemarle*, for she is the poorest ironclad in the Confederacy. Her sides are plated with four inches of iron, her spar deck is not covered at all, a portion of her flush deck forward is covered with one inch of iron, the other portion is not covered with anything. Her after flush deck is partially covered with one inch iron,

Top: **A rough sketch of Captain William W. Hunter, commander of the Savannah Squadron** (*Harper's Weekly* (1893). *Bottom:* **The ironclad CSS *Albemarle*** (*Battles & Leaders of the Civil War*).

the rest of it with ¼ inch sheet iron. She carries 2 6.4 inch Brooke guns, one pivoted forward, and the other aft.

We are living the same monotonous sort of life here as usual, nothing to eat scarcely, and no amusements. I wish you would give me a description of the *Water Witch* next time you write. I showed an extract from your letter to Commodore Pinkney, he was much pleased with it, etc.

I received my commission as Master a few days ago to date from June 2nd. How is Hillock's ironclad getting along? I should like to be ordered to her when she is completed. How are the torpedo boats getting along? When will they be completed? After the row is over here, I should like to be ordered to Savannah again if there is any chance of doing something there.

How is your suit progressing, does Miss L. treat you as coldly as ever, or does she give you a smile occasionally?

You must excuse me for not writing to you oftener, but this town is so far out of the world that I am almost unable to obtain writing material, and am totally unable to get postage stamps. I have sent home for some stamps, when they come I will write oftener. Remember me to Mr. Carnes, and Trimble. Write often.

Yours,
Long.

Savannah Is Lost

By the summer of 1864, Minor was bored and restless onboard the CSS *Savannah*. Admittedly, there was not much for a young midshipman to do. The *Savannah*, confined to patrolling the river between the city and the obstructions below Fort Jackson, offered little in the form of action or training. Because of this inactivity, Minor longed for an assignment to a cruiser on the open sea, or at least to some other vessel where he could sharpen his skills as a junior naval officer. He reasoned that his only hope of securing such a transfer was through the auspices of his cousin, Robert D. Minor. Writing from the naval hospital where he was temporarily confined, he pleaded with his cousin to effect his relocation.

C. S. Naval Hospital,
At Savannah, Ga.
Tuesday, *July 19th 1864*

Dear Cousin Bob,

I wish very much to go to sea, & want you to have me, if possible, ordered to the *Florida*, or the new vessel which Semmes is to have. Midn. Ed. Anderson was killed on the *Alabama*, & I wish to fill his vacancy. There is no use in my applying for orders to sea for they will not give them to me. Besides, there are midshipmen being ordered to sea, for one left here not long ago & I stood above him too at the school ship. I read your letter from the Va. [*Virginia II*] and thank you for it. You told me sometime ago that you could get me orders to sea, & I hope you can do it now. I write to you now as I would to my father were he in the Confederacy. I know he could have me ordered to sea, for he does most anything he wants. I could not keep my position on the *Water Witch*, as I had to do the duty of Watch Officer on the C. S. Str. *Savannah*. I think it quite strange that neither Trimble nor myself will be on board of the *Water Witch*. They have ordered the Midshipmen that were on the *Chattahoochee* on her & she is a vessel on which it is possible to learn something, & I think that Trimble & myself merit the benefit we might be able to derive from being on her. She has both fore & aft & square sails on her, & we might learn much about the standing rigging. Now that there is no prospect of my going on board of her, I wish to get away from this station as soon as possible & to go to sea above anything! I ought to be at sea, for I am now 19½ old the 7th inst. being my birthday. If I am ever to learn anything of my profession which I like, it is time I was about it. I am busy every day studying Bowditch & progress rapidly, so please let me go out upon the waste of waters soon. Now good-by. Remember me to Capt. Pegram. If I cannot get to sea, let me ordered away from here.

I am very Respectfully,
Your Obt. Svt.
Midn. H. T. Minor, Jr.

★★★★★

Minor continued his diary entries until the end of July, 1864, recounting his duties aboard ship, his attempts at study, and numerous visits with Annie. No entries were made from that point until November 1864. Sherman's forces were approaching the city and the *Savannah* was called upon several times to take up positions near Fort Jackson. With the ironclad guarding the approaches to Fort Jackson, Minor was among a group of men selected for an expedition against an enemy shore battery on Argyle Island. The city of Savannah was evacuated on December 21, 1864. Much of Minor's diary from this point on was evidently written hurriedly, and at times in lead pencil, making it extremely difficult to transcribe. I have included as much as I can, even if many words are unreadable, in order to give the reader a sense of what Minor was experiencing.

Tuesday, November 29, 1864

Got up at 7:30 & ate breakfast then went to quarters at 9:00 A.M. & exercised one of the guns of the division which I had charge of till yesterday. I have now but one gun. I learned yesterday that all of us were to be issued small arms, canteens, & haversacks, so thinking that I may need my infantry tactics soon, I today read over the 1st volume of *Hardee* [General William J. Hardee's *Rifle and Light Infantry Tactics,* published by Lippincott, Gramble & Co., 1854] & intend also to review the 2nd volume. The list of men above & along this book are the names of all the men who boarded the *Water Witch.* I found this book blank on board & used it for the purpose. They are all mainly in Mr. Pelot's. I had to await him & bring him down in the boat pulled down against the tide also in less than an hour. Relieved Trimble to supper & then read some little in *Hardee's Tactics in Battle* till 7 o'clock. I was ordered to take charge of 2 boats & to pull up the river & put up two globe lanterns in order that the ship which was to come up might know the channel. Fixed up my lights & then awaited the coming of the ship. It came up about 8, but owing to bad management on the part of the pilot, she got aground. I put up my lights on the objects the pilot told me to, but the night being foggy, he was deceived as to the distance they were from him. At 10:30 was called aboard & turned in to get up at 12 & keep the mid-watch. Had quite a disagreeable watch as I wanted rest & was relieved at 4 A.M. ... I wish to go on shore & fight Sherman for I do not think that this vessel will be of much effect when its crew are thrown on shore. I believe that Sherman intends really to attempt Savannah & if he finds it too much for him will go to the coast at Brunswick. We must not allow him to get to the sea coast for he will establish a base of operations which it will be impossible to move him from & then this state will be overrun at all times of the year. We have got him now & must capture the whole of his army. Went on watch at 12 & at 2:30 was relieved & ordered to take a boat & 12 men & pull as rapidly to town to take an order to Commodore Hunter & to bring down the pilot. Pulled up with my 12 oars in an hour & quarter against tide. Detained the *Firefly* by order till 4 in order that I might get the officers aboard & be towed back. Got all the officers aboard, out was relieved & turned in till 7.

Wednesday, November 30

    At 7 got up & dressed & then went on deck. We sent up for the *Sampson* to come down & pull us off the bar & at last she succeeded in doing so & we came up town. The *Sampson,* having gotten aground in pulling us off, was left to shift for herself, besides we could not afford her any assistance without again endangering the *Savannah* & she is the only vessel in this squadron that is worth a cent. After coming to an anchor, I was ordered to take the same boat I had yesterday & to go down to the ordnance officer & to get some small arms & _____ for the crew. Got back to the ship with them at 11 A.M. & then studied *Hardee's Camp & Drill.*

After dinner I again studied *Hardee* & at 4 P.M. went on watch. Wanted to go up to see Miss Annie Lamar today, but being on quarantine, could not. The 1st Lieut. thinks that the Capt. will release me tomorrow & if he does I shall go up. My uniform was to be ready today & I wanted to go get it but could not. At quarters I inspected the crew with small arms & then ate supper. Heard late this evening that the whole of Genl. Cleburne's division was here & if so would not be surprised to meet Uncle Dave. I do not think that the report is correct, however, & shall not then expect the pleasure I should have in meeting him. At 8 was relieved and turned in to get up at 4 A.M., & go on watch till 8.

Thursday, December 1, 1864

I spoke on yesterday to Vaughn [Master Henry L.] who has now the charge of *Water Witch* about the pet cat we found aboard of her & he told me that I might have her. I intend to take her to Va. with me. It is a most wonderful cat. It will fish & do many other things, it is also one of the most beautiful & the largest I ever saw. After 12 o'clock, got ready to go to town after dinner. Went to see Miss Annie Lamar & then walked with Miss Annie Sorell & herself a little way up the street. Miss Sorell came in to fulfill her engagement of taking a walk with Miss Annie. So I walked with them from Miss Annie's to where I could turn off to go to the tailors. Got my new coat & again went walking by myself out to the park. It was dark as I went out & I did not recognize many of the people. I met but did recognize Miss Jeanne Lamar, Mrs. George Mercer, & Miss Eliza Lamar. Slept up town tonight & got up & came down to the ship.

Friday, December 2

Our walk was quite a pleasant one & I enjoyed it much. Graves was with me. After eating breakfast, I took the deck till 12 & then was relieved & came below & studied some in *Company Drill* in Hardee. Relieved the officer of the deck to dinner & got ready & walked up town with Mr. Hudgins [Lieutenant William E.]. Went to the park & joined Miss Annie Lamar & Miss Jeanne. Walked home with them & they came down to the wharf & at 5:30 went up to ship. Ate supper & then took a nap till 8 when I went on watch till midnight, when I came below & turned in to get up at 7 A.M.

Saturday, December 3

After breakfast & quarters, studied Hardee till 12. Went on watch till 4 P.M., & then walked again to town with Hudgins & gave Miss Annie Lamar her veil which I had forgotten to give her yesterday when I told her good-by at her house. Joined Miss Jeanne McDonald & Miss Nina Anderson & walked home with Miss Jeanne, Mrs. Edward having joined Miss Nina. After tea went to see Miss Annie Lamar & found Miss Joe McD. with her. They, with Miss Lamar, were playing [the popular card game] euchre & I took a hand, Miss Annie & myself being partners. We beat them

The fountain in Central Park where Minor took many walks with Annie Lamar (Library of Congress).

badly, & at 9 I bid them good night & walked thru one of the darkest lanes I ever saw down to the ship, distant 2 miles. Got aboard at about 10 & & tried to go to sleep, but could not. At 12 got up & went on watch at 4 A.M.

Sunday, December 4

I was relieved & came below & went to sleep till 8:30. Got up, ate breakfast, & got ready to go to church. I went Presbyterian & heard quite a good sermon from Dr. Axton. Walked home with Miss Annie Lamar & parted from her not in the best of humor. Came down to the wharf, got in the boat, came up to the ship & after dinner went on watch at 4 & came off at eight then turned in to get up at 4 A.M.

Monday, December 5

After quarters, went to see Miss Annie Lamar & came away in quite good spirits. Went to Waley's by invitation & took a splendid dinner. Mr. Southerns was a nice host. After dinner we took a glass of sherry said to be 30 years old, but from its taste I should call it new wine. Then played 3 handed game of billiards with Southerns & Mr. Holst, then walked in the park & saw the ladies. After Tea went 'round to Mrs. George Mercers & we went to see Miss Eliza Lamar. Left soon & I went to bed at my room, got up early.

Tuesday, December 6

I walked down to ship. Received yesterday letter from her just one month after it was written. At 11:30 relieved Trimble to dinner & while on deck was seized with quite a bad chill. As soon as Trimble took the deck, I came below & turned in & having drawn up my feet my muscles contracted & I could not straighten. I suffered much from the pain. After my chills left me I had high fever which went off in time leaving me in a profuse perspiration. I then fell asleep & did not wake until....

Wednesday, December 7

Wednesday morning. I had read yesterday a note from Mrs. Babcock & with it a pair of socks for the little boy above attended to. I also read one from Mrs. Fairfax telling me that Miss Annie Lemar would leave for Augusta on Friday & wished to inform me of it. I got up & dressed this morning feeling quite well & went up {to} the city & to see Miss Annie till 11:30 then came aboard in order that I might not be left by the ship which was to have sailed at 12:30, but owing to the poorness of the rise in the tide we could not. At twelve I took the deck & stood watch till 4 P.M., then came below & studied Hardee. Went to bed at 8 & got up at 12. I could not sleep tonight till after 11. I had slept all the previous one. At 12 I went on watch till 4 & then turned in till 8 A.M.

Tuesday, December 8

Got up & went to breakfast then after quarters went to see Miss Annie Lamar. Had a splendid time & she told me that she did not intend to go to Augusta nor leave Savannah, at least not on the morrow & I was glad to hear it. At 2 I bid her good-by & came down to the ship & ate dinner meeting on my way down Midshipman Scharf & I brought him with me & we ate together. After dinner Scharf went ashore & at 4 P.M. I went on duty till 8. I was relieved after supper at 7:30 by Graves, & Trimble & myself went ashore & to see Miss Nina Anderson & Miss Georgia. We wanted them to go with us around to Miss Joe McDonald, but only Miss Nina could go, as Miss Georgia, having a composition to write, was not allowed to go. Miss Nina took one of my arms and one of Mr. Trimble's

& soon we were at Miss Joe's where we enjoyed ourselves. At 11 Miss Nina & myself came away from Joe's & I, after leaving her at home, walked down to the wharf, hailed the ship & came aboard & turned in to get up at 4 A.M. on Friday.

Friday, December 9

When I went on watch till 8 then came below & after dressing anew, ate breakfast & went ashore & to see if Miss Annie Lamar [was at home]. At first I was told that she had gone to Augusta, but just as I was moving away, she put her head out the window & told me she had not gone & I think it was quite evident. I went in & gave her, before I left, my little Smith & Wesson pistol which I had gotten from Paymaster Billings of the *Water Witch*. At about 2 I came away & down to the ship. After dinner again went to shore & to my room & then walked in the park, came out & as I was walking back met Miss Annie & Miss Jeanne L. & walked back with them there. After we got to Miss Annie's I went home with Jeanne & what she said amused me much & I shall remind her of it some of these days. After supper time I went to see Miss Annie & found Mr. L. all by himself. Miss Annie is leaving for a moment; gone over to the next house for a moment. After she _____ . She & all of them were going to Augusta tomorrow at 8. She said that they had intended to have done so, but the railroad being out, they could not. We played cutthroat chess till 10 when

A heavy Confederate gun in Fort McAllister (Library of Congress).

I came away but very reluctantly. She said something to me that garnered much pleasure.... I bid her goodnight, came down to my room, intend to get up at 7 A.M.

Saturday, December 10

Forgot to mention that last night went down to the *Sampson* at 11:15 to tell Mr. Carnes [Second Lieutenant William W., commander of the *Sampson*] good-by. He is ordered up the river & will leave tonight at 2 A.M. Mr. Carnes was asleep so I did not awake him but told all of my other friends onboard good-by & told Mr. Fairfax [Master Julian] to tell Mr. Carnes good-by for me & to tell him that I had come down to tell him myself. I think much of Mr. Carnes & have reason from what he says to others of me thinks a great deal of me, but both of us toward each other appear friends. I endeavor to disguise my feelings to him & he does the same. Walked down to ship after dressing which was not more than 4 squares & hailed, got in the boat, & went aboard. After eating breakfast went on watch at 8 & at 12 came off & seeing a stray wild goose floating about on the other shore, I got in a boat & pulled towards him. I knew my advantage would be to shoot him on the wing, so I determined to await till he should fly up & providing that he would fly straight for me. I got much nearer than I expected to before he flew & having my right barrel cocked, I pulled, but my gun snapped. I immediately cocked the left & let him have it & down he came. I shot him with ___ of shot & distance about ___ 55 or 80 yards. It was a splendid shot....

> [During this entry Minor began writing some portions by pencil and these are mostly too faint to transcribe.]

... have been skirmishing all day with Sherman & I am in hopes that soon they will order us out & give us a chance. General Sherman intends, I think, to first gain a position between Savannah & Fort Pulaski & he can easily do it & then to take the city. He cannot now have much ordnance & supplies of any kind & by gaining such a point he will have communication with his base for we cannot interrupt it. Once established at such a point as he doubtless will take Fort & then he can collect what he wishes in the way of supplies & also troops & will have a base of operations. Fort McAllister is in our possession, but it cannot be defended by land & must be evacuated if Sherman attempts it or surrendered. But I think we will hold Savannah & wish to do something. We ought to be thrown on shore for the obstructions & shore soldiers can do all the service necessary should a demonstration be made by water from the seaboard, & we can be useful on shore to boot, in fact, very useful. But enough. The first duty of a soldier or seaman is to obey orders & no matter how much I may regret it, I shall have to remain on board unless our Capt. sees fit to put us ashore. Tis hard that so many brave spirits as are in the navy here should all be liable to be kept idle & useless.... Should such be the case, we all would have to share the odium of not having assisted when we could & not be alone. This evening got up steam & started down the river, but running foul of a bar, we turned back as the tide was too low when we got clear. I kept the first watch tonight & heard the alarm guns fired, but could not discover any cause. They have been skirmishing all of this day & I expect that the ball will open tomorrow.

Sunday, December 11

Got up steam this morning & came down to our old anchorage at Fort Jackson. All of last night was quite.... I fear that Sherman has taken advantage of it to make an advantageous disposition of his forces. I think that an attack will be made from the seaward at the same time that he makes it from on the land. If so, we will have a plenty of work for we can dispose ourselves so as to engage two or three monitors at short range & so will have the advantage. Kept the watch from 12 to 4 P.M. My goose went splendidly for dinner. We had a plenty of stuffing & he was well cooked. I carved him & helped my messmates, all of whom were present. This has been quite a disagreeable day for a cold N.W. wind has been blowing since early this morning & bids fair for two or three days yet. Read some in the Bible which Annie gave me & then read Scott's *Lay of the*

View of the interior of Fort McAllister (Library of Congress).

East Minstrel. Turned in at 8 P.M. & got up & kept the mid-watch till 4 A.M.

Monday, December 12

Last night, or rather this morning, I was brought, by one of my watch, a fine pot of hot coffee & a hardtack & it warmed me up a great deal. Was relieved at 4 by Trimble & came below & smoked my pipe by a good fire & at 5 A.M. turned in to get up again at 7. The Capt. was today called up to see General Hardee & I am in hopes that something is to be done.

> Lieutenant General William J. Hardee was from Georgia and had been a prominent commander in the Army of Tennessee. He was now in charge of all forces in the Department of South Carolina, Georgia, and Florida.[12]

Heard this morning that on yesterday we killed 4,000 of the enemy & also that Jack Perry, the coxswain of Mr. Trimble's boat on the *Water Witch* expedition was killed. Jack was a good man & was wounded mainly in the same place as myself on the *Water Witch,* and I am sorry to hear of his death, but it is only rumor. I was told too by one of Wheeler's men that Uncle Dan C____ was one of the five generals said to be killed at the same time with Genl. Cleburne. I wanted to go today to see Miss Annie but could not. I hope it is only rumor that numbers my gallant uncle with the dead. I only wish that he would allow me to bear the colors of his brigade but hesitate to ask him.

> Five Confederate generals were killed at the Battle of Franklin, Tennessee, on November 30, 1864: Patrick R. Cleburne, States Rights Gist, Hiram B. Granbury, John Adams, and Otho F. Strahl. A sixth general, John C. Carter was mortally wounded.[13]

I should either distinguish myself or be extinguished, for that's

Lieutenant General William J. Hardee (*Miller's Photographic History of the Civil War*).

my motto. Fixed up my pistols today in order that they may be ready for service. At 4 P.M. went on watch & came off at 8. Learned some little seamanship during my watch from King our boatswains mate. Turned in to get up at 4 A.M. & keep the cold deck till 8. Last night got up steam & shifted our position this morning during my watch. Saw three white rockets & one red one & having reported them to the Capt. was ordered to beat to quarters. We remained at them till after daylight & at 8 I was relieved & got permission to go up town which I did at 9:30 & called on Miss Annie L. I had not been there long when Graves who had also come up to the city told me that the Capt. wanted me on board. I immediately came down to the *Isondiga* as instructed & got a boat & came on board *Savannah* & found that they were about to send out a boat expedition & I was expected to participate.

The following is what I desire to be done with my personal effects should I be killed or taken prisoner. I wish them to be sent to Bishop Elliot with the request that he will retain them till he can deliver them to some member of my family. All papers I wish to be secret & to be preserved till they can be done with as above desired.

{Signed} Midn. H. T. Minor, Jr.

P.S. All manuscripts and the matter herein contained, I wish to remain private & to be done with as the rest.

At 5:30 went off from the ship in charge of whale boat. Mr. Trimble & Dr. Stokley [Assistant Surgeon William S.] went with me. Mr. Marmaduke [First Lieutenant Henry H.] had the barge. The whale boat & barge of the *Ga.*[*Georgia*] were with us also. We went up the river all along the enemies' line of sharpshooters, but discovered none of the boats we were in search of. Our oars were muffled & we were not discovered by the sharpshooters, but it was rather ticklish business. Came back to ship at 2 P.M. & turned in to get up on Wednesday.

Wednesday, December 14

At 7:30 & after eating breakfast, went on watch at 8 till 12. Was relieved by Trimble & came below & being up the greater part of last night, laid down & slept till dinner then relieved Trimble. The *Isondiga* passed up & has been firing at the enemy's batteries. I laid down again after coming off deck, but could not go to sleep. The rumor today came of Sherman having taken Fort McAllister & it was confirmed this evening. I think now that we will evacuate this place & if we do I shall loose all of my clothes & a man may as well be dead as in the Confederacy without them. Should they evacuate we will be the last to leave for it will be left to us to cover the retreat of our army across the river. After supper I went on watch at 8 till midnight. At 9 P.M. saw 1 white rocket, later another & at ten Capt. Hunt of Hardee's staff came on board & the boatswain called away also. Heard up the river before 9 the report of a heavy gun. At 10:30 our boats shoved off manned as on the night before & we pulled up the river past the enemy's batteries distant as we passed some 200 yards. We got along finely with our muffled oars till we passed a line of the enemy's sharpshooters & soon after got aground with Mr. M's [Marmaduke's] boats. The enemy discovered us there & poured a rapid fire into us. It was quite foggy & by keeping quite we were not readily discovered except by the sound. The sharpshooters fired splendidly by that, however, for two shots took effect in my boat & one in Mr. M's. They were about a hundred yds from us & coming nearer. Our orders were to discover if the enemy were on Argyle Isle, & this was proof enough for we were opposite it. We soon got out of their fire by coming about & having gone below & waited a little while, again passed up & over to the Isle & discovered that they had retreated to the Ga. Shore. We remained there awaiting what we could hear or see till it was nearly 4 A.M., thus leaving just time enough before daylight to re-pass their batteries & make good our retreat. Our orders were not to go above the Isle. We came down without discovery & after a pull of nine miles again reached our ship at little before 6 & all turned in to get up at 7 & eat breakfast. After breakfast & quarters, I laid down & slept till 12 when I went on watch. At 12:30, called away armed boats & I was relieved & got ready. Went up to the *Isondiga* & was left there to await orders. The duty we were sent on was deemed too hazardous & Capt. Brent, having remonstrated with Genl. Hardee, I received at midnight, orders to return to the ship. I am sorry, for I wished to go very much. We were to land on shore under a battery of the enemy on Argyle Isle & then to take, if possible, the battery. There would have been much loss of life doubtless, but I think that we should have been successful. I had charge of one of the two boats & Mr. M. the other. The *Isondiga* was to open on the battery & we were to take it while she attracted their attention. The affair was to have come off in the night & must have succeeded. I do not say that I wish such work, but I do want the Navy to stand high as a gallant set of fellows as they are. I met on the *Isondiga* Parish Davis who came up in the boat that brought my orders. I put Mr. Graves, who was with me in the boat that came up & got into mine, shoved off to proceed 6 miles to the *Savannah*. Mr. M. had returned to the ship at 8:30 of the evening. Went to bed on board & slept soundly till 7.

Friday, December 16

Got up & got ready to go to town but could not go as no liberty was granted either to officers or men. So I wrote a note to Miss Annie L. & then asked permission to take twenty volunteers & Mr. Graves & go on the isle & sharp shoot the Yankees on the western end of it. This was refused me also & feeling in a very bad humor I came below & took up

Veile on "Field Fortifications and Artillery." Studied till I was sleepy & then went to sleep till dinner. Got up, ate it, & then wrote some letters till 4 P.M. & when I went on watch till 8. Heard that Genl. Hardee had made application to Capt. Brent for 5 officers & the Capt. said that he could not spare the officers. I am disgusted with the way affairs are managed here in the Navy. Tonight the Capt. has consented to let old Capt. Thorn___ and a lieut. of the *Georgia* & a lieut. on shore duty go with 20 men to man the battery. I heard that Maj. Poole had charge of the batteries & as I know him, I intend to ask him to let me have them & to make application for me. I also intend to ask the Capt. to let me go in the place of the lieut. form the *Georgia*. I have been drilled in heavy artillery & think that I can get along finely in it. If I once get them, I intend to have Graves if possible.

Saturday, December 17

The Capt. refused to let me go in place of Lieut. ___ this morning. I kept the watch from 4 till 8 & then came off duty & got permission to go to town. Went to see Miss Annie L. & also Mrs. Pollock & the Miss McDonald. After tea went to see Miss Anderson. Played Whist till 9:30 & then bid them good night. Came down to ship & turned in to get up at 8 A.M. of ...

Sunday, December 18

& go on watch till 12. Forgot to mention that on yesterday went to see Maj. Poole who told me that it was Col. Paul who had charge of the batteries. Maj. Poole promised to speak to Col. Paul about me & so did my sweetheart. I expect the application to be made for me & I have reason to hope from what Mr. Hudgins told me today that the Capt. will let me go. I think in fact that application was made for me last night. Late yesterday the Yanks demanded the surrender of the city & garrison. It was refused & my information is official. Should they evacuate as I now think they will they will attempt doubtless to run this ship to Charleston. I should like much to be on it if they do. If I know of it & I am out at the battery, I will come in immediately.

Monday, December 19
[illegible entry]

Tuesday, December 20

& having recd. orders to be party & the batteries got ready. I had nearly every thing. I had two walking canes .... what I intended to take to Granpa & Pa. Showed my sweetheart my letters ... & told her goodbye. Then walked about 10 miles to the batteries. The enemy were only 450 yards from us & I had to defend a narrow causeway. During the day, I was charged papers with some of my men. At 7:30 was ordered to evacuate & I destroyed all my _____ & then I left. Marched ahead of the column & were to my _____ wrote to tell my own good little _____ Goodby & having gotten _____ _____ clothes again, put out pressed _____ _____ at 10 o'clock & caught my command. Marched all night till....

Wednesday, December 21

When rested short time, & then continued the march till 5 o'clock in the evening. Saw Bishop Elliott on the road, today a refuge from his home. Slept all night on an empty stomach & dreamed of my Annie. I should like to know what she thinks of me now, whether she will always love me.

Thursday, December 22

Spent the whole day in camp. Saw on the road today Graves & Trimble. Am attached to Mercer's Brigade. Have been thinking of Annie all day. I wonder will I do as I have promised, love you always. Yes, I feel that I will, for you are the only one I ever met that appreciates me, & you know my every feeling. I love to think of you. I know you will write to me, but how can I ever write to you. I know that I would rather think of you than write of you. So I will lay here & think I am all by myself, my men being camped nearby. At 5:30 got on cars & started for Charleston. We will have to run the gauntlet by the Coosawhatchie [River] where the enemy have several land batteries & are able to bring their vessels into action. At 1:30 passed the batteries safely. One of their shells went directly over my head & if I had not been laying down would have killed me. Our trip on the cars has been very disagreeable all the time up to now, & this is....

Friday, December 23

At 10:30 A.M., we have been on flat open cars packed as closely as sheep. The *Savannah* was set on fire at 7:15 P.M. of Wednesday, & today I have been with her crew, having joined them on Thursday evening & the whole navy has been on this train. We are now about 45 miles from Charleston & we will reach there tonight I hope. I cannot help thinking of the separation. I have been compelled to _____ go from the one I love without even having an opportunity to tell her.

Saturday, December 24

Got _____ to Charleston at 6:30 & camped just where we got off cars. I went up to the city & got a good supper _____ _____. Slept in the dirt till morning then went to find Commodore Ingraham [Duncan N. commander of the Charleston Squadron] & Capt. Brent to find out what _____ to _____. Was ordered to march the men across the city from Ashley River to the Cooper & to put them on board the receiving ship *Indian Chief*. Some of us were quite uncomfortable & had no place to sleep & in the evening Mdns. Wilkinson came on board. He & I got a boat &

went onboard the *Palmetto State* ironclad. On this night met on this vessel Midshipman Inglis [John Henry] & Master Pearson [James M.]. Was introduced to Lieut. Bowen [Robert James] & Dr. Lynch [Arthur M.]. Master Banks [John S.] was aboard also. _____ _____ Paymaster _____ Brokenbrough [George L.], of the *Georgia*, a thorough scoundrel in the

Top: The Confederate evacuation of Savannah, December 21, 1864 (*Harper's Pictorial History of the Great Rebellion*). *Bottom:* Upon the evacuation of Savannah, the navy yard was set ablaze (*Frank Leslie's Illustrated Newspaper*).

steerage. They are having quite a merry Xmas eve, but I cannot enjoy one with them. Went to bed with Wilkinson and got up at 7:30.

Sunday, December 25

After eating breakfast, I went on board the *Indian Chief* with Wilkinson. I then came with him to James Island where we camped & commanded a detachment of naval pickets, _____ quite a dull Xmas & will turn into & get _____ hope much refreshed. Wish I could spend this Xmas at home enjoying it more than this night.

Monday, December 26

Got up 8 A.M. & went up town and onboard ironclad str. *Charleston.* Saw Otey Bradford [Lieutenant] & Dan Colcock [Master Daniel D.]. Then came on *Indian Chief* & went on watch

Commander Duncan Ingraham (Scharf: *History of the Confederate States Navy*).

at 12 till 4 P.M. In the evening was told that the Capt. wished me to act as his aid[e] & that I should be expected to go on shore every day. Wrote letter to my sweetheart, Miss Annie, but could find no way of sending it to her. Will do it doubtless by the blockade. Will write a letter to my mother & send it to Miss Annie to send to Ma for me. Had no _____ at all today, now goodnight.

Tuesday, December 27

Went up town & had quite a busy time. I ran all over the city for Commodore Tucker [Commander John R., commander of the ironclad CSS *Chicora*] & Capt. Brent. Met several young men from [the] *Savannah.* Wrote my letters to Miss Annie & Ma last night & gave them to Col. Waddy to send by flag of truce to Savannah. Col. Paul introduced himself to me at the time & told me that he got quite a touching note from Miss Annie about me. I told him that she told me she had written to him about me. He knows my father very well. Got orders to Richmond this evening & transportation will leave on Thursday for there. Intend to stop at Charlotte if possible & to see Cousin Mathew.

Wednesday, December 28

Do now recollect what occurred except that got on freight train Greensboro, North Carolina. Got on another then was put in charge of a box car, which Genl. [Samuel] McGowan in it & it was he that put me in charge. Got to Danville where I gave 80 dollars for enough for two people to eat of ham & eggs. There were four of us that partook of the fugal meal. This was....

Thursday, December 29

At 12 at night of this day got on the Danville cars & arrived at Richmond on Sunday, January 1, 1865. Looked all over the city for Uncle Will Hart & Bob

Captain John R. Tucker (Scharf: *History of the Confederate States Navy*).

Minor but could not find either of them nor a boarding house, so I took my _aps to Mrs. Barnes & then came back to the American Hotel where my companions stopped & took a room with them at the rate of 40 dollars a day. Went to bed early tonight & got up late on....

The End Approaches

Minor was now back in Richmond, a dreary and desperate city at this point of the war. The winter of 1864–65 was an intensely cold one with snow from three to six inches deep lying constantly on the ground. The James River became so clogged with ice that it became almost impossible for the ships of the James River Squadron, including the *Patrick Henry*, to maneuver. Grant's armies continued to tighten their hold on the city, and few supplies were getting through to the ragged gray soldiers in the trenches. Civilians also suffered as most store shelves in Richmond were bare. It was in this bleak atmosphere of a frigid city under siege that, at the urging of his cousin, Minor resumed his studies on the *Patrick Henry*.[14]

Richmond, Virginia
Monday, January 2, 1865

When I went to breakfast & then over to Messrs. G_ & A office to get some funds being entirely out & barefooted to boot. I got a pr. of boots $250.00 pr. having got the amount of $500.00 from the agents Messrs. _____ & Williams & gave the receipt in Pa's name as _____ collected for him the receipt received. Forgot to mention that on Sunday evening called at Mrs. Hernders to see Mrs. George Mercer from Savannah & then met however _____ & his son. Saw Miss Mollie & soon took leave. I told Mrs. Mercer all I knew of her husband. Was forced to spend this night at the American Hotel & will I hope tomorrow get off to Fredericksburg to see them all. Uncle Will is there too I imagine. I got leave on yesterday till the 8th Inst. when my examination comes off.

Tuesday, January 3

Concluded not to go to Fredericksburg till I saw Uncle Will, so after breakfast went round to Major Smith's office & the first man I met was Uncle Will. I then went to see Cousin Bob [Minor] at the Office of Ordnance & Hydrography. Saw him & he advised me to give up my furlough & to come onboard & to cram for my examination which I determined to do. So I went back to see Uncle Will & to tell him my determination. Stayed at his room tonight & in the morning of

Wednesday, January 4

Went to see Mrs. Marshall & Miss Ellen then wrote a letter to cousin Lou Scott & came on board of the ship & went straight to work at my books. Slept very uncomfortably this night & got up at 7 A.M.

Thursday, January 5

After eating breakfast went to study. Last night Mr. Blackey [Andrew Blackie] our boatswain gave us some lectures on seamanship & I hope improved us some little. Read over about one-half of my algebra & some little on steam. Studied the whole of this day & kept the mid watch at night. This evening I was thinking of going to Mr. Seddin [James A. Seddon, Secretary of War] & asking him to give me a commission as captain of light artillery & orders to join to the Trans Mississippi Department & get [to] my company. Got to thinking of Miss Stendod & thought how much she would think of me if I were the captain in Artillery.

Friday, January 6

Got up at 7 & went to study. Slept comfortably all last night before & after my watch. Continued the review of my algebra as I wish to be found posted one time at least & hope that I may be able to catch up in some of my other studies. Should have studied more at Savannah but when a man is in love how can he study[?]

Saturday, January 7

Kept the watch from 8 to 12 then dried my feet & socks which I had

gotten very wet on watch & my over coat. This has been quite a disagreeable day as it has been drizzling the whole of it. I had the watch from 4
to 8 also today as we are keeping days duty & relief. Did not have time to
do my studying till after dark, & then went to bed as I had to get up &
keep the morning watch till 8 when I came off duty & hope will remain
so for some time.

Sunday, January 8

I went up town & to church at St. Pauls [Episcopal Church] then
called with Uncle Will on the Herndons & spent quite a pleasant time. Went
round to Uncle Will's room & took dinner. Smoked & sat till 6:30 when I
came down & was going to see Cousin Bob Minor to ask him if he could
take care of me tonight when I met him on his way to church so I turned
back with him & went to church also. After church went round to Cousin
Bob's room & he told me all about his expedition & I told him about the
Water Witch. Went to bed at 10:30 & slept till 8 of next morning.

> The expedition to which Minor refers was a secret mission to capture the
> USS *Michigan*—the only armed Federal vessel on Lake Erie—and to release
> the Confederate prisoners being held on Johnson's Island. A commando
> group consisting of approximately fifteen officers and sailors was formed
> under the command of Lieutenant Robert D. Minor. At Wilmington, North
> Carolina, on the dark night of October 10, 1863, Minor, along with his fel-
> low commandos, filed aboard the blockade runner *R. E. Lee* which was com-
> manded by Lieutenant John Wilkinson. After a harrowing run through the
> Federal blockaders offshore, in which the *Lee* was struck and momentarily
> set on fire, the group reached Halifax, Nova Scotia, on October 16. Dividing
> into separate parties, the men set out overland through Canada with instruc-
> tions to rendezvous later in Montreal. Just when it seemed that their plan
> was assured of success, an informant betrayed them to U. S. Secretary of War
> Stanton, who immediately contacted the governor-general of Canada. Not
> wishing to incur the wrath of their neighbor to the south, Canadian officials
> broadcast a warning to all their military outposts to be on the lookout for the
> commandos. With the plan now revealed there was little possibility for its
> success, and the enterprise was called off. One by one the Confederate officers
> and men made their way back home, or to Europe for further assignments.[15]

Monday, January 9

When ate Breakfast & went to see Mr. [Stephen R.] Mallory, but
could not see him till after 12 so called on Miss Anna Dean & then went
again to see Mr. Mallory. Spent quite a pleasant time with Miss Anna but
was not much pleased with my interview with Mr. Mallory. I must resign
& that soon. Circumstance must control, however, & I know not what to
do just yet. Came down to ship at 1:30 & found letter for me from Cousin
Lou Scott which gave me much pleasure at the reading of it. Answered
the letter immediately. Will write to Edward Rives soon & let him know
that I contemplate paying him a visit soon after my examination comes

Top: The Confederate blockade runner *R.E. Lee* (Naval Historical Center).
Bottom: The USS *Michigan*, initial objective of the Johnson's Island expedition (U.S. Navy).

Lieutenant John Wilkinson, commander of the *R.E. Lee* on the Johnson's Island expedition (Naval Historical Center).

off. Studied some little in my algebra this evening till supper time.

Tuesday, January 10

Been a wet & disagreeable day till late in evening. Studied steam nearly all this day. Got an invitation to Miss McCans's party & will attend. I think it comes off tomorrow night. Went uptown tonight after study hours & played two or three games of billiards, turned in late & got up early. There is quite a freshet in the river & it has over flown its banks. Deposited with my wash woman $40 to be taking out in washing. Sent off my letter to Cousin Lou, wrote a statement of my expenses to Secretary Mallory & hope he will pay me the amount I request to be allowed. Will take it up to him tomorrow.

Wednesday, January 11

Spent the morning in study, in the evening got ready & went to Miss Anna McCan's Party, had quite a pleasant time. Left them at 2:30 & went to bed at uncle Wills room. Got up late & came down to ship & studied all of Thursday except the time it took me to take my account up for Mr. Mallory's approval. Slept quite uncomfortably tonight & got up early on Friday feeling quite unwell, feared am going to have another chill season. Must go, therefore, to the mountains & get well of them. Wrote a day or two ago to Edward Rives & will hear from him soon doubtless. Slept uncomfortably this night also for I had fever & awoke with it in the morning.

> The Naval Academy was not immune to the various ailments that were sweeping the James River Squadron. Midshipman James Morris Morgan, another student at the school, wrote concerning what we today would probably term as the "flu," that the chills and fevers were
>
> "not the fashionable "malaria," but regular old-time chills and fever, which first made the agonizing tremors pass through the frame and the teeth chatter and rattle, the chill only to be allayed by the heat of a burning fever, which always followed it. The mouth became parched and the dry tongue clove to the roof of the mouth. In those days it would have been considered a crime to give a sufferer from fever a drop of cool water!"

"It was my day and hour for a chill, so I sought out a quiet place on the deck, where the planks looked soft, and lay down to shake it off. This performance was not included in the routine of the ship, but was as regular as the beat to general quarters. As we slept in hammocks and they were stowed away in the daytime, we were allowed to lie down any place where we did not interfere with the routine of the ship. With the exception of some of the boys from the alligator states, most of us were sufferers from the cause, and many of them were also weakened from chronic dysentery brought on by the bad food they had to eat; but simple chills and fever were never considered of sufficient to allow one to be excused from either duty, lessons, or drills."[16]

Saturday, January 14

Studied some little in trigonometry & came in gaining spirit the whole day in study of some kind or other. Wrote to Mr. Carnes & to Buckell.

Sunday, January 15

Has been raining all day so, I did not go to church. Saw Captain [Benjamin P.] Loyall [Commandant of Midshipmen] who told me that he was going to allow the benefit of Practical Seamanship & I am glad of it.

Monday, January 16

Went aloft as a top sail yard man & liked the exercise very much. Had much more practical study today & learned how to signal. Pulled in the evening in the boats & I had charge of [a] launch. We were exercised as in fleet....

Wednesday, January 18

Practical exercises again & tonight lecture from Captain Loyall. Discussion on the strain on the mass necessary to raise one ton from the deck.

Thursday, January 19

Same routine as yesterday & lecture on mathematics tonight from Captain Loyall. Was asked to work on example

Midshipman James Morris Morgan (Naval Historical Center).

& at last succeeded in doing it. It was considered quite a difficult expression to get rid of.

Friday, January 20

Same thing as yesterday from 10 to 11:30 infantry tactics from 11:30 to 12:30, practical seamanship, from 12:30 to 1:30, drawing, then dinner and at 3 P.M. till 4 P.M., broad sword exercise from 4 to 5. Boat exercise & then parade & supper, then from 7:30 to 9:30, lecture from Captain Loyall. This routine will continue for some time & will in time be changed.

Saturday, January 21

Answered Ed. Rives's letter & then went uptown & had quite a disagreeable time as it was sleeting & has continued all day. There were no exercises today, but holiday as at school. I came down & did not feel very well so I turned in & did not get up to supper & am captain of a crew & will always have to account for 17 of the midshipmen.

Sunday, January 22

Did not go up to church today as I was not well & it has been quite a disagreeable day, for it has been drizzling all the time. Studied some little today in geometry & also wrote a letter by Flag of Truce to Miss Annie L. Went to see if she had written to me on yesterday but was again disappointed.

Monday, January 23

No exercises today on account of the weather. I am today acting adjutant, as Hogue [W. S. Hogue] is sick. I am ranking midshipman on board at the time & have been ever since I have been here & am one of the senior ones in the Confederacy.

Tuesday, January 24

Exercises in small arms & in Seamanship. No great gun exercise or boat exercise. I have been quite sick for last two or three days my bowels being out of order. Tonight I intend to take opium & hope it will do me some good.

Wednesday, January 25

Exercised in small arms as I was the captain, had no exercise in seamanship. At 12:30 went to drawing lessons then dinner after which exercised with broad sword then went up to the city to see Houge who is in the hospital. Met several of my class just from Mobile, they all rank me & I am sorry of it. I hope this time to stand above them & if I can study will do it. Had no boat exercise this evening.

Some of Minor's classmates from his previous tour on the *Patrick Henry* had been assigned to the naval squadron at Mobile, Alabama.

Thursday, January 26

Had an opportunity of writing home. Midshipman [J. Thomas] Scharf has resigned & intends to get a pay from secretary of war to go home. He is a Baltimorian & has promised to send my letters to their destination. I also wrote a long letter to Miss Annie L & received one from her today. It came through the lines. The letter is one I prize very much. At the same time it was handed me I received one from her Aunt Mrs. McLeod of Augusta telling me news that was gratifying except that Mr. L had taken the oath. Have message for Parish Davis & will send it to him as soon as I find out where he is. I do not recollect what has occurred during the days of this month up to the 1st of February, 1865. I have been quite sick for some time my bowels being out of order. On this day my class was relieved from all practical exercises & was notified that on the morrow the examination of it would take place.

Thursday, February 2, 1865

We were all examined on this day but some time will elapse before we will know our standing. This is Thursday & we all would leave after our examination but none of us could get it. I then went to Captain Parker & asked for leave for three days in order that I might go upon Friday evening & come back on Sunday evening & see my cousins. He would not give me leave because he said that he wanted me to study. I got, however, his permission to go up on Friday & come down on Sunday.

Friday, February 3

We all expect to be made passed midshipman in June & therefore I do not regret that I have to remain here 'till then for the purpose of preparing myself. At 1:30 today I went uptown & got ready for going upon the train at 3:30 P.M. I got from Uncle Will Hart $35, as I was out of money.

Sunday, February 5

I got to the depot & got on the train & came back to Richmond where I arrived at 3 o'clock & came aboard of the Ship. My bowels were not at all benefited by my trip & I am going on the sick list tomorrow.

Monday, February 6

Studied hard all day & went to the sick list.

Tuesday, February 7

Studied all of this day also & remained on sick list. Drew from paymaster 2 blankets & gave him certificate of when last paid. He owes me 20 yards of cloth & 1 blue cap.

Wednesday, February 8

Studied all of this day & remained on the sick list. Got a letter from

Lieutenant Carnes & shall answer it soon. He gave me some good hints for my improvement.

Thursday, February 9

Studied hard all day & have progressed some little. My previous studies have been mostly reviewed.

Friday, February 10

Spent this day in study also & practical exercises.

Saturday, February 11

Went up town but did not stay very long. Got from Grubbs & Williams 3 hundred dollars & receipted in my fathers name. I need this money for the purpose of getting some shirts & having some clothes made. I get the cloth from the government at a reduced price.

Sunday, February 12

Did not go up to church but stayed aboard & read something useful.

Monday, February 13

Studied all day till 4:30 when I went up town to have my cloth made up. I will get two pair [of] pants & a jacket made for $100.00 as every thing [is] furnished but the buttons & cloth by the tailor. Came back on time for study hours & supper & went to bed early to get up early at 4 A.M. & study till 7 A.M.

Tuesday, February 14

Went to work to prepare for inspection which came off at 8 A.M., then breakfast & then recitations & practical exercises till 1:30 when we had leisure till 2, then dinner & leisure till 3 when we had a recitation till 4, then practical exercise of some kind till ½ hour before supper which came off at 6:30. This was the general routine every day & is full of interest.

Wednesday, February 15

Spent like the former & so was Thursday the 16th. Forgot to mention that on Wednesday I received a letter from Edward Rives telling me that his sister was in town & that she would be glad to see me. Will call on her tomorrow.

Friday, February 17

Studied all of this day. Late this evening requested to be allowed to go up to see Miss Rosalie Rives, but it was refused. Went to bed early, got up early, had two recitations one in seamanship & one in gunning then went up town. Called on Miss Rives, spent quite a pleasant time. Came back a few squares [&] took dinner with Willie Hart, then we both walked up town. I went to see Uncle Will but he had gone up to Caroline County so I missed him. Walked out Franklin Street, saw all of the pretty young ladies & bowed to several of them. After supper time went to see Cousin Bob Minor. Met Captain Brooke [John M. Brooke, chief of Naval Ordnance and Hydrography], Captain [John McIntosh] Kell, & Cousin Nonie. Came down to sleep at 10:30 & went to bed having first asked permission to be allowed to go down the river.

Sunday, February 19

My request was refused, so on Sunday I got permission to pull down with several other gentlemen, but we could not remain away long enough to enable us to get back within the required tide, so we had to give it up. Captain Parker refused

Captain John McIntosh Kell (Naval Historical Center).

to give us the permission that I shall ever think he should have given. Did not go to church today as I could not go on Shore.

Monday, February 20

Spent the day in study. After muster went up town & got my clothes. My Jacket fits me quite well but my pants were both pair ruined as they were cut badly. Came aboard after paying 100 dollars for them & went to studying. Several very pretty ladies came aboard today. I was introduced to them & requested to show them the ship. They stayed till after muster & parade & then went ashore.

Tuesday, February 21

Studied hard all day long & made good recitations. There is a rumor afloat that we are to be put in the Army. Received a letter from Edward Rives telling me that his sister, Miss Rosalie, was in the city & would be glad to see me. Will go up at the first opportunity.

Friday, February 24

Asked permission to go up to see Miss R. after supper but did not get it. Willie Hart came down to see me. I wrote to Savannah by Flag of Truce to Miss Annie L.

Saturday, February 25

Went up town after exercises were over. Called to see Miss Rosalie Rives & felt a great deal of curiosity to test the saying of the Man of the World in Bulwers, "What will he do with it that an object once loved when looked on again after an elapse of years causes not the emotion of yore." I once loved or imagined that I loved Miss R, but think that the man of the world speaks truly & that both Darrell & Bulwer are at fault in many cases where they assert that an object once loved will always be so. Spent quite a pleasant time with Miss R. & then came down to Willie Hart's quarters & took dinner with him, then we both walked up town & upon Franklin street where I met & bowed to the Miss Dunlaps, & Miss McCan, Miss Dean, & Mrs. Herndons. Came down to the ship after seeing Cousin Bob Minor, Cousin Nonie, & Captain Kell who was the executive officer of the *Alabama*, [CSS *Alabama*] also went to see Uncle Will but he had gone up to Uncle Frank Scotts so I did not see him.

> John McIntosh Kell was at this time commander of the ironclad CSS *Richmond* of the James River Squadron.

Sunday, February 26

Spent this day on board as I could not go up to church.

Monday, February 27

Do not know what I did on this day nor on the succeeding days so I shall commence from today the 19th of March, 1865. Have been quite sick for the last week. Had intermittent fever. The navy has become defunct, & it is my duty I think to resign & go into the Army. If Pa were south I think he would be willing for me to do so. Will try to go into the Army with a commission if possible, should I get orders to sea I shall not resign because I will then be serving my country but they must not expect me to remain here & let others fight it out for me. I would be unworthy of my father were I to do so, & I will not do it. This is Sunday. On yesterday I went to see Mr. Thomas Snead, but did not see him. Saw him day before yesterday & he promised to assist me all he could. Will see him again on Monday & get him to go with me to the secretary of [the] navy & secretary of war. If Mr. Mallory will order me to sea, I will not go to the secretary of war at all.

Monday, March 20, 1865

Do not recollect what took place on this day, nor any of the succeeding ones till....

Sunday, April 2, 1865

On this day every thing was in a stir about Richmond & I was sent to the hospital having suffered for nearly two weeks with dysentery, all of my passages being bloody. At 6 P.M. all of the midshipman left Richmond for Danville as did many other persons & it was rumored that Richmond was being evacuated. I was in Belvins Block on 13th street so I determined to get down to the Danville depot by 6:30 on Monday morning so I went to work & put up 2 white undershirts, 1 flannel overshirt, & a Jacket, & pair of pants with a towel, & my shawl, & a blanket this being all I could possibly carry in my weak state. I then had my trunk, two overcoats & a pair of blankets carried to Messrs. G & Appersons office & left them with Mr. Apperson who was in. It was now about 9:30 P.M., & I wanted to leave my things with Messrs Grubbs & Williams but their office was not open so I drew from Mr. Apperson $300 dollars giving him an order on Grubbs & W. for its payment then went to bed at the hospital & got up early.

> Ordered to guard the Confederate archives and treasury which was to accompany the president and cabinet on their exodus from Richmond, the midshipmen from the *Patrick Henry* were responsible for the security of nearly half a million dollars in gold, silver specie, and bullion. Because he was ill, Minor was not able to join his comrades on this important mission.

Monday, April 3

Went down to the Danville depot. Wanted to have written some letters & left them to be sent by the mail but felt too sick to do so. When I got to the depot I was told that the last train had left. I knew this to be a humbug so I went over to Manchester & found there several trains & got aboard of one of them. Last night nearly every store in Richmond was

The evacuation of Richmond, Virginia, April 2, 1865 (National Park Service).

broken into & robbed & this morning many large buildings were on fire. Warricks large flourmill was the most perfect fire I ever saw from its very bottom to high above its top was one continued sheet of flame. Did not get off till nearly nine & then the Yankees were in the city.

The evacuation of Richmond was a traumatic and catastrophic event in the life of the Confederacy. Captain Parker, writing after the war, has left a graphic account of this frantic evacuation:

"The next morning I walked down to Rocketts, and went on board my ship. We had the customary Sunday muster and inspection, and as we piped down I observed a company of Home Guards going out in the direction of Wilton, and I wondered at it. Shortly after I received a dispatch from the Secretary of the Navy which read as follows: "Have the corps of midshipmen, with the proper officers, at the Danville depot to-day at 6 P.M., the commanding officer to report to the Quartermaster General of the Army."

"Sending for Captain Rochelle I directed him to carry out the order and to have three days provisions cooked to carry. He asked me if I would go myself. I told him no; that he would go in command and I would remain and take care of the ship; that he would probably be back in a few days. While preparations were being made, it struck me that it would be as well to go to the Navy Department myself and obtain more definite information. I landed, and as I passed Rocketts (the landing-place of our river steamboats) I met a large number of prisoners on their way to the boats to be sent down to be exchanged. It passed through my mind at the instant that in the case of the evacuation of Richmond this was just what would be previously done, and it had not been the custom to send them off in the middle of the day—they were always sent off at daylight. However I pursued my way up Main street and in a few moments met a clerk who inquired of me how he could get down to Drewry's Bluff. I told him, and observing him to be excited inquired if there were any news. "Why don't you know," said he with his eyes starting out of his head, *"Richmond is to be evacuated this evening!"* I at once returned to the *Patrick Henry* and gave orders for all hands to be at the Danville depot at 6 o'clock with the exception of Lieutenant Billups and ten men whom I left to burn the ship. I then went to the Navy Department and saw Mr. Mallory. He told me the news. The city was to be evacuated that evening, and my command was to take charge of the Confederate treasure and convey it to Danville. Everything was being packed up for carrying off about the departments, though a good many things had been sent away in March in anticipation of this event. In the city those who had anything to do were at work at it, and yet in the midst of all the excitement there was a peculiar quiet—a solemnity—I have never ceased to remember; perhaps the pale, sad faces of the ladies aided to bring it about—they knew it was impossible for them to leave, and they prepared to share the fate of their beloved city with the same heroism they had exhibited during the past four years. The provost marshal had given orders to his men to seize and destroy all the liquor they could find in the stores, and they did so—a wise precaution. I went to the depot at 6 o'clock and found the treasure packed in the cars, and the midshipmen under Captain Rochelle in charge of it. So far as I know there was about half a million of dollars in gold, silver and bullion; at least that is what the senior teller told me, as well as I recollect. I saw the boxes containing it many times in the weary thirty days I had it under my protection, but I never saw the coin. The teller and his assistant clerks had charge of the money, and the corps of midshipmen guarded and eventually saved it. In addition to the Confederate money, there was also some belonging to the Richmond banks. It was in charge of their officers, and traveled with us for safety. I had nothing to do with it, but, of course, gave it our protection."

"At the depot, the scene I find hard to describe. The President's train was to precede mine, which was expected to be the last out of the city; both trains were packed—not only inside, but on top, on the platforms, on the engine,— *everywhere,* in fact, where standing room could be found and those who could not get that "hung on by their eyelids." I placed sentinels at the doors of the depot finally, and would not let another soul enter."

"While waiting in the depot I had an opportunity of seeing the President and his Cabinet as they went to the cars. Mr. Davis preserved his usual calm and dignified manner, and General Breckenridge (the Secretary of War), who had determined to go out on horseback, was as cool and gallant as ever— but the others, I thought, had the air (as the French say) of wishing to be off. General Breckenridge stayed with me some time after the President's train had gone, and I had occasion to admire his bearing under the circumstances. The President's train got off about 8 P.M.; but there was much delay with mine. Hour after hour passed and we did not move."

"The scenes about the depot were a harbinger of what was to come that night. The whiskey, which had been "started" by the Provost guard, was running in the gutters, and men were getting drunk upon it. As is the case under such circumstances (I noticed it, too, at the evacuation of Norfolk), large numbers of ruffians suddenly sprung into existence—I suppose thieves, deserters, etc., who had been in hiding. These were the men who were now breaking into stores and searching for liquor. To add to the horror of the moment (I say horror, for we all had friends who had to be left behind), we now heard the explosions of the vessels and magazines, and this, with the screams and yells of the drunken demons in the streets, and the fires which were now breaking out in every direction, made it seem as though hell itself had broken loose. Toward midnight, hearing the rumbling of artillery crossing the bridge below us, I sent an officer to see what it was. He returned with the information that it was *Lightfoot's* battery and the rear guard of the army. I thought the name suggestive. Shortly after, to our relief, our train started and crossed the bridges; and after a short delay in Manchester we steamed away at the rate of some ten miles an hour."[17]

Tuesday, April 4

Traveled all of this day & did not eat a thing as I had no appetite. My disease troubled me much & I had to climb on top of the cars & then down between them & stand on the joints for the connecting link of the two cars to have my passages which were all of blood.

Wednesday, April 5

Spent this day traveling just like the former & suffered much. Eat nothing but a piece of hardtack.

The horrors of war: A street in Richmond after the evacuation (Library of Congress).

Thursday, April 6

Arrived at Danville on this morning early & went up to my camp which was here a few yards from the depot guarding the specie. I was immediately put upon the sick list & was gladly welcomed by all of my friends who thought me a prisoner. I remained here for several days when we left for Charlotte, [North Carolina] where we arrived on the 12th at 7 P.M., my sickness having grown worse.

Thursday, April 13

Went up to a hotel this morning & got our breakfasts, all of us the government paying for it, & while there met doctor Williams asked him

This photograph, taken at the end of the war, was purported to be of the burned-out hulk of the CSS *Patrick Henry* (Library of Congress).

if I could go to the hospital anywhere & he told me that I could. I then went & got a certificate from our surgeon recommending that I should remain in Charlotte till able to resume my duties, & while waiting for my dinner at the hotel, saw Henry my brother standing at the hotel door & I immediately went up to him & found that he had heard of my being in town & was looking for me. He walked out to the hospital with me & promised to come in from his camp which was a few miles out of the city to see me in the morning.

Friday, April 14

Went down town from Dr. [John W.] Ashby's hospital & learned that I would have to leave unless I wished to be taken prisoner. I went back to

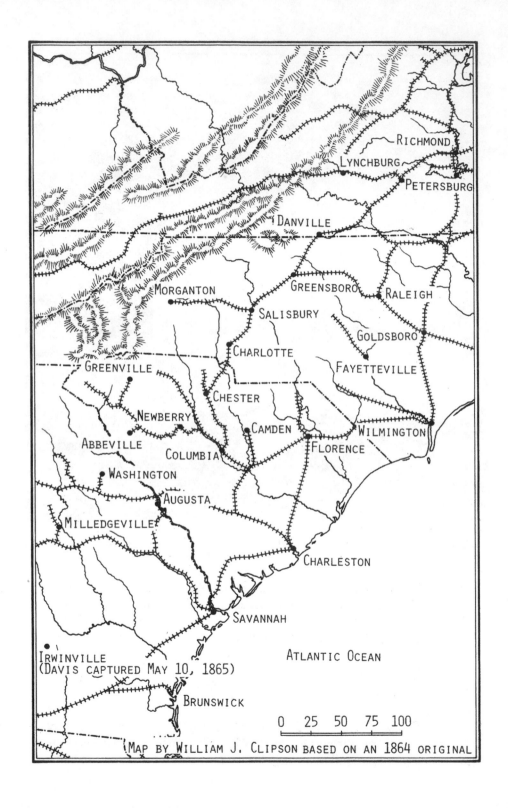

RICHMOND
LYNCHBURG
PETERSBURG
DANVILLE
MORGANTON
GREENSBORO
RALEIGH
SALISBURY
GOLDSBORO
CHARLOTTE
FAYETTEVILLE
GREENVILLE
CHESTER
NEWBERRY
CAMDEN
WILMINGTON
ABBEVILLE
FLORENCE
COLUMBIA
WASHINGTON
AUGUSTA
MILLEDGEVILLE
CHARLESTON
SAVANNAH

ATLANTIC OCEAN

IRWINVILLE
(DAVIS CAPTURED MAY 10, 1865)

BRUNSWICK

0   25   50   75   100

MAP BY WILLIAM J. CLIPSON BASED ON AN 1864 ORIGINAL

the hospital told Dr. Ashby, who was a whole souled Virginian, & finding my brother then, he wished the Dr. to allow me to make my way with him & he gave me an order to do so. [Records indicate that Minor was discharged from Way Hospital No. 6, Charlotte, North Carolina for reason of the "near approach of the Enemy to this place."] I could not go with my Company of which I was captain, I mean the midshipmen, for they would in all possibility have to walk & I could not walk any distance whatever without fainting or rather breaking down. About 5 in the evening we left the city I riding my brother's horse & he walking. My brother got a prescription from the Dr. to have filled for me, but I do not think it will do me any good. We traveled 5 miles, my brother's camp having moved on account of the near approach of the enemy to Charlotte, across the Catawba River distant from Charlotte 15 miles the greatest portion 3 miles....

Even though Minor's diary ended on April 14, 1865, a letter to Annie, which was dated April 24, was found with his papers that revealed him still near Charlotte, where he was staying at a friend's house while recovering from his illness. In the letter he recounts how only a few days before, Federal soldiers had seized his sword but for an unknown reason had not taken him prisoner. Perhaps they did not want to be bothered by a sick captive. As soon as he felt well enough, he told Annie, he would start for Augusta, Georgia.

Within a short time after this letter, however, the war ended and Minor enrolled in the 1865 session at the University of Virginia. In 1867, he and Annie Lamar were married, and by 1870 they had two children, Harriet and Benjamin. That same year Annie died, and four years later Minor was dead at the age of 29.

Opposite: Map of the eastern portion of the Confederacy showing the area traveled by Minor and the midshipmen while guarding the Southern archives and specie (collection of R. Thomas Campbell).

5

Some Final Thoughts

When the Confederate Congress authorized the establishment of a naval school, no one contemplated the possibility that a war-torn future might be in store for the Academy and its midshipmen. Conceived in the prolific mind of naval secretary Stephen R. Mallory, and nurtured and supported by the innovative John R. Brooke, the Confederacy's Naval Academy came into being during the midst of a cruel and bloody war for survival. The reality that the school existed at all is simply astounding.

Even more remarkable is the success that the school enjoyed in spite of the terrible war that raged around it. School boys one day, soldiers the next; and yet through it all, the Academy was able to train and graduate boys such as Hubbard T. Minor as junior naval officers who were second to none. No doubt they were superior to many, for their classroom instruction had been supplemented by active operational experiences.

When Minor was assigned to the CSS *Savannah* at Savannah, Georgia, he quickly discovered that the skills he had acquired during the gun exercises on the *Patrick Henry*, including the knowledge and discipline needed to direct a gun-crew, were essential qualities for a junior officer in time of battle. While his duties onboard were typical, Minor spent much of his off-duty hours writing about his longings and experiences ashore. In his attendance at church, his visits with friends, and his courting of the ladies, he was no different from his contemporaries of the time. His pleadings with his cousin, Robert D. Minor, to arrange for a transfer were not born out of a desire to shirk his duty. His discontent was the product of plain boredom, for the Savannah Squadron had little to do until the approach of General Sherman's hosts near the end of 1864. When that time came, Minor was eager to strike a blow for his struggling country.

While there were tranquil and sometimes boring months, the lives of all midshipmen became very stressful and dangerous as the winter of 1864 stretched into 1865. The constant calls to man portions of the trenches or the rotations to the ironclads of the James River Squadron were not very conducive to scholastic learning. After the evacuation of Savannah, Charleston, and Wilmington, Minor found himself back aboard the *Patrick Henry*. He fretted over the fact that other midshipman were being called upon to serve on the ironclads or man the heavy guns along the James River, while he sat studying.

Hampered by illness, Minor prepared for the evacuation of Richmond as best he could. Unable initially to join the other midshipmen who were detailed to guard the gold and archives of the Confederate government, he traveled the evacuation route to Danville, Virginia, on his own, and he finally caught up with the cadets guarding the specie. After a torturous trip to Charlotte, North Carolina, with his illness growing worse, Minor's war was soon over.

Today, little remains of the Confederate Naval Academy. The site of the landing at Rocketts, where the *Patrick Henry* was converted into a school ship, is today the departure dock for the cruise ship *Anabel Lee*. Visitors to Richmond can enjoy an evening dinner as they sail those same waters that not long ago were all astir with the black smoke and hissing steam of the James River Squadron. Parker's yellowed and faded textbooks are still preserved in a few archives.

Drewry's Bluff still exists, though only a shadow of its formidable self. Preserved by the National Park Service, it is administered as part of the Richmond Battlefield. Not far from its frowning face lie the remains of the *Patrick Henry*. At Savannah, Fort McAllister is now a tourist attraction, while Minor's ship, the CSS *Savannah*, sleeps beneath the river of the same name.

Pieces of china used on the school ship, a midshipman's desk, a few old photographs, and some odds and ends; these are all that remain to remind us of a fascinating Naval Academy and the vibrant young men who entered through her portals.

Fortunately, we can still get a fleeting glimpse of the tumultuous lives of these Southern naval cadets through the diary and letters of Hubbard T. Minor.

Appendix A: Regulations of the School Ship CSS Patrick Henry

Prepared by Lieutenant William H. Parker, CSN, Commanding

Chapter I

Organization

1. The C. S. School-Ship, Patrick Henry, shall be under the supervision of the officer in charge of the office of Ordnance and Hydrography, and he shall personally inspect the vessel at least once a year.

2. A commandant, of rank not lower than that of a lieutenant, will have the immediate government and command of the school-ship, and will be held responsible for its discipline and good management. All communications to the Navy Department on subjects connected with, or relating to the ship, are to be made, or forwarded the commandant to the officer in charge of the office of Ordnance and Hydrography.

3. An executive officer shall also be attached to the ship, whose rank shall not be below that of 2d lieutenant. He shall be the executive officer of the school-ship, and also in charge of either the department of seamanship, gunnery, or navigation.

4. There shall be attached to the ship two officers, of rank not lower than that of master, who, in addition to the duties of the ship shall have charge, each, of one of the departments of seamanship, gunnery, or navigation.

5. No officer of the navy shall exercise military command on board the school-ship unless subordinate to the commandant, excepting the

officer of the navy who may at the time be in charge of the office of Ordnance and Hydrography.

6. There shall be attached to the school-ship, a surgeon or assistant
surgeon, paymaster or assistant paymaster, master, secretary, and such
warrant and petty officers, and other persons of inferior ratings, as may
be authorized by the Secretary of the Navy.

7. There shall also be attached to the ship the following professors, viz:

One Professor of Mathematics.
One Professor of English Studies.
One Professor of Modern Languages.

8. The relative rank and precedence of the members of the academic
staff to be determined by the date of commission or appointment.

Chapter II

Academic Board

1. The Academic Board shall be composed of the following officers
and professors, viz:

The Commandant.
The Executive Officer.
The Second Lieutenant.
The Third Lieutenant.
The Professor of Mathematics.
The Professor of English Studies.
The Professor of Modern Languages.

2. The commandant, or, in his absence, the executive officer, shall
preside at the meetings of the Academic Board. In the event, however, of
the absence of both, from illness or otherwise, then the senior officer present shall preside; but all reports, returns, &c., of the board, under such
circumstances, shall be made to or through the commanding officer as
usage or the nature of the case may seem to require.

3. The Academic Board shall be convened for the transaction of business as often as the commandant may judge necessary.

4. A majority of the board shall constitute a quorum for the transaction of business; but a less number may constitute a quorum for the
examination of candidates for admission, provided at least three members be present.

5. Unless called on by the Navy Department to act upon other matters, or by the commandant to do so upon other affairs concerning the
school, the Academic Board shall confine duties to the examination of

candidates for admission, and of students, at the times prescribed by regulations; the preparation of necessary papers, reports, or returns, connected with examinations; the arrangement, for the approval of the Navy Department, of the order of instruction in the several branches of each course of study, and the time to be employed in each branch; the arrangement of the order in which the several classes and their sections composed of midshipmen are to present themselves at a December or June examination; the recommendation of students, found deficient, for further trial; also of individuals for restoration to the service; the recommendation, for the approval of the Navy Department, of the textbooks best suited for each department of instruction; the recommendation for purchase of all such books, maps, models, instruments, and apparatus as may be necessary in the different departments of instruction for the purposes of tuition; to reporting, from time to time, on the system of studies and instruction pursued and proposing any improvements therein that experience may suggest; and to granting certificates of graduation.

6. In questions of order at the Academic Board, relating either to the propriety of deportment of a member, observance of decorum, or routine of business, the presiding officer is to decide upon his own motion; but in cases which involve a consideration of the course and order of proceedings, a vote of the board is to be taken.

7. The adjournments of the Academic Board will be directed by the presiding officer.

8. The commandant will designate a member of the Academic Board to act as its secretary, and keep a correct record of its proceedings, which record shall be carefully kept in the office of the commandant, and transmitted by him to his successor. In case, however, of the illness or absence of the member so designated, at a time a meeting of the board is held, the presiding officer will then appoint another member to act in such secretary's stead for the time being.

9. Any officer connected with the school-ship, or any member of the academic staff not a member of the Academic Board, may be required by the commandant, in the name of the Academic Board, to attend its meetings for the purpose of giving information, or expressing opinions; but such individual is not to vote in any decision of the board.

Chapter III

Rules of Admission

1. Application for admission to the school-ship, addressed to the Secretary of the Navy can be made at any time, by the candidate himself or by his parent, guardian, or any of his friends, and his name will be at once

placed on the list of applicants; but the registry of a name does not give any assurance of an appointment. No preference will be given on account of priority of application. No application for an appointment as acting midshipman will be considered where the candidate is under or over the prescribed age; where the precise age and actual fixed residence are not stated or where the applicant is not a resident of the congressional district of the State from which he applies.

2. The law limits the number of midshipmen, and requires that they shall be divided among the several States and Territories with reference and in proportion, as near as may be, to their number of representatives and delegates to Congress; that appointments shall be made from those States and Territories which have not their relative proportion on the navy list; that appointments from each State shall be apportioned, as nearly as practicable, equally among the several congressional districts therein; and that the person so appointed shall be an actual resident of the congressional district of the State from which appointed, and be recommended by the member of Congress representing the district in which he resides.

3. The selection of candidates is made semi-annually, and candidates who receive permission will present themselves to the commandant of the School in January and July when they will be examined by a board of medical officers, and by the Academic Board of the school, as to their qualifications for admission.

4. No candidate will be admitted on board the school-ship unless he is found, in the opinion of a medical board, to be composed of the surgeon of the school-ship, and two other medical officers to be designated by the Secretary of the Navy, qualified to discharge the arduous duties of an officer of the navy, both at the time of his examination, and probably, during the rest of his life, until age shall disable him; and shall have passed a satisfactory examination before the Academic Board.

5. Any one of the following conditions will be sufficient to reject a candidate, viz:

First. Feeble constitution and muscular tenuity; unsound health, from whatever cause; indications of former disease; glandular swellings, or symptoms of scrofula.

Second. Chronic cutaneous affections, especially of the scalp, or and disorder of an infectious or immoral character.

Third. Severe injuries of the bones of the head; convulsions.

Fourth. Impaired vision, from whatever cause; inflammatory infection of the eye-lids; immobility, or irregularity of the iris, or fistula lachrymalis.

Fifth. Deafness; copious discharge from the ears.

Sixth. Loss of many teeth, or teeth generally unsound.

Seventh. Impediment of speech.

Eighth. Want of due capacity of the chest, or any other indication of a liability to a pulmonic disease.

Ninth. Impaired or inadequate efficiency of one or both of the superior extremities on account of fractures, especially of the clavicle, contractions of a joint, extinuation, or deformity.

Tenth. An unnatural excurvature or incurvature of the spine.

Eleventh. Hernia.

Twelfth. A varicose state of the veins, of the scrotum, and spomatic cord (when large) sarcocele, hydrocele, hemorrhoids, fistulas.

Thirteenth. Impaired or inadequate efficiency of one or both of the inferior extremities on account of varicose veins, fractures, malformation, flat feet, lameness, contraction, unequal length, bunions, overlying or supernumerary toes.

Fourteenth. Ulcers, or unsound cicatrices of ulcers likely to break out afresh.

6. Candidates must be over fourteen and under eighteen years of age at the time of examination for admission; must be of good moral character; able to read and write well—write from dictation and spell with correctness; and to perform the following elementary operations of arithmetic, viz: numeration, and the addition, subtraction, multiplication, and division of whole numbers; all of which must be established to the satisfaction of the Academic Board.

7. A candidate who has passed the required examinations will receive the appointment of an acting midshipman, become an inmate of the ship, and be allowed his traveling expenses from his residence to Richmond. If, on the contrary, he shall not pass both examinations, he will receive neither an acting midshipman's appointment nor his traveling expenses.

8. A candidate who has once presented himself for examination under the authority of the Navy Department, and been rejected, cannot be allowed to present himself for examination a second time.

9. No one who may be admitted on board the school-ship under these regulations shall receive a warrant as a midshipman in the navy, unless he graduate thereat.

10. When candidates shall have passed the required examinations, and have been admitted as members of the school, they must, if not already supplied, immediately furnish themselves, and at all times keep themselves supplied with the following articles, viz:

One complete suit of steel gray uniform.

Two pairs white pantaloons.

Six white shirts.

Six pairs of socks.
Four pairs of drawers.
Six pocket handkerchiefs.
One black silk handkerchief or stock.
One mattress.
One pillow.
One pair of blankets.
One bed cover or spread.
Two pairs of sheets.
Two pillow cases.
Six towels.
Two pairs of boots or shoes.
One hair brush.
One tooth brush.
One coarse comb for the hair.
One fine comb for the hair, and
One thread and needle case.

Messmates will jointly procure for their common use and will keep their room at all times supplied with one looking-glass, one wash-basin, one water-pail and one slop-bucket.

11. On admission, each acting midshipman will be credited with his actual and necessary traveling expenses, and if they do not amount to the sum of fifty dollars, he will be expected to make up the deficiency by a deposit of money current in Richmond. This sum will be expended, under the direction of the commandant, for his further equipment.

Chapter IV

Uniform

1. All officers attached to the school-ship, shall wear their service dress uniforms at all times while on duty, unless the commandant should, on any occasion, direct the officers to appear in some other particular kind of uniform prescribed for their respective grades.

2. The uniform of an acting midshipman to be the same as that now authorized for midshipmen.

3. A service or fatigue dress of the same color and form, but of coarser and stronger fabric; jumpers of gray flannel, pantaloons of gray flannel, and straw hats and white jackets, may be worn when authorized by the commandant.

4. Changes of clothing from gray to white, or the reverse, suggested

by different seasons of the year, are not to be made by students until directed by the commandant.

5. Students appointed to act as officers of crews, companies, &c., shall wear such badges of designation on the sleeves of the jacket as the commandant may prescribe.

6. No student shall be allowed to wear on board the ship, or in the city of Richmond, or its immediate vicinity, any article of clothing, or wearing apparel, not permitted to be worn with, or as a part of, his uniform.

Chapter V

Course of Instruction

1. The studies which shall be pursued, and the instruction which shall be given on board the school-ship, are comprised under the following departments and branches:

FIRST DEPARTMENT—SEAMANSHIP, NAVAL TACTICS, AND STEAM.
> *First Branch—Seamanship.*
> *Second Branch—Naval Tactics.*
> *Third Branch—Steam.*

SECOND DEPARTMENT—GUNNERY, FIELD ARTILLERY, AND INFANTRY TACTICS.
> *First Branch—Theory and Practice of Gunnery.*
> *Second Branch—Field Artillery.*
> *Third Branch—Infantry Tactics.*
> *Fourth Branch—The Art of Defense.*

THIRD DEPARTMENT—ASTRONOMY, NAVIGATION, AND SURVEYING.
> *First Branch(Astronomy.*
> *Second Branch(Navigation.*
> *Third Branch(Surveying.*

FOURTH DEPARTMENT—MATHEMATICS.
> *First Branch—Arithmetic.*
> *Second Branch—Algebra.*
> *Third Branch—Geometry.*
> *Fourth Branch—Trigonometry.*
> *Fifth Branch—Application of Algebra and Trigonometry to the mensuration of planes and solids.*

FIFTH DEPARTMENT—ENGLISH STUDIES.
First Branch—English Grammar.
Second Branch—Descriptive Geography.
Third Branch—Physical Geography.
Fourth Branch—History.
Fifth Branch—Political Science.

SIXTH DEPARTMENT—MODERN LANGUAGES.
First Branch—French.
Second Branch—Spanish.

2. The foregoing studies shall be distributed into four annual courses, and the acting midshipmen shall be arranged in four classes, each class pursuing one of these courses; and each class may be subdivided into convenient sections, according to the relative standing of the members in the several branches of study.

3. The studies for the fourth class shall be: Practical Seamanship, Gunnery and Artillery and Infantry Tactics, Arithmetic and Algebra to Equations of the first degree, English Grammar and Descriptive Geography. For the third class: Practical Seamanship, Gunnery and Artillery and Infantry Tactics, Algebra, Geometry, Plane and Spherical Trigonometry, Physical Geography and History—French. For the second class: Seamanship and Steam, Gunnery and Field Artillery, Astronomy and Navigation, Application of Algebra and Trigonometry to the mensuration of planes and solids, Political Science, French. For the first class: Seamanship and Naval Tactics. Gunnery and Infantry Tactics, Navigation and Surveying, French and Spanish.

4. The professors and heads of departments of instruction, in order to ascertain the proficiency of the sections entrusted immediately to their assistants, the relative merits and qualifications of the students of the whole class: and the manner in which the assistants have performed their duty, shall, occasionally, instruct each of the sections entrusted to the assistants.

5. Professors and instructors will be held responsible for the regular and orderly conduct of their respective classes and sections whilst under their immediate instruction. They will not allow any student to absent himself from the recitation room, unless for satisfactory reasons; nor will they fail to report the wants of preparation, the absence or misconduct of any student at recitation.

6. Each professor, instructor, or assistant, shall keep daily notes of the progress and relative merit of those in the classes or sections under his charge. The assistants shall make weekly reports of such notes to the heads of departments to which the classes or sections respectively belong. These reports shall be rendered weekly to the commandant by the head

of each department, accompanied by a similar report of his own section or sections, with such explanatory remarks as may be necessary to show the relative progress in the sections; and he shall, at the same time, recommend the transfers which should, in his judgment, be made from one section to another.

7. Monthly reports shall be made up according to Form C, for every academic month in the academic year, and be signed and forwarded to the Secretary of the Navy by the commandant. These reports shall show the relative standing of the members of each class in the different studies in which they have been instructed, and their conduct or demerits. For the months in which there has been an examination, these reports shall be based on the weekly reports and the results of those examinations, and for other months upon the weekly reports only.

8. The academic month shall be understood to terminate on the Saturday which may happen to fall nearest the last day of the month, whether such Saturday precede or follow that day. Monthly academic returns will be made to the commandant by the professors and heads of departments accordingly.

9. The academic year shall begin on the 15th of January, and end on the completion of the following December examination. The academic year shall be divided into two terms; the first to commence with the academic year, and to terminate at the close of the June examination; and the second to commence on the 15th July, and to terminate with the close of the December examination, or the end of the academic year.

Chapter VI

Academic Examinations

1. An annual examination of all the classes shall be held by the Academic Board, commencing on the first day of December; (the second when the first falls on Sunday.) This examination shall be sufficiently thorough to enable the board to decide upon the proficiency and the relative merits of the members of the several classes; and it shall embrace all the studies, theoretical and practical, pursued by the several classes during the year, except such as may have been completed before the previous June.

2. A semi-annual examination of the same kind, of all the classes, shall also be held by the board, commencing on the first day of June; (the second when the first falls on Sunday.) This examination shall be sufficiently thorough to enable the board to decide upon the proficiency and relative merits of the members of the several classes; but the board may, at its discretion, omit the examination of the first class in any depart-

ment of study not completed before the period assigned for their semi-annual examination to commence.

3. Those who may be found by the board, at either an annual or semi-annual examination, deficient in any department of study, shall be so reported to the Secretary of the Navy, for his decision, whether they shall be dropped from the Navy List and returned to their friends, or be allowed to continue on board the school-ship for further trial. If there should be circumstances attending the case of any student thus found deficient, entitling him, in the judgment of the board, to a longer continuance on board the school-ship, they shall be duly stated in the report of the board to the Secretary of the Navy, upon the report by Form D.

4. Any acting midshipman may be advanced to any class which he may be qualified to join, either upon his admission or at any subsequent examination; and he may be graduated at any December examination at which he shall be found fully qualified to pass a graduating academic examination.

5. Every acting midshipman who succeeds in passing a graduating examination in December, will receive from the Academic Board a certificate of graduation which will entitle him to a warrant as a midshipman in the navy; bearing the same date as that certificate.

6. When the exigencies of the service so require, acting midshipmen who succeed in passing a graduating examination, may be promoted to the grade of passed midshipman, master, or lieutenant.

7. No acting midshipman who shall have been dismissed from the school-ship, or dropped from the Navy List in consequence of being found deficient in studies at an academic examination, or deficient in conduct at any time, will be restored to the school-ship, except upon the recommendation of the Academic Board. In the event of such restoration, the Secretary of the Navy, after considering the report and recommendation of the board, will prescribe the class the individual is to join, and the other conditions under which he is to be received.

8. The examination in each department will be made or directed by the professor or head of that department; and during the time any class or section is under examination in any branch, not only the professor but also the immediate instructor of the class or section, shall be present with the Academic Board, and he may, under the direction of the head of the department to which he belongs, make the examination of his class or section.

9. The Secretary of the Navy will, when expedient, annually invite not less than five persons, such as he may judge well qualified, to attend on board the school-ship during the December examination, as a board of visitors, for the purpose of witnessing the examination of the several classes, and of examining into the state of the police, discipline, and gen-

eral management of the institution, the result of which examination they will report to the Secretary of the Navy.

Chapter VII

Merit Rolls

1. The relative weight, or the maximum numbers, which are to be assigned to each of the " principal branches of study, and to conducts in each of the several classes, in forming the merit rolls, will be as follows, viz:

DEPARTMENT.	BRANCHES.	First Year, or 4th Class.	Second Year, or 3rd Class.	Third Year, or 2nd Class.	Fourth Year, or 1st Class.	Graduating Maxima.	Maxima of the several departments.
Seamanship, Naval Tactics, and Steam, ...	Seamanship, . .			50	100	150	215
	Naval Tactics, .				30	30	
	Steam, . . .			35		35	
Gunnery, Artillery and Infantry Tactics, ...	Gunnery, . .			50	100	150	215
	Field Artillery, .				30	30	
	Infantry Tactics, .				35	35	
Astronomy, Navigation and Surveying, ...	Astronomy, . .			50		50	160
	Navigation and Surveying, . .				110	110	
Mathematics, . . .	Mathematics, . .	40	60	80		180	180
English Studies, .	Grammar, . . .	10				10	90
	Geography, . .	15	15			30	
	History, ...	20				20	
	Political Science,			30		30	
Modern Languages,	French, ...		30	30		60	90
	Spanish, . . .				30	30	
Conduct, ...	. . . . . .	5	10	15	20	50	50
Aggregate. . . .	. . . . . .					1000	1000

2. If any students shall, at any June or December examination, fail to pass satisfactory examinations, in any of the principal branches of study in which they have been instructed, or shall have recorded against them respectively more than two hundred demerits since the commencement of the academic year, the Academic Board shall prepare a report of the same, to be transmitted to the Secretary of the Navy, according to Form D, showing the habits of study, aptitude for study, &c. If the Academic

Board should consider any of them thus reported deserving of being allowed to remain on board the ship for further trial, they shall designate the individuals, and assign upon the report their reasons for recommending their continuance.

3. At every December examination, the Academic Board shall form a "General Merit-Roll" for each class, in the following manner, viz: Of those members of each class who shall have passed a satisfactory examination, the individual having the highest standing in any principal branch for that year, shall receive the maximum number assigned to it for that class and year in the table of weights of this chapter, and the one having the lowest standing, shall receive the minimum number, which, in every case, shall be one-third of the maximum for the same branch and class. The members of the class having intermediate standings, shall receive numbers proceeding by equal differences from the maximum to the minimum, in the order of their relative merit as fixed by their "class merit rolls." Of those who have not two hundred demerits recorded against them, such as have no demerits shall receive the maximum number allowed for that class and year, and the others shall have that maximum diminished by one three-hundredth part of it for every demerit recorded against them. All the numbers which shall be thus assigned to the several members for the several branches of study, and for conduct, shall then be added together, and the names of the members shall be arranged in each class according to the aggregates thus obtained, the highest number being placed first on the list, and the others in their order. Only those who shall have passed in all the principal branches of their classes, and have not exceeded two hundred demerits recorded against them, are to be included in the "general merit roll."

4. At the December examination, the Academic Board shall also form the "graduating merit rolls," for the graduating class, by adding the aggregate numbers which each member of the class shall, have received on the several "general merit rolls" for December during the four years, and arranging the order of the members according to the aggregates, placing the highest first.

Chapter VIII

Final Examination of Midshipmen

1. A Board to consist of five Captains and Commanders, of whom at least three shall be captains, will convene, annually, on the first day of December, (the second, if the first should fall on Sunday,) at such place as the Secretary of the Navy may direct, for the purpose of making the "final examination" of Midshipmen to ascertain and decide upon their qualifications for promotion.

2. Candidates must produce certificates from their respective commanding officers of their good conduct and attention to duty, together with journals of all their cruises; and, besides, watch, quarter and station bills of at least one of the vessels in which they have served, in their own hand writing.

3. The examination by the Board will embrace Seamanship, Naval Tactics, Steam, the theory and practice of Naval Gunnery, Field Artillery Infantry Tactics, Navigation, and French; but the relative standing of the candidates will be decided by their standing in Seamanship, Gunnery and Navigation, unless their relative standing in these branches shall be equal; in which case, superior proficiency in the other branches shall be entitled to precedence.

4. In assigning numbers to candidates on their final examination, the number 402 is to be considered as expressing the maximum, and 134 as the minimum, to be allowed; and the Board will assign to such candidates as shall, in its opinion, be duly qualified for promotion, the number within those limits which, in the judgment of the Board, will fairly express their relative qualifications.

5. In the case where the candidates have not graduated from the school-ship, the numbers so assigned will determine their standing as passed midshipmen; otherwise, the numbers thus assigned, when added to the numbers which have already been assigned to them respectively on the "graduating merit roll" of the school-ship, will determine their standing as passed midshipmen; the highest number, in both cases, to take precedence.

6. The Secretary of the Navy will cause the Board of Examiners to be furnished with the numbers which had been assigned by the Academic Board to each of the midshipmen, to enable the Board of Examiners to determine the relative standing of those whom they may examine as required in the next preceding article.

7. As many of the same graduating class as can be conveniently assembled, will be ordered before the same Board for their "final examination;" but should it be necessary to examine members of the same graduating class by different Boards, then a majority of the members of each of those Boards will, when practicable, be composed of the same officers.

Chapter IX

Conduct Roll

1. For offenses not considered deserving severe punishment, the following classification of delinquencies shows the numbers which are to be

marked as *demerits* against the students on board the school-ship, in making up the conduct rolls:

First class of delinquencies counting ten demerits.—Repeated neglect of orders; overstaying verbal leave; absent from room at night after "taps;" and violation of articles 5, 7, 11, 12, and 15, of Chapter X.

Second class of delinquencies counting eight demerits.—Light in room after "taps" at night; and violation of articles 10 and 14 of Chapter X.

Third class of delinquencies counting six demerits.—Absence without authority from parade; roll-call; drill; quarters; inspection; exercise; muster; recitation; or other prescribed duty. Also, improper noise in rooms or steerage; unnecessary or unauthorized absence from room during study hour; out of prescribed uniform when on duty, &c.

Fourth class of delinquencies counting four demerits.—Slovenly dress at parade, inspection, or recitation; talking at recitation or in ranks; loud talking or rude conduct at mess; being superintendent of the steerage and failing to keep it in proper order, or allowing it to be in disorder; or to report visits to it in study or other prohibited hours; or to report a breach of regulations occurring therein.

Fifth class of delinquencies counting two demerits.—Late at any exercise, recitation, or other duty; inattention on drill, or at recitation; out of uniform when not on duty.

Miscellaneous class of delinquencies, to count from one to ten demerits according to the circumstances of each particular case. Disrespectful, ungentlemanly, disorderly, insubordinate, or unmilitary conduct; willful neglect of studies or other duties; and violation of such regulations of the school-ship as are not specifically mentioned in the course of this chapter, and which carry with them no positive penalty.

2. In all cases of delinquencies where demerits positively attach, the commandant will, after due inquiry, determine whether those reported to him for record shall be placed thereon; and in cases of a "miscellaneous" character, he is to decide upon the number of demerits, between one and ten, to be assigned to each of such cases.

3. The total demerits of each student will be expressed by the sum of all the demerits standing against him upon record.

4. Whenever a student shall have a number of demerits recorded against him greater than two hundred during any one academic year, he shall be declared deficient in conduct, and be immediately reported to the Secretary of the Navy for his decision, whether he shall be dropped forthwith from the Navy or otherwise.

5. The commandant may reduce or remit recorded demerits upon satisfactory explanation in writing being made in reference to a particular case, or upon satisfactory assurance in writing, or well-grounded hopes

of future good conduct; but all such reductions or remissions must be stated in the first monthly report to the department of delinquencies after they are made.

Chapter X

Discipline

1. The laws for the government of the Navy of the Confederate States are to be strictly observed by every person attached to the school-ship.

2. The commandant being charged with, and held responsible for, the good order and discipline of the school-ship, all persons attached thereto, for any purpose, are to give implicit obedience to his commands.

3. Any student who shall be intoxicated, or shall use, or bring into the school-ship, or have in his quarters, or elsewhere within the limits of the ship, any spirituous, vinous, fermented, or other intoxicating drinks, may be dismissed from the navy.

4. Any student who shall leave the ship without permission first duly obtained, shall be dismissed from the naval service.

5. Profane, obscene, or vulgar language, is strictly prohibited.

6. Any person attached to the school-ship who shall publish, prepare or submit for publication, in any manner or form, any matter relating to transactions or occurrences, official or private, which have taken place within the ship, or are in any wise connected with it, without permission previously obtained from the Secretary of the Navy or the commandant, shall be dismissed.

7. No firearms or fireworks of any description, or gunpowder in any form, shall be introduced by any student on board the ship; nor shall the same be used by any person on board, without the sanction of the commandant.

8. Students are strictly forbidden to contract debts while connected with the school-ship, unless with the sanction of the commandant.

9. All combinations, under any pretext whatever, are strictly prohibited.

10. Students must never present themselves to the commandant or to any other superior officer set over them, or at their offices or quarters, to make known a complaint, or for any other purpose, except by invitation, in greater numbers than three at a time.

11. Students are not only required to abstain from all vicious, immoral, and irregular conduct, but are enjoined to conduct themselves upon every occasion with the propriety and decorum which characterize the society of gentlemen. Those guilty of conduct unbecoming an officer and a gentleman, may be punished by dismissal from the service.

12. No student is to visit the room of another, or to absent himself unnecessarily from his own room, during the hours of recitation or study.

13. No student shall remove from the mess assigned him without the authority of the commandant.

14. No student shall introduce any improper character on board the ship; nor shall he introduce any person into the students quarters at any other time than during the hours of recitation prior to the time prescribed to commence evening studies.

15. No student shall answer for another at any roll-call, or muster of any kind.

16. The customary salute of officers in addressing or passing each other, is to be strictly observed on board. The junior or inferior will be the first to extend the salute, and the senior or superior will be scrupulously careful in returning it.

17. No person shall be excused from the performance of his duties on the plea of sickness, unless so excused by the surgeon; and no person whose name is on the sick-list, will be permitted to leave the ship, unless it be recommended by the surgeon and approved by the commandant.

18. Any student who shall, when absent from the ship, commit any immoral or disgraceful act, may, on satisfactory proof, be punished as though the offense had been committed on board, even to dismissal, if necessary, from the naval service.

19. Officers and others having cause of complaint against any person connected with the ship, or employed in any capacity on hoard, will make the same known to the commandant; and they are not to undertake to address a complaint to a higher authority, unless the commandant should fail promptly to notice the same, or the decision given by him should be unsatisfactory.

20. It shall be the duty of every officer, professor, and instructor attached to the ship, having knowledge of any violation of a law or regulation, or of any crime, irregularity, neglect, or other improper conduct of which a student or any other person has been guilty, to report the same without delay to the commandant.

21. No student shall use any reproachful or provoking speech or gesture towards another, or shall by any means traduce or defame another, or strike, or in any manner offer violence to another, without subjecting himself to the severest punishment which the offense may require.

22. The punishments to which students shall be liable for offenses they may commit whilst borne on the rolls of the school-ship exclusive of those resulting from demerits, or such as may proceed from judicial investigations by courts-martial, or courts of inquiry, will be distributed among the following three classes.

First Class.—Confinement to the limits of the ship; private reprimands; deprivation of recreation within the ship; confinement to room or apartment; reprimand to be read on parade; suspension from recitations and from all drills and exercises.

Second Class.—Confinement in guard-room.

Third Class.—Dismissal, unless the offender avail himself of a privilege that may be granted to him of resigning; public dismissal.

23. Punishments of the first or second class, just mentioned, may be directed by the commandant, or the commanding officer of the ship for the time being; but, unless in an extreme case, the circumstances of which are to be communicated to the department with all proper dispatch, "deprivation of recreation within the ship" shall not be prolonged beyond *twenty days;* "suspension from recitations and all drills and exercises" beyond *fourteen days,* or "confinement in the guard-room" beyond *one week,* without the direct sanction of the Secretary of the Navy.

24. "Confinement in guard-room" shall only be ordered upon those who, in the judgment of the commandant or commanding officer, shall be guilty of highly insubordinate, riotous, or mutinous conduct, or who shall not conform to the conditions imposed when ordered to confine themselves to their rooms, apartments, or to other limits which may be prescribed to them.

25. Any student who shall leave the guard-room without express permission, when placed there for punishment, may be regarded as guilty of the very serious military offense of *breach of arrest.*

26. Removal from the service, either with or without permission to resign, will only be authorized or ordered by the Secretary of the Navy, with the sanction of the President of the Confederate States.

27. While a student is under the punishment of "confinement to the limits of the ship," he is, on no account, to go out of the ship, either in a boat or otherwise, unless *ordered* so to do by a superior officer.

28. When a student is under the punishment of "deprivation of recreation within the vessel," he is, on no account, to absent himself from his room or apartment, except during the times absolutely necessary to enable him to attend the recitations of his studies, meals, parades, drills, exercises of small arms, swords, or great guns, and to answer the calls of nature.

29. While a student is under the punishment of "confinement to room or apartment," he is, on no account, to absent himself from his room or apartment, except during the times absolutely necessary to enable him to attend meals, and to answer the calls of nature.

30. While a student is under the punishment of "suspension from recitations and all drills and exercises," he is, on no account, to absent

himself from his room or apartment, except during the times absolutely necessary to enable him to answer the calls of nature.

31. Any student who shall hesitate or refuse to submit to any of the foregoing punishments of the first or second class, when ordered so to do by the commandant, or the commanding officer for the time being, may be dismissed forthwith from the naval service; and if any student or students shall, individually or collectively, decline or refuse to convey into confinement, either to a guard-room or other designated place, any other student or students, when ordered so to do by competent authority, or shall not obey the order promptly and literally, he or they may likewise be so dismissed.

Chapter XI

Leaves of Absence

1. No person connected with the school-ship shall go beyond the limits of the ship without a general or special permission of the commandant.

2. As a general rule, no student will be allowed to leave the ship for the purpose of visiting Richmond or its vicinity, except on Saturday; and then for a period not to exceed twenty-four hours.

3. Not more than one-half of the students attached to the ship shall be absent on leave at the same time, and those only who have merited it by general good behavior shall receive this indulgence.

4. On very particular occasions, the commandant may grant leave during the week to those who shall have deserved such indulgence by exemplary conduct.

5. The commandant, during the academic year, may grant to students leave of absence, upon an application in writing, for not exceeding forty-eight hours. He may also grant, upon similar application, leave of absence to professors and instructors for forty-eight hours, or for a period of time which shall not at all interfere with the regular recitations. All applications for longer time must be submitted for the decision of the Navy Department.

6. At the close of each term, the commandant, when authorized by the Secretary of the Navy, may grant leave of absence to such of the students as can be spared from the duties of the ship; provided their conduct has been satisfactory, and they have not received more than one hundred and fifty demerits during the academic year. No extension of this indulgence beyond the 10th of the following July or January, will be granted.

7. Leave of absence may be granted by the Secretary of the Navy to the professors, assistant professors, instructors, and other officers attached to the ship, from the close of one academic term to the com-

mencement of another; provided their services are not required for duties pertaining to their respective positions or departments.

8. Any person connected with the ship who shall overstay his leave of absence, verbal or written, must be reported to the Navy Department; and unless he produces satisfactory evidence of his having been detained away by sickness, or other unavoidable cause, he will be subject to punishment according to the circumstances of the case.

9. When a student of the ship applies for leave of absence on account of ill health, his application must be accompanied by a certificate of the senior medical officer present after the following form:

_____, midshipman (or acting midshipman) of the C. S. School-ship, having applied for a certificate on which to ground an application for leave of absence, I do hereby certify that I have carefully examined his case, and find that [here the nature of the disease, wound, or disability, is to be fully stated, and the period during which the individual has suffered under its effects.] And, in consequence thereof, he is, in my opinion, unfit for duty. I further declare my belief that he will not be able to resume his duties in a less period than [here state explicitly an opinion as to the period which will probably elapse before the individual will be able to resume his duties. When there is no reason to expect a recovery, or when the prospect of recovery is distant and uncertain, it must be stated.]

Dated at _____, this _____ day of _____, 18__.

[Signature of the medical officer.]

Which certificate is to be forwarded to the Navy Department, through the commandant, for its orders in the case.

10. When a student, absent on leave, is prevented by ill health from re-joining the ship, he must, on the first day of each month, transmit a certificate of the state of his health, in the foregoing form, to the commandant, which shall be signed by a medical officer of the navy when practicable; but, should there be none in the vicinity, a resident physician of the place must sign the same, whose standing must be attested by a magistrate, or some person known to the authorities at the School.

11. Students, on obtaining leave of absence, will report to the commandant their intended place of residence, and, during their leave, any change of such residence.

Chapter XII

Hospital

1. The surgeon, will, if he discovers in any student diseases or defects, which are enumerated as causes to prevent the admission of a

candidate for the service, or any bodily or mental defect disqualifying in its consequences, report the case to the commandant, who will forward the report to the Secretary of the Navy, that he may order an examination and a report to be made by a medical board, for his decision whether such student shall be retained in the service or dropped from the navy.

2. The surgeon will have the immediate control of the hospital, hospital steward, and hospital attendants, as well as of all who are sick in the hospital, or in their own quarters.

3. He will be responsible for all expenditures of medicines and stores belonging to the hospital department of the ship. No article of medicine, of diet, or of drink, shall be issued from the dispensary or hospital department without his order.

4. The police regulations of the hospital shall be established by the surgeon, subject to the approval of the commandant.

5. The surgeon shall report to the commandant, daily, by 10 o'clock, A.M., the names of those whose condition of health unfits them for any academic duty, or renders it desirable that they should be excused from employment as a means of recovering their health. He shall also furnish to the commandant a daily "sick list," and an "excused list," of those to be excused from military drills and exercises only.

6. When a student is ill enough to be excused from attendance at mess formations, morning and evening roll calls, or recitations, his name must appear on the regular sick-list, and not on the list of those excused only from military drills and exercises.

7. No person whose name is not on the sick or excused list will be excused from duty in consequence of alleged indisposition.

8. No person will be permitted to visit any patient in the hospital without the sanction of the surgeon.

9. No student shall visit any patient in the hospital without a written permission, signed by the surgeon and approved by the commandant. Every such permission must be left with the hospital steward.

10. The hospital steward shall obey all orders he may receive from the surgeon, and observe such police regulations as may be established for the hospital.

11. No patient in the hospital will be permitted to exercise any authority over the hospital steward, or over any nurse or other attendant. Every instance of neglect or inattention towards any patient may be reported to the surgeon.

12. No person shall be employed in the hospital without the approbation of the commandant. All persons employed in the hospital as nurses, cooks, and servants, shall obey the orders of the hospital steward.

13. No student who is on the sick-list, and directed to remain in quarters, shall leave there except at such times as the surgeon may have prescribed; but no student whose name is on either the sick or excused lists shall, for any purpose, be absent from his room or sick-apartment when one is assigned him, during any drill, parade, roll-call, exercise, or other duty of a military cast, from which he shall have been excused by the surgeon's list.

14. When more than one medical officer shall be attached to the ship, both shall not be absent at the same time.

15. The sick in the hospital shall conform to the directions of the surgeon, and to all the police regulations of the hospital.

16. Any person feigning disease may be dismissed from the service by order of the Secretary of the Navy.

17. There shall be a sick-call, every morning throughout the academic year, half an hour after the breakfast call, when all the sick, not in the hospital, who are able to attend, shall report to the surgeon until discharged by him.

Chapter XIII

Secretary

1. The Secretary, under the direction of the commandant, will keep all the records of the school, viz: rolls of the school, which shall contain a list of the students, with the date of each admission, place of birth, age, whence appointed, residence, and name of parents or guardians, results of class reports, conduct and general merit rolls; an inventory of public property of every description, and records of requisitions. He shall also make out all consolidated reports of conduct, and of merit, for the Navy Department, and file and preserve the public correspondence, and other papers of the school-ship.

Chapter XIV

Pay Master

1. The commandant may, from time to time, authorize the pay master to pay for or to the students such small sums of money due them as he may deem proper.

2. The remainder of the pay of the students will be kept to their credit by the paymaster, on the payrolls of the school, and paid to them when they shall be detached, or shall graduate.

3. The pay master shall present to the commandant, at the end of

each month, a statement of the account of each student, showing the amount paid and the balance due.

Chapter XV

Miscellaneous

1. All communications to the Navy Department, from persons connected with the school, must be made through the commandant, whose duty it shall be to forward them, accompanied with such remarks as he may deem proper.

2. The Executive Officer will carefully inspect, at least once a day, the mess and recitation rooms, quarters, and the ship; and his principal, assistant will also visit the students' quarters daily, and more frequently, if necessary, to preserve good order and strict obedience to regulations. In event of discovering anything damaged or out of place, the Executive Officer will have it repaired or adjusted, unless it be a matter of serious moment, or involving expense of importance, in which case he will report the same to the commandant, and receive his orders upon the subject.

3. After "Taps" at night, no lights are to be allowed in any part of the students' quarters, except by the authority of the commandant.

4. Students shall, when passing up and down the ladders, always do so in an orderly manner. Loud talking, scuffling, or unnecessary noise of any kind, is never to take place in their rooms. Boisterous behavior is prohibited everywhere within the limits of the ship, and in the boats when beyond those limits.

5. Each professor and instructor at the head of a separate department shall have charge of, and be accountable for, the instruments and apparatus supplied for the use of his department.

6. No student shall address his instructor upon the subject of his recitation marks without the permission of the commandant.

7. One of the students of each mess will perform the duties of superintendent of that mess for one week at a time, and be held responsible for the cleanliness and general neat arrangement of the room; the preservation of the public property in it; and for the strict observance there of all the regulations of the ship.

8. Officers to whom special duties are not assigned by these regulations, are to perform such as may be directed by the commandant; and when special duties are herein assigned the commandant may require the officer to perform other duties when circumstances shall, in his opinion, render it advisable.

9. All regulations necessary for the interior police and discipline of

the school-ship, not inconsistent with the foregoing, will be established by the commandant and shall be duly observed and obeyed.

The foregoing regulations are approved and are to be observed by all persons to whom they are applicable.

S. R. MALLORY.
Secretary of the Navy.
NAVY DEPARTMENT.

Appendix B: A Realistic War College

James Morris Morgan. "A Realistic War College." Annapolis: U.S. Naval Institute, *Proceedings*, March 1916, pp. 543–554.

In 1862 I ran the blockade at Charleston and proceeded to Europe, where I was detailed to the Confederate commerce destroyer (by some called *pirate*) *Georgia*. I was 16 years of age and a midshipman. I had been in many battles and considered myself a veteran—if experience in actual war makes a veteran I surely was one. I was away from the Confederacy for two years, and then, returning to my native land, ran through the blockade again, this time at Wilmington. When I received my new orders I hoped that I would at least find instructions to report aboard a small gunboat as a watch officer, for naval officers were scarce in the South. One can imagine my consternation and disappointment when I discovered that I was to be sent to school! I wondered if the Secretary of the Navy knew that I was all of 18 years of age, and that I was engaged to be married. I fretted and fumed, but now know that if there was one thing I needed more than another, it was a little schooling.

During my absence from the Confederacy a naval school for midshipman had been established. One might well indeed ask where in the world the Confederate States could locate a naval academy? But the Southern naval officers were a resourceful lot, who could build gunboats in cornfields out of yellow pine trees found in the neighborhood, and make armor out of rails and scrap iron; so to them a naval academy was a very simple thing to evolve. The Old Dominion Line side-wheel steamship *Patrick Henry*, which had formerly plied between New York and Norfolk, was lying at Richmond. She carried guns and was square rigged on her foremast, which would allow the midshipman to be taught how to reef and furl sail. Two little pine board recitation rooms were erected on her hurricane deck between the paddle boxes. What more could be asked for in those days? Here was a fully equipped naval academy ready to hand. Lieutenant William H. Parker, who before the war had been detailed as a professor of seamanship at Annapolis, was made superintendent of the new institution, and he was assisted by several naval officers and civilian professors who, in the face of many trials and difficulties, struggled in an effort to educate some forty or fifty lads, between the ages of 14 and 18, who were restlessly champing at the bit because they wanted to take a more active part in the fray which was going on around them. Among these boys was a young brother of Mrs. Jefferson Davis, a nephew of General R. E. Lee, a son of General J. C. Breckenridge, a son of Mr. Mallory, Secretary of the Navy; a son of Captain Semmes of *Alabama* fame, and many other scions of the most prominent families in the South.

One would think that the school should have been located in some quiet bend in the river, out of range of the shells of the contending forces, but there were no such places on that river; and besides, the Confederate naval officers were utilitarians, and the school ship was a very important factor in the defense of Richmond. She was anchored at "Drewry's Bluff" the main fortification on the river, situated about seven miles below the city. Through the obstructions in the river a passageway for our own boats had been left open. If the Union gunboats attempted to force their way through, as they had once before done, it was the appointed duly of the school to scuttle itself in this narrow channel. There were no defenses, on the river between "the Bluff" and Richmond, and should the enemy succeed in getting by the capital would have fallen. The *Patrick Henry* also served as a guard boat as well as a receiving ship, and all day signal men stood on top of her makeshift recitation rooms, thrashing the atmosphere with their little wigwag flags, sending and receiving messages from the naval land batteries located on the river below Drewry's Bluff, one of which was continually engaged, night and day, in shelling the Dutch Gap Canal which General B. F. Butler was engaged in digging. Opposed to these naval batteries were a number of strong fortifications on the north side of the river.

When prisoners were exchanged the flag of truce boats were always required to stop alongside the school ship on their way to or from Richmond or Harrison's Landing (within the Federal lines), where the Union prisoners were delivered, and the Confederates embarked when released. I met with a mortifying *contretemps* on one of these occasions, when a cartel loaded with Confederate prisoners came alongside of the *Patrick Henry*, and discharged her human freight on to our deck. They were a pitiful looking lot of human wrecks. I was busily engaged in assisting the officer of the deck in keeping the gang plank clear, as each poor fellow wanted to stop and have some conversation with the first men they had seen in gray uniforms for many months. Some of the poor fellows wanted news, and the more affectionate wanted to embrace me; but the executive officer, standing on the quarterdeck, had his eye on me, and I was compelled to be stern, as well as to repel their affectionate demonstrations. I was busily engaged repeating again and again: "Pass forward, my man; I will attend to you in a moment; but don't block the gangway—let these men come aboard," etc., when the raggedest and most forlorn looking of the lot approached me. His matted hair reached to his shoulders. His clothing was not only ragged, but dirty, and it was evident that he had not luxuriated in a bath tub for many a long week. There was a certain assurance in his manner as he approached which, despite his haggard and wretched appearance, should have warned me to be careful; but, as I have said before, I was busy. The poor fellow asked me very politely "who was in command of the *Patrick Henry*?" and I replied with the stereotyped, " Pass forward, '*My Man*'; don't block the gang-way!" His eyes suddenly blazed in indignation, and to my consternation the dilapidated looking creature drew himself up and with suppressed wrath said: "Mr. Morgan, I will apply for you when I get a ship, and I will show you, sir, who goes forward! I am Commander Kennon!"

I had known Commander Kennon well when I served in the same flotilla with him on the Mississippi in 1861–2. To say that I was mortified faintly describes my feelings when I realized that I had ordered a commander "forward." If the deck had opened and let me drop into the coal bunkers, where my embarrassment would not have been so conspicuous, I would have been grateful. The last time I had seen Kennon was when he was in command of the old side wheel steamer *Governor Moore*, with which he rammed and sunk the U. S. sloop-of-war *Varuna* when Admiral Farragut passed the forts below New Orleans. Immediately after he struck the *Varuna*, the *Hartford*, *Brooklyn*, and the frigate *Mississippi* closed in on him and shooed him ashore with their heavy guns. They set fire to the *Governor Moore* and blew her up almost instantly. The last the Confederates saw of Kennon he was struggling in the river. Now I submit that by all the rules of the game, after not hearing of him for more than two years, I had a right to suppose that he was dead, and I do not think it was right for him to come back in disguise to confound a poor midshipman who was obeying orders and trying to do his duty. Several years after this *contretemps* I again served with Kennon, this time in the Egyptian army, and he seemed to take a fiendish delight in recounting to the army officers how he was once ordered "forward" by a "d—d midshipman!"

Life at that naval academy was necessarily one of privation. The clothing of the midshipmen was made of the coarsest materials. We slept iii hammocks slung as closely together as sardines in a box. Our food was scanty and unappetizing—a little lump of fat pork or a slither of meat which from its toughness aroused the suspicion that it had been carved from very close to the horns of some half-starved animal, a "hardtack," generally infested with weevils or worms, to be washed down by a tin cup full of hot water colored with chicory or burnt grains of ground corn. This decoction was brevetted coffee. There was no variety—the same menu served for breakfast, dinner and supper. But if we were short on rations, we had plenty of excitement to make us forget the emptiness of our stomachs. Drills, study and recitations went on continually, the latter punctuated by the booming of the guns and the bursting of the shells. A section of midshipmen with camp stools under their arms would enter a recitation room where would be seated the professor on a rough cane-bottom chair. He would order one of the youngsters to "take the blackboard," and commence the business of the hour by giving out the problem. "If x equal 10," but frequently he got no farther before a crashing of great guns aroused his curiosity and he would request one of the young gentlemen to step outside and see which one of the batteries was using a particular rifle gun or a heavy smoothbore. Having received the information, he would attempt to resume the recitation, when he would again be interrupted by a message from the captain to send two or three midshipmen to assist in working the guns of some battery which was short of officers. After the artillery duel was over these boys would return to the ship and continue their studies. On other occasions they would be detailed to go down the river and assist in laying mines and anchoring spar torpedoes. The bushes on the bank of the river were infested with sharpshooters. Then there were expeditions in small boats to cut out Federal warships and carry them by boarding, as they succeeded in doing on several occasions. It was useless to ask for volunteers, as every midshipman on the *Patrick Henry* would clamor for permission to go, so these details were given as rewards for good conduct.

For the expedition to board the U. S. gunboat *Underwriter*, lying in Albemarle Sound, a number of midshipmen were fortunate enough to get details, among them Daniel M. Lee, a younger brother of Fitzhugh Lee, and Palmer Saunders. It was moonlight the night of the attack, but the clouds obscured the moon. With muffled oars the Confederate row-boats approached the doomed craft, and before they were discovered they were so close that the broadside with which the warship had intended to annihilate them passed harmlessly over their heads. Lee and Saunders were in the same boat and boarded at the gangway, where a Jacob's ladder had been left hanging against the side. Saunders tripped gayly up the ladder, only to meet a sailor armed with a cutlass; this the man brought down on the poor boy's head with such terrific force that it literally split his skull into two parts, one-half of his head resting on his shoulder as he dropped dead and fell into his boat. Lee, who was closely following Saunders, leaped lightly onto the deck and tackled a sailor at close quarters. The sailor threw him down and fell on him. The sailor was trying to use his weapon, but Lee was holding him so tightly he could not manage it. Some Confederates rushed to Lee's assistance, and one of them placed the muzzle of a navy revolver against the Yankee sailor's back and was about to pull the trigger when Dan Lee called out: "Don't shoot, you fool! Can't you see how thin this man is? I am under here!" Those who know Lee believe that he would have had his joke even if the man's cutlass had been in him.

The conflict on the deck of the *Underwriter* was brief and bloody. Her crew made a gallant fight for their ship, but were assailed from all sides and to add to their difficulties, the *Underwriter* was on fire. Wounded and prisoners were put into the boats, and the gunboat was left to her fate. The midshipmen of the expedition, with the exception of the much-loved Palmer Saunders, returned to their school, where they resumed their studies while awaiting another opportunity to show their metal.

I remember one morning that, shortly, after daylight, we received the information that a portion of General Grant's army had surprised and captured Fort Harrison, which was situated on the north side of the river, about two miles front where we lay. Fort Harrison was one of the most important defenses on that line of fortifications. About 7 o'clock in the morning we discovered that a pontoon bridge was being thrown across the river a short distance above where we lay. The bridge was soon completed, and then we saw Hoke's famous division crossing it. These were the best dressed soldiers in the Confederate army, as the state of North Carolina had the forethought to buy for itself several blockade runners, which kept their troops decently clothed.

It was evident to all of us that our soldiers were going to try to retake Fort Harrison. Several of the midshipmen, myself among the number, obtained permission to accompany the troops so that we could see the fight to greater advantage. Arriving at the selected spot, Hoke's division was drawn up in line of battle. We were within range of the enemy's artillery, but not a shot was fired at us while the formation was going on. We were much pleased at this, as we thought it showed weakness. No sooner had our line completed its formation than it opened at intervals to allow batteries of light artillery to pass to the front. At the gallop they went for several hundred yards, arid then, wheeling, they unlimbered and opened fire. Soon the smoke was so dense that we could no longer see them, and then suddenly the firing ceased and they burst through the smoke on their way back to us. All of this time Fort Harrison and its outlying fortifications were ominously silent. As soon as our artillery had repassed through our lines, the infantry received the order to move forward, and shortly afterwards came the command to charge. The car-splitting rebel yell rent the air as the gallant fellows rushed at the works, but, alas! as they got within a hundred yards or less of the fort, out of the bushes and undergrowth a long line of bluecoats arose and poured a withering fire into the ranks of our men, while the great guns of the fort sprinkled grapeshot and canister among them. Soon we midshipmen saw a few skulkers and slightly wounded men coming to the rear, and then the whole line seemed to suddenly give way and they fell back, but not in much disorder. When we reached the point from which we had started, the division was reformed, and suddenly the men burst into cheers. At first we could not understand what had caused the wild outbreak of enthusiasm, but soon we saw a stately figure mounted on a white horse coming down the line. It was General R. E. Lee! As he passed near where we were standing we could distinctly hear him telling the men that they "must retake that position for him, as it was the most important on the line, and he was sure they could do it if they would only try."

Again our artillery roared, and under cover of the smoke we again advanced, only to meet with a similar reception to that given us on the first attempt. Again we came back, but in somewhat greater disorder than on the previous occasion. Again they reformed at the same place, and again General Lee, hat in hand his splendid silvery head uncovered, rode down the line imploring his men to make one more effort for him. I had always had the idea that General Lee was a cold, unemotional man, but he was excited that day—even the staid and stately "Traveller," his war horse, was prancing. Well, to cut the story short, we advanced for the third time on the works which had been ours but were now in the possession of the enemy. The charge was not as enthusiastic as the two previous ones, and when our men were again repulsed they broke and fled in disorder. I may have been a web-footed sailor, but I did not notice any infantrymen pass me on the way back to our second line of defense.

As soon as the division reformed General Lee again rode down the line, thanking his troops for their gallant effort and begging them not to be downhearted over their failure, as they had, done all that it was possible for men to do, and that anyhow the position was not as important as he had at first thought it was.

On our way back to the ship a "sawbones" caught one of the middies and made him hold a wounded man's leg while he (the surgeon) cut it off.

As the sun went down we midshipmen returned to our school and chills and fever—not fashionable "malaria," but regular old time chills and fever, which first trade the agonizing tremors pass through the frame and the teeth chatter and rattle, the chill only to be allayed by the heat of a

burning fever, which always followed it. The mouth became parched and
the dry tongue clove to the roof of the mouth. In those days it would have
been considered a crime to give a sufferer from fever a drop of cool water!
It was my day and hour for a chill, so I sought out a quiet place on the
deck, where the planks looked soft. and lay down to shake it off. This performance was not included in the routine of the ship, but it was as regular as the beat to general quarters. As we slept in hammocks and they were
stowed away in the daytime, we were allowed to lie down any place where
we did not interfere with the routine of the ship. With the exception of
some of the boys from the alligator states, most of us were sufferers from
this cause, and many of them were also weakened from chronic dysentery brought on by the bad food they had to eat; but simple chills and
fever was never considered of sufficient importance to allow one to be
excused from either duty, lessons or drills.

In the autumn I passed my examination and was promoted to the dig-
nity of passed midshipman. I received my orders with delight, as they did
not take me far from Richmond. I was sent to a perfect inferno, a naval
battery called "Semmes," situated on a tongue of land by the river, and
in a semi-circle, completely enfilading it, were the Bohler, Signal Hill, the
Crow's Nest, Dutch Gap and Howlet House batteries. All day the big guns
boomed and all night the mortar shells exploded; but I could get away on
Saturday evenings, and spend a night in town, so what did I care, at my
age, for the inconveniences of the rest of the week?

The winter of 1864–5 was a very cold one, and the snow lay deep on
the ground for most of the time. When the early spring at last arrived my
commanding officer surprised me by ordering me to report to the Secretary of the Navy, and advised me to take my belongings with me. As I
had none besides the clothes, ragged and torn, I stood in, and my sword
and pistol, which I always wore, it did not take me very long to pack my
effects.

While trudging along through the mud on my way to Richmond I
very- seriously pondered over all my sins of commission and omission,
as I could not understand why a Secretary of the Navy would want to see
a passed midshipman unless it was for the purpose of giving him a rep-
rimand(?). Judge of my surprise when I was ushered into the august presence of the, so far as I was concerned, all-powerful man, and he simply
informed me that I was to accompany Mrs. Jefferson Davis' party south.
It then suddenly dawned upon me that the Confederate cause was doomed
and that Richmond was about to fall.

Mrs. Davis' party consisted of herself, her children, her sister, Miss
Howell; three daughters of Mr. Trenholm, Secretary of the Treasury;
Colonel Burton Harrison, Mr. Davis' private secretary, and myself. We
boarded a train at the station and the President joined us there to bid

good-bye to his family. The train stopped every few miles to let troop trains pass by, and it was a wearisome and uncomfortable journey. The news of the fall of Richmond caught up with us on the way, and when we at last arrived at Charlotte, N. C., nothing could induce Mrs. Davis to go a foot farther until she could hear from her husband.

The superintendent of the Confederate States Naval Academy was among the very last to be informed that Richmond was being evacuated. This information was conveyed to him in an order directing him to land the midshipmen, blow up the school ship, and proceed south with his command. The midshipmen had not proceeded very far on their way to Richmond before they heard the magazines of their late home tearing the old ship into atoms, and as they trudged along the river bank one terrific explosion after another shook the ground under their feet as the ironclads were destroyed. Arriving in Richmond, they found the gutters running with whiskey which the frightened inhabitants had attempted to destroy in that way to keep it from falling into the hands of the Federal soldiers—instead of which, much of it went down the guzzles of a mob composed of the riffraff of the city, skulkers, deserters and dazed Negroes. The midshipmen, marching like the veterans they were, crossed the bridge to Manchester, where they were to entrain for the south.

On arriving at the railway station they found the officials of the Treasury Department in a great state of trepidation, owing to the fact that they had under their charge all the gold belonging to Confederacy, some half a million of dollars. The mob had learned of it, and were rapidly gathering with the object of looting, and not a soldier in sight to afford them protection. When the mob saw a lot of young boys with guns file onto the platform alongside the train that was to carry the kegs of specie they cheered derisively. Captain Parker ordered his command to fix bayonets, and in less time than it takes to tell, had cleared the station of that crowd of ruffians. Putting the gold on the train with his midshipmen in charge of it, he pulled out of the station, bound he did not know where.

At Charlotte it was learned that General Sherman's troops were approaching from several directions, and that there was grave danger of Mrs. Davis falling into their hands. It was decided that with the treasure she should leave at once under the protection of the midshipmen. They went as far as Chester, S. C., and detrained there, the specie being loaded on commandeered wagons in which Mrs. Davis and her family also rode—a midshipman guard on foot preceding and following, as well as marching on each side of the unique traits; and thus they plodded on their weary way over the wretched country roads.

When night overtook them at the end of their first day's journey they found shelter in a rough, pine-board, wayside church, where Mrs. Davis and her little children slept on the bare floor. Captain Parker, as commanding officer, spent the night in the pulpit, and the middies who were not on guard lay their wearied young bodies down anywhere and went to sleep.

Day after day this peculiar cavalcade continued its march, in all kinds of weather, over those roads which one moment were ankle deep in mud or sand, and the next so stony that the unshod mules were lamed and the feet of the midshipmen were cut and bruised—there was hardly a sole left to a shoe in the command, and many of the youngsters had no shoes at all before then reached the end of their tramp. Throughout this trying journey Captain Parker attests that he never heard a single complaint uttered by any one in the command. The long marches were very trying on another account. Constant vigilance had to be maintained, as on their flanks were constantly hovering gangs of deserters watching for an opportunity to swoop down on the coveted booty.

It was impossible for Mrs. Davis to obtain shelter at any house, as the natives feared that "the Yankees" would destroy their property if they heard she had received hospitality. When finally she arrived in Abbeville, Colonel Armistead Burt put his house at her disposal, and when she declined his kind offer, telling him that "if she accepted his hospitality she feared his house would be burned," the noble old aristocrat made her a profound bow saying: "Madam, I know of no better use my home could be put to than to be burned in such a cause!"

The midshipmen left Mrs. Davis at Abbeville and resumed their march to Augusta, Ga., still escorting the gold. Augusta was only eighty miles away, and when they arrived there it was to learn that the place was being evacuated and that they must get away from there as quickly as possible. So back to Abbeville they tramped.

Captain Parker was determined, if possible, to put that gold into the possession of Mr. Davis, but when he returned to Abbeville Mr. Davis had not yet arrived. But Mr. Mallory, the Secretary of the Navy, had and he ordered the gold turned over to the tender care of the soldiers, and also ordered the Confederate States Naval Academy disbanded! Each midshipman received a copy of the following order:

Abbeville, S. C., May 2, 1865.

SIR: You are hereby detached from the naval school, and leave is granted to visit your home. You will report by letter to the Hon. Secretary of the Navy as soon as practicable.

Paymaster Wheless will issue you ten days' rations, and all quarter masters are requested to furnish you transportation.

Respectfully your obedient servant,

(Signed) Wm. H. Parker,
Commanding.

It was in this way that these ragged and weary boys were turned loose on the world. Many of them were a thousand miles from their homes. The homes of others had been destroyed. The quartermasters who were expected to furnish transportation immediately became invisible, as they had already fled in an effort to save themselves, and could they have been found, Sherman's army had destroyed the railroads which were to furnish the transportation. It was a tragic ending for a unique institution of learning.

One might ask what became of the men who received their only education under such extraordinary circumstances. The answer is that the after careers of many of these boys would compare favorably with that of many youths graduated from the most celebrated universities. They became lawyers, doctors, civil engineers, planters, bankers, and business men. Several of them became millionaires. Three of them became judges; one a distinguished member of Congress; several were members or state legislatures; and two of them were afterwards captains of large merchant ships. Two of them became mayors of great seaport cities, and one of them was appointed United States Consul General to Australia, while still another one was a United States Minister to Russia.

One interesting incident in the careers of three of these little midshipmen who were together on the school ship *Patrick Henry*, and whose combined capital at that time probably would not have exceeded 15 cents in Confederate money (and gold was at a 100 for 1 premium), occurred when they met some thirty years afterwards on a commission to settle the long litigated question concerning the debt due bondholders by the States of "old" Virginia and West Virginia. One of them was Clarence Cary, of the prominent law firm of Cary & Whitridge, representing Brown Brothers and the bondholders of the North; another was Bartlet Johnson, banker and broker, representing the bondholders of Baltimore and that section of the business world; and the third was Virginius Newton, president of a great national bank and representing the interests of the Virginia and Southern bondholders. It is true that there were only a score or two of millions involved, but it goes to show the prominence achieved in the business world by some of the graduates of the Confederate States Naval Academy.

Appendix C: Johnson's Island Expedition

A letter from Lieutenant Robert D. Minor, C. S. Navy, to Admiral Franklin Buchanan, C. S. Navy, giving a detailed account of the expedition for the relief of Confederate prisoners on Johnson's Island, Lake Erie, in the fall of 1863. *Official Records of the Union and Confederate Navies in the War of the Rebellion*. Washington, D.C.: Navy Department, 1894–1927, series I, vol. II, pp. 822–828.

Naval Ordnance Works,
Richmond, Va., February 2, 1864.

My Dear Sir: Enclosed I send you the express company's receipt for a package of cloth, forwarded several days since to your address at Mobile. Before leaving the Confederacy in October last I wrote to say good-bye, and with the hope that before my return you would have heard of our success abroad, but the fortunes of war were against us, and all the consolation we have is the consciousness that we did our best, and that our efforts have been appreciated. You will pardon the prosy story I am about to tell you of our expedition, but as it were one designed to do much good to our poor fellows at the North, and through their release to be of great benefit to our country, I have thought that it would be interesting to you to know something of its details.

Early in February of last year Lieutenant William H. Murdaugh, of the Navy, conceived the plan of a raid on the Northern Lakes, based on the capture by surprise of the U.S.S. *Michigan*, the only man-of-war on those waters, and on mentioning his views to Lieutenant Robert R. Carter and myself, I need not tell you how cordially we entered into them, and endeavored by every means in our power to carry them into execution; but it was only after repeated efforts that the Government was induced to take any active part in promoting the expedition, though Mr. Mallory, the Secretary of the Navy, was in favor of it from the inception of the plan, but money, or rather the want of it, seemed to be the cause of delay, which, however, being eventually provided to the amount of $25,000, we, together with Lieutenant Walter It. Butt, one of our wardroom mess on board the old *Merrimack*, were at last ordered to hold ourselves in readiness to proceed on the duty assigned us, when suddenly the order was changed, it having been decided in Cabinet council that our operations on the lakes might embarrass our relations with England, and thus prevent the completion of the ironclad and other vessels building for us in the private shipyards of that country. So the plan was foiled at the last moment, and, as we learned, by order of his Excellency President Davis, who was apprehensive on the score of foreign complications. With the expedition thus broken up, Murdaugh, disheartened, sought other duty, and he, Carter, and Butt were ordered abroad, leaving me here on my regular ordnance duty, as the only representative of a scheme whose prospects were so inviting and so brilliant. Late in the spring, I believe it was, that our enemies made Johnson's Island, in the Bay of Sandusky, Ohio, a depot for our officers, their prisoners, and after the surrender of the Post of Arkansas, Vicksburg, and Port Hudson, some 1,500 or 2,000 were imprisoned there, whom it became an object to release, as the balance was, and still is, strongly against us. With this view I found myself one day in August last closeted with Mr. Seddon, Secretary of War, and Mr. Mallory, who asked me to give my views on the contents of a letter, a part of which Mr. Seddon read to me, containing a proposition for the release of our poor fellows.

As a cruise on the lakes in the *Michigan* and the destruction of the enemy's very valuable commerce has been my study for months past, I assented at once to the plan, and remarked that "I need not inform you, gentlemen, how much pleasure it would give me to be engaged upon such duty." Well, sir, nearly a month of precious time passed away without my hearing another word on the subject, when one day I was sent for by Mr. Mallory, who told me to organize the expedition, select the officers, make all the necessary preparations, and then concluded by offering me the command of it, which, however, I waived in favor of my friend John Wilkinson (who was in a manner somewhat committed to the plan by the letter which I have mentioned as being shown to me by Mr. Seddon, the Secretary of War), with this proviso, however, that on our arrival in Canada, in the event of adopting two lines of operations, I was to have one of them as my command.

As soon as it was definitely settled that the expedition was to go (for the President said it was better to fail than not to make the attempt, as it had been vaguely talked of in Montreal), our preparations were made.

Thirty-five thousand dollars in gold, or its equivalent, was placed at our disposal by the Navy Department, and a cargo of cotton which was subsequently sold at Halifax for $76,000 (gold) by the War Department—in all, some $111,000 in gold, as the sinews of the expedition. The officers selected were John Wilkinson, lieutenant commanding, myself, Lieutenant B. P. Loyall, Lieutenant A. G. Hudgins, Lieutenant G. W. Gift, Lieutenant J. M. Gardner, Lieutenant B. P. [F. M.] Roby, Lieutenant M. P. Goodwyn, Lieutenant Otey Bradford, Acting Master W. B. Ball (colonel of Fifteenth Virginia Cavalry), Acting Master William Finney, Acting Master [H.] W. Perrin, Lieutenant Patrick McCarrick, Acting Master Henry Wilkinson, Chief Engineer [J.] Charles Schroeder, First Assistant Engineer H. X. Wright, Second Assistant Engineer Tucker, Assistant Paymaster [P. M.] DeLeon, Assistant Surgeon Von [William] Sheppardson, Gunners Gormley and Waters, John Tabb, and a man named Leggett, who subsequently left us at Halifax. Of coarse our plan was kept secret, only Wilkinson, Loyall, and myself knowing its objects, and we did not attempt to contradict the report that we were going to England, where many of the officers and our friends on shore supposed we were bound.

The party consisted of twenty-two all told, and on the 7th of October we left Smithville, N. C., on the Cape Fear River, in the blockade steamer *R. E. Lee*, with Wilkinson in command, and after successfully running the gantlet of the blockading squadron of river vessels (not, however, without getting a shell in our starboard bulwarks, which exploded on board, set the cotton on fire, wounded three men, and broke a small hoisting engine into smithereens), we arrived at Halifax, Nova Scotia, where our arrival was at once telegraphed all over the country as being en route for England. Dividing the party, we left Halifax as soon as possible, taking two routes for Canada, one via St. John, New Brunswick, and thence up through the province via Fredericton and Grand Falls to Rivière du Loup, on the St. Lawrence, to Quebec and Montreal, and the other via Picton, through the Northumberland Strait to Bay of Chaleurs, via Gaspé, up the St. Lawrence to Quebec, and thence by railroad to Montreal, where we all met under assumed names about the 21st of October.

As it was of vital importance that the utmost secrecy should be observed, the officers were directed to take lodgings in quiet private boarding houses, to avoid the hotels, not to recognize each other on the street, and not to be absent from their rooms for more than half an hour at a time. Finding Marshal Kane and some of our friends in Montreal, we set to work to prepare and perfect our arrangements the first object of the plan being to communicate with the prisoners on Johnson's Island, informing them that an attempt would be made to release them. This was effected through a lady from Baltimore, a Mrs. P. C. Martin, then residing with her husband and family in Montreal, and whose husband did all in his power to aid us in every way. She brought a letter from Baltimore which General [J. J.] Archer (who, with Major-General [I, R.] Trimble, was a prisoner at Johnson's Island) had sent there to Beverly Saunders, esq., telling us to communicate with him through the personal columns of the New York Herald, which Wilkinson very promptly did, telling A. J. L. W. that his solicitude was fully appreciated, and that a few nights after the 4th of November a carriage would be at the door, when all seeming obstacles would be removed, and to be ready. The obstacles alluded to were the U. S. S. *Michigan* and the prison guard. Our original plan was to go on board one of the lake steamers at Windsor, opposite Detroit, as passengers, and when fairly out on the lake to play the old St. Nicholas game, and by rising on the officers and crew take possession and run her to Johnson's Island, trusting to the prisoners to overpower the guard, while we would be ready to receive them on board for transportation to the Canada shore; but finding that the steamers seldom and at irregular intervals stopped at Windsor, or at any point on the Canada side, we changed the plan at the suggestion of a Canadian named McCuaig, who was introduced to Kane by Mr. Hale, of Tennessee, as a good and reliable Southern sympathizer, engaged in running the blockade, and occupying a high commercial position in Canada. He entered into our views with enthusiasm, and we believe that up to the last moment he was heart and soul with us; but more of him directly. A reliable man was sent to Sandusky to ascertain the strength of the garrison, position of the guns, etc., and on his return we were delighted to bear that the U. S. S. *Michigan*, under Jack Carter, was lying at anchor about 200 yards from the island, with her guns (having six reported as mounted) bearing upon the prison; that there were but 400 troops on the island, and no artillery save two small howitzers, one of which was upon a ferryboat plying between the island and the city. Two small 9-pounders were quietly purchased; Colt furnished us with 100 navy revolvers, with an ample supply of pistol ammunition, of course through several indirect channels. Dumb-bells were substituted for cannon balls, as it would have excited suspicion to have asked for such an article in Montreal; powder, bullets, slugs, butcher knives in lieu of cutlasses, and grapnels were obtained, and all preparations made to arm the escaped Confederate officers and soldiers, who, to the number of 150, we were promised could be induced to act with us in any way to benefit our cause; but when the time came for them to come forward only 32 volunteered, and with our party thus augmented to 54 we determined to make the attempt on the *Michigan* on the following plan: From Ogdensburg, in New York, there is a line of screw steamers plying to Chicago in the grain and provision trade, and as they return nearly empty to Chicago, and some times carry the Adams Express Company's safe, we decided to take deck passage on board one of them as mechanics and laborers bound to Chicago to work on the city waterworks there, and with this view one of our clever privates, named Connelly, was sent over to Ogdensburg, who paid the passage money for 25 of us in advance, to be taken on board at some point on the Welland Canal, and while doing so he made an agreement to take as many more laborers as he could obtain, their passage being fixed at the same price, to which the New Yorker consented, and gave him the ticket to show to the captain of the boat. We were then to assemble at St. Catharines, on the canal, go on board the steamer (one of our men, apparently entirely unconnected with us, having charge of the guns, powder, pistols, etc., boxed up in casks, boxes, etc., and marked "Machinery, Chicago," going on board the same steamer with us), and when fairly out in Lake Erie, and well clear of British jurisdiction, we were to rise on the officers and crew, overpower them, seize the steamer, mount our two 9-pounders, arm the men, secure the prisoners, and push on for Sandusky, timing our arrival so as to reach the *Michigan* about daylight, collide with her, as if by accident, board and carry her by the cutlass and pistol, and then with her guns, loaded with grape and canister, trained on the prison headquarters, send a boat on shore to demand an unconditional surrender of the island, with its prisoners, garrison material of war, etc. upon penalty of being fired into and the prisoners being released without restraint upon their actions. Major [W. S.] Pierson, the commanding officer, is said to be a humane man, and seeing the disadvantage at which we would have him, with the prisoners by this time clamorous for their release, he would have been compelled to surrender, and with the half dozen steamers at the wharf in Sandusky we could have speedily landed the whole 2,000 prisoners on the Canada shore, distant only some 40 miles; and then with the *Michigan* under our command, and she the only man-of-war on the lakes, with a crew composed of our 54 and some 50 others of such men as the Berkleys, Randolphs, Paynes, and others among the prisoners, we would have had the lake shore from Sandusky to Buffalo at our mercy, with all the vast commerce of Lake Erie as our just and lawful prey. So confident were we of success and so admirable were our arrangements that we had all assembled at St. Catharines, on the canal, waiting in hourly anticipation the arrival of the steamer, when the storm burst upon us in the shape of Mr. Stanton's telegram to the mayors of the lake cities to be on their guard against a Confederate raid, which he had been notified by the governor-general of Canada (Lord Monck) had been organized in Canada for operations on Lake Erie. Thus, my dear admiral, with victory, and such a victory, within our grasp, we were foiled, and so anxious were the British authorities to keep on good terms with their detested neighbors (for they do detest them) that the troops who were about to be removed from Port Colborne, the Lake Erie terminus of the canal, were ordered to remain at that place, with instructions to arrest any vessel passing through the canal with a suspicious number of passengers on board. With our plan thus foiled, and with the lake cities in a fever of fear and excitement, and with the rapid advance of reinforcements, both naval and military, to reinforce the garrison at Johnson's Island against our compact little band of 52 Confederates, we had, as a matter of course, to abandon the design, and leave Canada as soon as possible, but to do so in a dignified and proper manner. Wilkinson, Loyall, and I (Coleman, Kelly, and Brest) remained in Montreal from five to ten days, giving to the Canadian authorities every opportunity to arrest us, if it was thought proper to do so, but Lord Monck was satisfied with having frustrated our plans, and did not care to complicate the matter or to show his zeal for the Yankees in any other shape than the very decisive one of informing on us. And thus we came away, leaving our poor fellows to bear the increased hardships of their dreary prison life for months to come.

And now for the sickening part. It appears that McCuaig, whom I believed to have been earnestly with us, became alarmed at the last moment, when our success seemed so certain, and fearing the ultimate bearing of it upon his own individual fortunes, involving perhaps failure, exile, loss of position and imprisonment, betrayed us to Mr. Holden, a member of the provincial cabinet, who at once communicated it to the governor-general, and hence the discovery.

So, but for treachery, which no one can guard against, our enterprise would have been the feature of the war, and our little Navy another laurel wreath of glorious renown. Leaving Quebec we traveled in open wagons and buggies through the wilds of Lower Canada and New Brunswick, often looking into the houses on the Maine side of the river, with a desire to do to them as their people do to ours; but as our policy is different, and as we carry on the war more on principles of civilization, the feeling was a childish one, though the contempt one felt for the cowardly dogs who crossed the line to avoid the dreaded draft was only natural, and still more so when their daily papers poured such venom on our cause and all connected with it. Taking the steamer at the small village of Tobique, we came down the St. John River, and at St. John we went on board the steamer *Emperor*, in which we crossed the Bay of Fundy to the village of Windsor, in Nova Scotia, and thence by railroad to Halifax, where I volunteered for and obtained the command of the captured steamer *Chesapeake*, then supposed to be making her way to the port of St. Mary's, about 70 miles to the eastward of Halifax, but before I could get to her with my crew and officers, with the idea of making her a regular cruiser, she had been forced by stress of weather to put into a British port, where her arrival was telegraphed, and, as a great excitement had been made over her novel capture, both English and Yankees were endeavoring to get her; and as I had but a forlorn hope of ever reaching her in a dull, heavy-sailing collier, the attempt was abandoned, and thus I lost my chance of a command afloat, when I had invitingly open before me the prospect of so much damage to the enemy's coasting trade. At Bermuda (where we arrived on the morning of the 17th of December in the royal mail steamer *Alpha*) I found Bob Carter, of the Navy, in command of the Navy Department blockade-running steamer *Coquette*, purchased by Commander Bulloch, of the Navy, to run in naval supplies and out cotton for our service. Finding some cloth on board for you, I brought it over with me in the little steamer *Presto*, but by whom it was sent I do not know. After a very rough and exciting passage of four days, during which I did not have my clothes off, we succeeded in eluding the blockading squadron and reached Wilmington in safety on the 7th of January, our little steamer, under John Wilkinson, being the only one of four leaving about the same time that succeeded in getting into port, the others being wrecked on the coast. On the day of my return to Richmond with important dispatches from abroad my former position as lieutenant commanding the ordnance works was offered me and accepted, with more work ahead of me than I can do justice to.

I hope, my dear sir, that you have entirely recovered the use of your leg, and that you suffer no pain or inconvenience from your wound, and that you have recently had good news from Mrs. Buchanan. Captain Mitchell delivered your very kind message a day or two since; for which please accept my thanks, and if I can assist you in any way my services are entirely at your command.

I remain, my dear admiral, very truly, your friend,

R. D. Minor

Admiral Franklin Buchanan, C. S. Navy
Commanding Naval Forces, Mobile, Ala.

Appendix D: Initial Report of Lieutenant Commander Austin Pendergrast, Federal Commander of the USS Water Witch

Official Records of the Union and Confederate Movies in the War of the Rebellion (Washington, D.C.: Navy Department, 1894–1927), series I, vol. xv, pp. 474–475 and 477–479.

C. S. Naval Hospital,
Savannah, Ga., June 9, 1864.

SIR: Through the kindness of Commodore William W. Hunter, commanding the Confederate States naval forces at this place, I am permitted to report to you the capture of the U.S.S. *Water Witch*, at 2 A.M. on the morning of the 3d instant, by being boarded by seven of the enemy's boats whilst lying in Ossabaw Sound, Georgia. It affords me great satisfaction to state that the vessel was well defended, and we had only to succumb to superior numbers, and I have but little doubt we would have succeeded in beating the enemy off had it not been that the majority of the officers, including myself, were wounded early in the attack. Of the crew, 49 men and 13 officers are now prisoners.

The wounded are well cared for in this hospital, the surgeons manifesting much kindness toward us. At some future day I will make out a report in detail, when I hope to be able to give such an explanation of this sad affair as will prove satisfactory.

I hope and beg in the most expressive terms that the Department will take such steps as will effect an early exchange of the officers and crew for reasons which I shall be able to give when that event occurs.

I have the honor to be, very respectfully, your obedient servant,

Austin Pendergrast,
Lieutenant-Commander, U. S. Navy,

Hon. Gideon Welles,
    Secretary of the U. S. Navy, Washington, D.C.

Additional report of Lieutenant-Commander Pendergrast,
Federal commander of the USS *Water Witch*.

Washington, D. C., *October 22, 1864.*

SIR: In conformity with the desire expressed in my official report of June, 1864, to make a full statement of the capture of the U. S. S. *Water Witch*, I have the honor to submit the following:

On the morning of June 3, 1864, about 3 A.M., we were attacked by the enemy in 7 launches, containing, according to rebel accounts, 145 officers and men of the rebel Navy. Owing to the darkness of the night, and the carelessness of the officer of the deck, Acting Master's Mate E. D. W. Parsons, the boats were allowed to approach within 30 yards of us before the alarm was given, which was done in such a slight manner as to have but little effect in assembling the men at quarters. On hearing a noise, I sprang up the companion way and inquired of the officer of the deck what was the matter, but received no reply except from the rebels, who were shouting the word "Rebels! Rebels!"

I immediately gave the order to slip and start the engine ahead, and send everybody on deck, and then jumped to my stateroom to get my arms and some clothing. Upon regaining the deck, while making my way to the hurricane deck, I was struck by a cutlass on the head and rendered insensible.

Upon recovering my faculties I went on the hurricane deck and rang the bell to go ahead on the engine in hopes of swamping the boats of the enemy. The engine made half a revolution and then stopped for some unaccountable reason. Soon after ringing the bell I fell on the deck from loss of blood.

During this time all of the officers, with the exception of the engineers, and Acting Master's Mate Parsons, who, I believe, left the deck and went below without being relieved, were fighting with great bravery and success upon the quarter-deck, not only keeping the enemy from boarding, but dropping two out of four boats that attacked us aft, astern, two of which were so much cut up as to be unable to return to the attack, but drifted helpless until they reached the enemy's batteries at Beaulieu, while the fourth boat made but few efforts to board. Of the number that gained our decks, but one succeeded in reaching the engine room.

A few of the men, with Coast Pilot R. B. K. Murphy, were fighting the enemy forward, but were soon wounded and rendered unfit for action by loss of blood. The enemy then meeting no resistance was able to gain our deck, and after securing the hatches poured aft in such numbers as to soon overpower the few officers left engaged in repelling the enemy on the quarter-deck.

The men seemed paralyzed with fear, and remained under the hurricane deck without giving the officers the least support, though they were ordered out by Acting Assistant Paymaster Billings and Acting Ensign Hill. I found it impossible to discover the whereabouts of the men, owing to the darkness, and there was but little opportunity for the officers to give many orders, as all were engaged in combat the moment they reached the deck, and continued to fight until struck down.

I regret to say the watch below evinced no desire to come on deck and defend the ship. Had the crew but emulated the noble example shown them by their officers, the result would have been far different.

I am at a loss to explain the behavior of the men, unless they were dissatisfied with being detained over the term of their enlistment, as nearly all of them were. I had already sent home for discharge 20 of my best men, by order of Rear-Admiral J. A. Dahlgren, leaving me short in my crew, also 2 watch officers (an acting master and acting ensign) had been detached from me, as well as an acting master's mate rendering it necessary for me to order the acting master's mates to stand watch alone.

I regret to say that the engineers acted in the most cowardly manner. They were the only officers who surrendered and that to one man. Had they obeyed my orders to work the engine, the enemy would have been unable to board us, but so far from fighting rebels they surrendered at the first summons and thereby lost the ship.

While a prisoner of war, Acting First Assistant Engineer Samuel Genther has conducted himself in the most disgraceful manner, having openly declared that as he considered himself no longer an officer in the United States Navy, he did not fight, and that the rebels ought not to hold him as a prisoner of war, and while confined at Macon, Ga., he made the same statement to Colonel George C. Gibbs, commanding prisons, asking to be released from confinement on those grounds.

That the enemy paid dearly for their victory their long list of killed and wounded will evince, numbering 32 officers and men. Among their killed [were] their commanding officer, Lieutenant Pelot, and the only pilot they had to depend upon for the Savannah River. Soon after the capture of the vessel she was run up into Green Island Sound, where she ran aground, and when the last of the officers left her, she had only 18 inches of water under her. Late the same evening she was got off by lightening her, and succeeded in getting under the guns of Beaulieu battery. The officers and crew were then sent to Savannah; the wounded were well taken care of at the naval hospital at that place. The remainder were sent to Macon and Andersonville, Ga.

Notwithstanding the defeat which I have sustained, I can not close this report without recommending to the kind consideration of the Department the gallant conduct of those officers and men who so bravely defended their ship.

To C. W. Buck, acting master, Acting Ensign Chase Hill, Ensign A. D. Stover, Acting Assistant Paymaster L. G. Billings, Acting Master's Mate C. P. Weston, Coast Pilot R. B. K. Murphy, Henry Williams, captain of hold, John Williams, captain of afterguard, John Parker, gunner's mate, Jarvis T. Hazelton, coxswain, I am indebted for a cordial support in the defense of the ship, and though every one of them was wounded, and many of them threatened with instant death unless they would say that they surrendered, I am proud to say that not one of them disgraced himself by doing so.

The enemy with the aid of a greatly superior force, assisted by the neglect of duty on the part of the officer of the deck, and by the questionable conduct of the engineers, was enabled to take possession of the ship, but she was never surrendered to them.

I have the honor to be, very respectfully, your obedient servant,

Austin Pendergrast,
Lieutenant-Commander, U. S. Navy,

Hon. Gideon Welles,
Secretary of the Navy, Washington, D.C.

Appendix E: Officers Assigned to the CSS Savannah through December, 1864

Name	Grade
Baker, Thomas	Gunner
Barclay, A. A. E. W.	Master's Mate
Berrien, Thomas M.	Midshipman
Blackie, Andrew	Boatswain
Caldwell, George W.	Second Assistant Engineer
Carnes, William W.	Second Lieutenant
Carter, Barron	Midshipman
Comstock, William V.	First Lieutenant
Curdy, Joseph	Second Assistant Engineer
Dallas, Moses	Pilot
Dalton, Hamilton H.	First Lieutenant
Doak, Algernon S.	Midshipman
Fairfax, Julian	Master
Golder, Hamilton	Master's Mate
Goode, William D.	Midshipman
Hogan, John J.	Carpenter
Hudgins, Willam E.	First Lieutenant
Johnston, Oscar F.	First Lieutenant
Jones, C. Lucian	Assistant Paymaster
Jones, J. Pembroke	First Lieutenant
Jones, William C.	Assistant Surgeon
Keim, Charles W.	Assistant Paymaster
Kollock, E. C.	Flag Officer's Secretary

Name	Grade
Long, James C.	Master
McGrath, J. W.	Third Assistant Engineer
Minor, Hubbard T.	Midshipman
Pinkney, Robert F.	Captain
Porter, Thomas K.	First Lieutenant
Sanford, John W., Jr.	Assistant Surgeon
Trimble, John D.	Midshipman
Worth, James M.	Paymaster's Clerk
Younge, Bragg	Third Assistant Engineer

Appendix F: Report of Commander Brent, C.S. Navy, Regarding Operations Connected with the Evacuation of the City of Savannah

Official Records of the Union and Confederate Navies in the War of the Rebellion (Washington, D.C.: Navy Department, 1894–1927), series I, vol. XVI, pp. 483–485.

CHARLESTON, S. C., December 24, 1864.

Sir: I enclose the copy of a dispatch I received from the Secretary of the Nary, dated Richmond, December 14. The original, which I retain, is dated Charleston, December 15, and forwarded to you by General Beauregard, with the request that Lieutenant-General Hardee would have it deciphered and transmitted. I enclose a copy of a letter dated December 17, I received from the office of orders and detail, at Hardeeville. I was most anxious to carry out the instructions of the Department in relation to the escape of the vessels from Savannah after its occupation by the enemy, and with this view was making preparations to put the *Savannah* in a fit condition for sea. I directed Lieutenant McAdam, Provisional Navy C. S., the officer who laid the torpedoes, to remove with all possible dispatch those that obstructed the passage to sea by the way of Turner's Rocks. In his report, dated the 20th, he states that he immediately proceeded to the C. S. S. *Savannah*, where he was furnished with two boats and their crews, but after every endeavor he found that with all the appli-

auces at his command, grapnels, etc., he was unable with the motive power
of boats to remove any one of then, the anchors to which they are attached
being, too firmly embedded in the sand. The steam tender *Firefly* towed
the boats. Finding it impossible, with the means at my command, before
the time fixed upon for the evacuation of the city, to remove the torpedoes, I determined that it would not be proper to attempt the passage of
the river in that direction, and the passage by the North Channel was-
effectually obstructed. Under those circumstances it did not seem to me
possible to carry out the instructions of the Department in regard to taking the *Savannah* to sea and fighting her way into this or some other port.
As to the *Isondiga*, she was a very inferior vessel in speed and her magazine was very much exposed. I therefore thought her best chances of
escape would be to attempt to go up the river if a passage could be found
not commanded by the enemy's batteries. The *Water Witch* was burned
on the 19th, after consultation with the commanding general and by his
advice, to prevent her falling into the hands of the enemy. In a conference
I had with Generals Beauregard and Hardee a few days before the evacuation, the plan was fixed upon that the *Savannah* should attempt to get
to sea by Wassaw Sound, and the *Isondiga* and *Firefly* up the river. This
proved to be impracticable, principally on account of the torpedoes, as
before stated. General Hardee requested me to remain after the evacuation of the city until Thursday night, the 22nd instant, to protect valuable stores at Screven's Ferry, and which could not be sooner removed,
and informing me that Major-General Wheeler had been directed to keep
in constant communication with me to inform me of the movements of
the enemy, and if those movements should render my position unsafe that
I should be advised by General Wheeler. I was happy to have it in my
power to render very important service in the construction of pontoon
bridges with detachments of the crew of the *Savannah* and *Georgia*, under
Boatswain McCalla. On the morning of the 21st the enemy, in possession
of the city, opened upon the ship a well-directed fire of field artillery from
the bluff near the gas works. I was unable to give my guns sufficient ele-
vation to reach them when I returned the fire. On the evening of the 21st
Captain Quirk [Manning J. Kirk?], the commanding officer, and having
charge of the transportation at Screven's Ferry, informed me that he
intended evacuating that night by 8 o'clock, and asking me if I could land
my command by that time. The city and commanding positions being in
possession of the enemy, every outlet of escape closed except that by
Screven's Ferry, and my supply of provisions getting short, I considered
it my duty to destroy my ship to prevent her from falling into the hands
of the enemy, and to save the officers and crew. Accordingly, at about 7:30
P.M., the ship was fired, having previously landed her officers and crew,
except the firing party under charge of the executive officer, Lieutenant

Hudgins. I left with the last boat. Upon landing at Screven's Ferry, the wharf there was fired, and the *Firefly*, which was alongside of it.

I then proceeded with the officers and men in a march of about 18 miles to Hardeeville. Nothing was saved except what was carried about the person, and no transportation could be obtained from the army except a wagon to carry the sick, who could not march. On the morning of the 22nd I arrived with my command at Hardeeville, where I received by the hands of Lieutenant Ingraham, Provisional Navy C. S., the letter from the Navy Department referred to at the commencement of this letter. It was then too late to carry out the orders of the Department, even had it been in my power to do so. I found at Hardeeville Lieutenant Dalton, with the officers and crew of the *Isondiga*, which he had burned, on account of her getting ashore above the pontoon bridge in Back River, after the enemy had possession of the city, and whilst he was coming down the river to communicate with me. His report will be enclosed if ready before the closing of this dispatch. Upon application to Lieutenant-General Hardee, I obtained transportation for the officers and crews of the vessels to this place, leaving Hardeeville on the evening of the 22nd and arriving here on the night of the 23rd. I immediately reported to Flag-officer Ingraham, through whom the sick were sent to the naval hospital, and on the following morning to Flag-Officer Tucker, who placed the officers and crew on board the receiving ship. On the 24th I telegraphed my arrival to the Navy Department and am awaiting orders. On yesterday, the 25th, Flag-Officer Tucker asked me to place 100 men under Lieutenant Dalton, principally composed of the crews of the *Isondiga* and *Georgia*, with the marines of the *Savannah*, under Lieutenant Pratt, to reinforce Fort Johnson, threatened with an attack by the enemy. The rest of the command, consisting of about 300 men, under Lieutenant Hudgins, of the *Savannah*, were kept in readiness if required. I send this under charge of Third Assistant Engineer T. O. McClosky, with orders to report to you. I have transmitted a copy of this report to the Navy Department.

I am, sir, very respectfully, your obedient servant,

THOS. W. BRENT,
Commander.

Flag-Officer W. W. HUNTER,
Commanding Afloat, Savannah River.

Appendix G: The Gold and Silver in the Confederate States Treasury

Southern Historical Society Papers, vol. XXI, 1893, pp. 304–308.

I was an officer of the United States Navy from 1841 to 1861. In the latter year I entered the Confederate Navy as lieutenant. During the years 1863–'64–'65 I was the superintendent of the Confederate States Navy Academy. The steamer *Patrick Henry* was the school-ship and the seat of the academy. On the 1st day of April, 1863, we were lying at a wharf on the James river between *Richmond* and *Powhatan*. We had on board some sixty midshipmen and a full corps of professors. The midshipmen were well drilled in infantry tactics, and all of the professors save one had served in the army or navy.

On Sunday, April 2, 1865, I received about noon a dispatch from Hon. S. R. Mallory, Secretary of the Navy, to the following effect: "Have the corps of midshipmen, with the proper officers, at the Danville depot to-day at 6 P.M.; the commanding officer to report to the Quartermaster-General of the army."

Upon calling at the Navy Department I learned that the city was to be evacuated immediately, and that the services of the corps were required to take charge of and guard the Confederate treasure.

Accordingly at 6 o'clock I was at the depot with all my officers and men—perhaps something over one hundred, all told—and was then put in charge of a train of cars, on which was packed the Confederate treasure, and the money belonging to the banks of Richmond.

About Half a Million

I will here remark that neither the Secretary of the Treasury, nor the Treasurer were with the treasure. The senior officer of the Treasury present was a cashier, and he informed me, to the best of my recollection, that there was about $500,000 in gold, silver, and bullion. I saw the boxes containing it, many times in the weary thirty days I had it under my protection, but I never saw the coin.

Sometime in the evening the President, his Cabinet and other officials left the depot for Danville. The train was well packed. General Breckenridge, Secretary of War, however, did not start with the President. He remained with me at the depot until I got off, which was not until somewhere near midnight. The General went out of the city on horseback.

Our train being heavily loaded and crowded with passengers—even the roofs and platform-steps occupied—went very slowly. How we got by Amelia Courthouse without falling in with Sheridan's men, has been a mystery to me to this day. We were unconscious of our danger, however, and took matters philosophically. Monday, April 3d, in the afternoon, we arrived at Danville, where we found the President and his Cabinet, save General Breckenridge, who came in on Wednesday. On Monday night Admiral Semmes arrived with the officers and men of the James River squadron. His was the last train out of Richmond.

We did not unpack the treasure from the cars at Danville. Some, I believe, was taken for the use of the government, and, I suspect, was paid out to General Johnston's men after the surrender, but the main portion of the money remained with me. The midshipmen bivouacked near the train.

In the Mint

About the 6th of April, I received orders from Mr. Mallory to covey the treasure to Charlotte, N. C., and deposit it in the mint. Somewhere about the 8th, we arrived at Charlotte. I deposited the money-boxes in the mint, took a receipt from the paper officials, and supposed that my connection with it was at an end. Upon attempting to telegraph back to Mr. Mallory for further orders, however, I found that Salisbury was in the hands of the enemy—General Stoneman's men, I think.

The enemy being between me and the President (at least such was the report at the time, though I am not sure now that it was so), and the probability being that he would immediately push for Charlotte, it became necessary to remove the money. I determined, on my own responsibility, to convey it to Macon, Ga.

Mrs. President Davis and family were in town. They had left Richmond a week before the evacuation. I called upon her, represented the danger of capture, and persuaded her to put herself under our protection. A company of uniformed men, under Captain Tabb, volunteered to accompany me. These men were attached to the navy-yard in Charlotte. Most of them belonged to the game little town of Portsmouth, Va., and a better set of men never shouldered a musket. They were as true as steel.

Having laid in, from the naval storehouse, large quantities of coffee, sugar, bacon, and flour, we started in the cars with the treasure and arrived at Chester, S. C. This was, I think, about the 12th of April.

Formed a Train

We here packed the money and papers in wagons and formed a train. We started the same day for Newberry, S. C. Mrs. Davis and family were provided by General Preston with an ambulance. Several ladies in our party—wives of officers—were in army wagons; the rest of the command were on foot, myself included.

The first night we encamped at a crossroads "meeting-house." I here published orders regulating our march and made every man carry a musket. The Treasury clerks, bank officers, and others made up a third company, and we mustered some one hundred and fifty fighting men. Supposing that General Stoneman would follow, we held ourselves ready to repel an attack by day and night.

At sunset of the second day we went into camp about thirty miles form Newberry, S. C., and breaking camp very early the next morning, we crossed the beautiful Broad river on pontoon bridge at noon, and about 4 P.M. arrived at Newberry. The quartermaster immediately prepared a train of cars, and we started for Abbeville, S. C., as soon as the treasure could be transferred.

Always Ahead

On the march across the state of South Carolina we never permitted a traveler to go in advance of us, and we were not on a line of telegraphic communication; yet, singular to say, the news that we had the Confederate money was always ahead of us. [See Sir Walter Scott's remark on this point in "Old Mortality."] We arrived at Abbeville at midnight, and passed the remainder of the night in the cars. Mrs. Davis and family here left me and went to the house of the Hon. Mr. Burt, a former member of Congress. In the morning we formed a wagon train and started for Washington, Georgia. The news we got at different places along the route was bad; "unmerciful disaster followed fast and followed faster." We "lightened ship" as we went along—throwing away books, stationery, and perhaps Confederate money. One could have traced us by these marks, and have formed an idea of the character of the news we were receiving.

From Abbeville to Washington is about forty miles, and we made a two days' march of it. The first day we crossed the Savannah river about 2 P.M. and went into camp. The next day we arrived at Washington. Here we learned that General Wilson, United States army, with 10,000 cavalry, had captured Macon, and was on his way north.

After a day's deliberation and a consultation with some of the citizens of Washington, I determined to go to Augusta.

Heard of the Surrender

On the 18th of April, or thereabouts, we left in the train, and at the junction, while we were waiting for the western train to pass, we heard of General Lee's surrender. This we did not at the time credit. We arrived at Augusta in due time, and I made my report to General D. B. Fry, the commanding general. General Fry informed me he could offer no protection, as he had few troops, and was expecting to surrender to General Wilson as soon as he appeared with his cavalry. However, Generals Johnston and Sherman had just declared an armistice, and that gave us a breathing spell. The money remained in the cars, and the midshipmen and the Charlotte company lived in the depot. While in Augusta, and afterwards, I was frequently advised by officious persons to divide the money among the Confederate, as the war was over, and it would otherwise fall into the hands of the Federal troops.

The answer to this was that the war was not over as long as General Johnston held out, and that the money would be held intact until we met President Davis.

Declined to Disband

While waiting in Augusta I received a telegraphic dispatch from Mr. Mallory directing me to disband my command; but under the circumstances I declined to do so.

On the 20th of April, General Fry noticed me that the armistice would end the next day, and he advised me to "move on." I decided to retrace my steps, thinking it more than probable that President Davis wold hear of Mrs. Davis being left in Abbeville. Accordingly we left Augusta on the 23d, arrived at Washington the same day, formed a train again, and started for Abbeville. On the way we met Mrs. President Davis and family, escorted by Col. Burton N. Harrison, the President' private secretary. I have forgotten where they said they were going, if they told me.

Threats Made to Seize It

Upon our arrival at Abbeville, which was, I think, about the 28th, we stored the treasure in an empty warehouse and placed a guard over it.

The town was full of paroled men from General Lee's army. Threates were made by these men to seize the money, but the guard remained firm. On the night of May 1st I was aroused by the officer commanding the patrol, and told that "the Yankees were coming." We transferred the treasure to the train of cars which I had ordered to be kept ready with steam up, intending to run to Newberry.

Just at daybreak, as we were ready to start, we saw some horsemen descending the hills, and upon sending out scouts learned that they were the advance guard of President Davis.

About 10 A.M., May 2, 1865, President Davis and his Cabinet (save Messrs. Trenholm and Davis) rode in. They were escorted by four skeleton brigades of cavalry—not more than on thousand badly-armed men in all. These brigades were, I think, Duke's, Dibrell's, Vaughan's, and Ferguson's. The train was a long one. These were many brigadier-generals present-General Bragg among them-and wagons innumerable.

Turned Over to General Duke

I had several interviews with President Davis and found him calm and composed, and resolute to a degree. As soon as I saw Mr. Mallory he directed me to deliver the treasure to General Basil Duke, and disband my command. I went to the depot, and there, in the presence of my command, transferred it accordingly. General Duke was on horseback, and no papers passed. The Charlotte company immediately started for home, accompanied by our best wishes. I have a dim recollection that a keg of cents was presented to Captain Tabb for distribution among his men, and that the magnificent present was indignantly declined.

The treasure was delivered to General Duke intact so far as I know, though some of it was taken at Danville by authority. It had been guarded by the Confederate midshipmen for thirty days, and preserved by them. In my opinion this is what on other organization could have done in those days.

A Gallant Corps

And here I must pay a tribute to these young men-many of them mere lads-who stood by me for so many anxious days. Their training and discipline showed itself conspicuously during that time. During the march across South Carolina, footsore and ragged as they had become by that time, no murmur escaped them, and they never faltered. I am sure that Mr. Davis and Mr. Mallory, if they were alive, would testify to the fact that when they saw the corps in Abbeville, way-worn and weary after its long march, it presented the same undaunted front as when it left Richmond. They were staunch to the last, and verified the adage that "blood will tell."

The officers with me at this time were Captain Rochelle, Surgeon Garrleson, Paymaster Wheliss, and Lieutenant Peek, McGuire, Sanxay, and Armistead. Lieutenants Peek, McGuire, and Armistead are living, and will testify to the truth of the above narrative.

Immediately after turning the money over to General Duke I disbanded my command. And here end my personal knowledge of the Confederate treasure.

What Became of the Money

On the evening of May 2d, the President and troops started for Washington, Ga. The next day the cavalry insisted upon having some of the money (so its is stated), and General Breckinridge, with the consent of the President, I believe, paid out of them $100,000. A least, that is the sum I have seen stated. I know nothing of it myself. It was a wise proceeding on the part of the General, and it enabled the poor, worn-out men to reach their homes.

Its Disposition

The remainder of the treasure was carried to Washington, Ga. Here Captain M. H. Clark was appointed assistant treasurer, and in a frank and manly letter to the Southern Historical Society Papers, for December, 1881, he tells of the disposition of a portion of the money. Some $40,000, he says, was intrusted to two naval officers for a special purpose-to take to England, probably-but I happen to know that this was not done, and this money was never accounted for, and moderate sums were pair to various officers, whose vouchers he produces. Thus, it seems, he paid $1,500 to two of the President's aids, and the same amount to my command. That is, he gave us who had preserved the treasure for thirty days the same amount he gave to each of the aids. I do not know who ordered this distribution, but we were very glad to get it, as we were far from home and penniless. It gave us each twenty days' pay.

Never Accounted For

In my opinion a good deal of the money was never accounted for, and there remains what sailors call a "Flemish account" of it.

The Mysterious Box

Several years ago I read in the papers an account of a box being left with a widow lady who lived, in 1865, near the pontoon bridge across the Savannah river. It was to this effect: The lady stated that on May 3, 1865, a party of gentlemen on their way from Abbeville to Washington, Ga., stopped at her house, and were a long time in consultation in her parlor. These gentlemen were Mr. Davis and his Cabinet beyond a doubt. Upon leaving, they gave the lady a box, which, they stated, was too heavy to take with them. After they were gone the lady opened the box, and found it to be full of jewelry. Somewhat embarrassed with so valuable a gift, the lady sent for her minister (a Baptist) and told him his circumstances. By his advice, she buried the box in her garden secretly at night. A few days after, an officer rode up to the house, inquired about the box, and said he had been sent back for it. The lady delivered it up, and the man went off.

Now, I believe this story to be true in every respect, and I furthermore believe that the box contained the jewelry which had been contributed by patriotic Confederate ladies. The idea had been suggested some time in 1864, but was never fully carried out. Nevertheless, some ladies sacrificed their jewels, as I have reason to know.

As for the man who carried off the box, whether he was really sent back for it or was a despicable thief, will probably never be known, but to say the least, his action was, as our Scotch friends say, "vara suspicious."

Capture of President Davis

Mr. Davis was captured on the morning of May 9th, just a week after my interview with him at Abbeville. There were with him at the time Mrs. Davis and three children; Miss Howell, her sister; Mr. Reagan, Postmaster-General; Colonels Johnston, Lubbock, and Wood, volunteer aids; Mr. Burton Harrison, secretary, and, I think, a Mr. Barnwell, of South Carolina. There may have been others, but I do not know. Of these, all were captured save only Mr. Barnwell.

It is not my intention to write of this affair, as I was not present, and besides, Colonels Johnston and Lubbock, Judge Reagan, and others have written full accounts of it. I only intend to tell of the escape of my old friend and comrade, John Taylor Wood, as I had it from his lips only a few months ago in Richmond. It has never appeared in print, and I am only sorry I cannot put in the graphic language of Wood himself.

But this is what he told me, as well as I recollect:

Colonel Wood's Escape

The party was captured just before daybreak on the 9th of May. Wood was placed in charge of a Dutchman, who spoke no English. While the rest of the Federal troops were busy in securing their prisoners and plundering the camp, Wood held a $20 gold piece (the universal interpreter) to his guard, and signified his desire to escape. The Dutchman held up two fingers and nodded. Wood gave him $40 in gold, and sole off to a field, where he laid down among some brushwood. The Federals (under a Colonel Pritchett, I think), having finished their preparations, march off without missing Colonel Wood.

Started for Florida

After they were out of sight, Wood arose and found a broken-down horse, which had been left behind. He also found an old bridle, and mounting the nag, he started for Florida. I have forgotten his adventures, but somewhere on the route he fell in with Mr. Benjamin, Secretary of State, and General Breckinridge, Secretary of War. Benjamin and Breckinridge owed their escape to Wood, for Wood was an old naval officer and a thorough seaman. On the coast of Florida they bought a row-boat, and in company of a few others they rowed down the coast, intending either to cross to Cuba or the Bahamas.

A Close Call

Landing one day for water and to dig clams they saw a Federal gunboat coming up the coast. Wood mentioned as an evidence of the close watch the United States vessels were keeping, that as soon as the gunboat got abreast of them she stopped and lowered a boat. Thinking it best to put a blood face on the matter, Wood took a couple of men and rowed out to meet the man-of-war's boat. The officer asked who they were. They replied: "Paroled soldiers from Lee's army, making their way home." The officer demanded their paroles, and was told the men on shore had them. It was a long distance to pull, and the officer decided to return to his ship for orders. As he pulled away Wood cried to him: "Do you want to buy any clams?"

Upon the return of the boat she was hoisted up, the gunboat proceeded on her way, and our friends "saw her no more." Proceeding on her way to the southward, the party next fell in with a sail-boat, in which were three sailors, deserters from United States vessels at Key West, trying to make their way to Savannah. Wood and party took their boat, as she was a seaworthy craft, put the sailors in the row-boat, and gave them sailing directions for Savannah.

Wood then took the helm and steered for Cuba. In a squall that night he was knocked overboard. There was but one man in the boat who knew anything at all about managing her, and it looked black for him. Fortunately he caught the main sheet, which was trailing overboard, and was hauled in. It was providential, for upon Wood depended the safety of the entire party.

After suffering much from hunger and thirst they arrived at Matanzas (I think) and were kindly cared for by the Spanish authorities, from whom they received most respectful attention as soon as they made themselves known.

William H. Parker
Richmond, Va.

Appendix H: Confederate Naval Cadets

Southern Historical Society Papers, vol. XXXII, pp. 159–163.

It may not be known generally that the Confederate government had established and conducted through the last three years of its existence a regularly organized and well perfected naval school for the education of naval officers. Early in 1862 a prospectus appeared in one of the Richmond papers announcing the formation of an academy for the instruction of midshipmen; and soon after, by regular congressional appointments, the various district of the Confederacy were enlisted.

The school was under the command of Captain William H. Parker, a lieutenant of the old service. Assistant instructors in the various departments were detailed, some of them ex-students of Annapolis, and other men of high scholarship selection from the army. The steamer Yorktown, which, a few months before had participated in the conflict of the *Merrimac* and the *Monitor* as a tender to the former ship, was fitted up, given the name of *Patrick Henry*, and anchored off the shore batteries at Drewry's Bluff, where the school was quartered in cottages built for the purpose. Here she remained for a short time, and was then towed up the river to within two miles of Richmond, where she lay for nearly a year, with the entire academy on board, and finally, about eight months previous to the surrender, was moved up to this city and lay at Rocketts, where she perished in the flames of the 3d of April, 1865.

In March, 1865, the health of the crew became impaired by the foulness of bilge water, and the midshipmen were removed from the ship and quartered in a large tobacco factory on the corner of 24th and Franklin streets. The writer, in company with twelve or fifteen others, had been sent to the naval hospital in the city some two weeks previous.

On Sunday, the 2d of April, there were anxious looks upon the faces of medical officers of the hospital, and about 4 o'clock in the afternoon a midshipman, coming into the ward to see a sick comrade, met the jeers and amused expressions of many of us because he war armed and equipped as an infantry soldier instead of the dainty dress of the Confederate "Middy." The visitor informed us that at 2 o'clock that day orders had been issued for the corps to be armed as infantry, and that they had been marched to the naval storehouse in double-quick time and supplied with all the necessary accoutrements. Other rumor came in that members of the senior class and some passed-midshipmen had been seen as officers in infantry marching through the streets, and that a naval brigade had been formed ant the iron-clad squadron at Drewry's Bluff had been abandoned.

Then began a bustle in and about the wards, and at sundown the statements was freely bandied around that the President and cabinet had left the city, and that it was to be evacuated at once. At 8 o'clock the writer and two comrades drove in the hospital ambulance to the quarters of the midshipmen at the factory and found it empty. On one of the upper floors was the mahogany table and the silver table service of the wardroom, watched over by an old boatswain's mate, and, sitting in solemn state at the bottom of it, drinking, and eating crackers, was the second lieutenant. To him we mentioned the rumors, asked where the boys had gone, and requested to have the sailors transport our baggage to the depot from which the school had started. These he met with ridicule, denied the evacuation of the city and said the "Middies" had gone to Chapel Hill, N. C., which would be the seat of the naval academy for the rest of the war. He told us to return to the hospital and retire, and the next day leave with him and two other midshipmen for Chapel Hill. We did so, and on the next morning were awakened by the explosion of the magazines. Dressing rapidly, we proceeded to the surgeon's office and received our discharge from the hospital, with "permission to leave the city."

On going out into the street it appeared as if the final day of doom was upon us. The air was filled with smoke and sparks, and the darkness of twilight was over and about the city. Stores were being broken open and rifled; dead men—shot down in the attempt to rob—were lying at intervals, while Negroes fought over barrels of provisions that had been rolled from burning warehouses. Mingled with the roar of flames came the appalling crash of exploding magazines and the rumble of falling walls. Rapidly as possible we forced our way through the frantic masses and gained the Danville Railroad bridge, only to find it in flames at different points, and no evidence of trains on the southern side. Retracing our steps, we sought egress from the north side of the city. When crossing Main street we noticed two blocks below us, advancing on a trot, a regiment of Federal cavalry. They overtook us and rode by without observing us, although we were gorgeous in full uniform, but without side arms or accoutrements, save small haversacks, in which we had stored all the crackers we could get. By means of a locomotive, obtained under compulsion, and with the assistance of two army officers, we rode twenty-five miles from Richmond, and then, having no experienced engineer, and the steam being exhausted, we abandoned it on side track and reached the Valley of Virginia after days of tiresome progress of foot.

The Confederate Treasury

Going back now to the departure of the midshipmen from the warehouse, we can trace the connection of the Naval Academy with the fleeing treasury of the Confederacy. For the following accurate narrative we are indebted to the diary of Midshipman R. H. Fielding, then a zealous and efficient young officer, and now a Presbyterian minister of prominence in Virginia. He says: "We left our quarters at the tobacco factory at 4 P.M. on Sunday, and proceeded rapidly to the Danville depot. On reaching it we were formed in line and were addressed by Captain Lowall, the commandant of midshipmen, who told us that we had been selected by the secretary, because he believed us to be brave, honest and discreet young officers and gentlemen, for a service of peculiar danger and delicacy; that to our guardianship was to be committed a valuable train, containing the archives of the government, with its money. We were then marched into the depot, where our train, in company with others, was receiving freight. Guards were placed at all entrances, and the squad, with fixed bayonets, cleared the building of loafers and citizens.

"The train left the depot at midnight, and two midshipmen, with two loaded revolvers, were placed in each car containing the government boxes, one to sleep while the other watched, in these and their personal baggage. The next day we reached Danville, and on the 5th of April Admiral Semmes, with the men of the James River Squadron (the ironclads had been blown up on the night of the 2d) reached the point and were assigned to its defense. Midshipman Semmes was here detailed to his father (Secretary of Midshipman Breckenridge accompanied his father, Secretary of War) as his personal aid. Our train stood on the track not far from the depot, and our encampment was in a grove not far from the train.

"On the 9th of April, we left Danville and reached Greensboro, N. C., about 4 P.M., the 10th; then on to Charlotte. While there the money was placed in the mint and the midshipmen feasted at the leading hotels. On the 13th we were off to Chester, S. C. Here the government's specie, papers, treasury clerks and their wives, etc., were placed in wagons for a march across country to the railroad at Newberry. I saw the cargo transferred to the wagons, and there were small, square boxes, which we supposed contained gold, or bullion, and kegs, resembling beer kegs, which we inferred contained silver. The train was not a long one. Mrs. Davis and child and nurse occupied a large ambulance. I do not know whether she joined us at Greensboro or Charlotte. We marched to Newberry, reaching there on the 15th of April, and the same day took cars for Abbeville. Left Abbeville with wagon train on the 17th, and reached Washington, Ga., on the 19th. We went to Augusta, Ga., on the 20th, and here the money was placed in the vaults of a bank. Some of it, I know not how much, was sold to citizens; at least men crowded around with Confederate currency to get gold. On the 26th we were ordered back to Washington, Ga., the things going along with us. (It seems the "middies" had playfully dubbed the specie boxes, the things.)

The Coin

"On the 27th midshipmen who desired them were offered furloughs, which were accepted by all but five Virginians—Quaries, Hudson, Slaughter, Carter and Fleming. The things were again put in wagons, and across the country we marched on the 19th of April at Abbeville, S. C., where the things were put on board some cars that stood at the depot. We had no guard duty to do after leaving Washington, Ga. On May the 2d President Davis and Staff and Cabinet reached Abbeville, coming, I imagined, from Charlotte, on horseback. On that day we five Virginians were discharged, as per the following order, probably the last official act of the navy of the Confederate States:

"ABBEVILLE, S. C., May 2, 1865.

"'Sir,—You are hereby detached from the Naval School, and leave is granted you to visit your home. You will report by letter to then Hon. Secretary of the Navy as soon as practicable. Paymaster Wheless will issue you ten day's rations, and all quartermasters are requested to furnish transportation.

"'Respectfully, your obd't servant,

"'WILLIAM H. PARKER,

"'Commanding.'"

In continuation, Mr. Fleming does not know when the money left Abbeville, but thinks it was on the morning of the 1st of May. Some money was paid to the soldiers at Greensboro, how rattling did not know, but says he observed soldiers en route home rattling coins in their pockets and singing, "One dollar and fifteen cents for four years' service." The President and staff left on the night of the 2d. A committee of five discharged midshipmen, through Captain Parker, requested Secretary Reagan before leaving to pay them in gold sufficient to enable them to reach home. He obtained several hundred dollars to be distributed pro rota among the naval officers, and the midshipmen received forty dollars apiece. They remained in Abbeville until May 7, when they started homeward. A few days before the remaing specie had been placed in charge of some general of the army, and there personal knowledge of it ends.

This is the high testimony of a man who had followed closely the fortunes of the Confederate cause in its death throes, and who adhered until the last feeble nucleus of an organization had dissolved, In the close of a private communication recently received from him he says, referring to the imputations against President Davis and his connection with the government money: "I have no word of commendation for his accusers. Mr. Davis was never with the specie train a single day during our connection with it."

We contribute this as a subject which has never been referred to in any written records of the war, and it possibly contains a more succinct history of the route pursued by the heads of the government after the 3d of April than any yet given.

We have ever regarded the safe transit of this treasure through so large an area of country as a tribute to the honesty and law-abiding spirit of the Southern people. It will not be forgotten that the region through which it passed, with its little guard of forty boys, was filled with stragglers and unofficered bands of scattered and suffering soldiers—men knowing all the pangs of hunger and destitution of clothing and utterly hopeless of the success of their cause, yet men who obeyed through their sense of right when no law existed, and kept their hands free from the stain of robbery while boxes of this treasure lay in their midst, with only the lives of its slender little bodyguard between them and its possession.

(The coin belonging to the Richmond banks was upon the same train, but on a different car. It was under the charge of the officers of the banks, we believe. EDITOR CONFEDERATE COLUMN.)

Biographical

Dr. John W. Harris was born in Augusta county, Virginia, July 16, 1848. His father was Dr. Clement R. Harris, M.D., surgeon in charge of the gangrene ward in Dellivan Hospital, at Charlottesville, Va. His mother was Eliza McCue, of Scotch descent. His early boyhood was spent near Brandy Station, Culpeper county, Va. This home was broken up by the war. In 1863–'64 he entered the Confederate States service from Washington and Lee University, Lexington, Va., enlisting with Mosby. He could, in his vivid and versatile manner, tell of his experience with this command, which was varied and oftentimes savored of hairbreadth escapes. In January, 1865, he received from his congressman the appointment as midshipman in the Confederate States Navy. He passed in examination before Secretary Mallory and went aboard the school ship, *Patrick Henry*, at Rocketts, James river, Richmond, Va., where he remained until a few days before the evacuation of Richmond, when, with many of the ship's crew, having contracted dysentery, he was sent to the old Belleview Block Hospital, at which place the ever-memorable morning of the 3d of April, 1865, found him somewhat improved, though by no means sufficiently strong for the journey to his home, after receiving his discharge. He, with two of his shipmates, began a forced and weary tramp, however, up the old Central Railroad for Staunton, Va. They tarried and rested a few hours with his friend, Mr. Pratt, at the University of Virginia, and in due time they reached the old homestead at Mount Solon, Augusta county.

We all know what those days were to older hearts and heads than his, but he carried with him to the end the consciousness that he had stood by his State through her dreadful ordeal. While at the University of Virginia, three years after the war, he formed a lasting friendship with his classmate, the late lamented Henry W. Grady, whose untimely death he deeply mourned. These two friends died of the same disease, only one month apart. Dr. Harris studied the problems of unity between the North and south, and thought that Grady's genius was the touchstone that would be a power in formulating this unity of interest.

During the prevailing epidemic of la grippe, which appeared in Staunton in 1890, Dr. Harris was engaged in taking care of others, and in thus exposing himself to the weather, he contracted cold, which was followed by acute pneumonia, which resulted in heart failure, which was the immediate cause of his death, January 24, 1890. He fell with his "harness" on in the faithful discharge of his professional duties.

Notes

Chapter 1

1. Civil War Centennial Commission of Tennessee. *Tennesseans in the Civil War*, vol. 1 (Nashville: Civil War Centennial Commission of Tennessee, 1964), pp. 233–242.

2. Ezra J. Warner, *Generals in Gray* (Baton Rouge: Louisiana State University Press, 1959), pp. 248–249.

3. "Muster Roll, Co. E, 42nd Tennessee Inf." Washington, D.C.: National Archives.

4. Warner, p. 216.

5. *Official Records of the Union and Confederate Armies in the War of the Rebellion*, series I, vol. XLV/I (Washington, D.C.: Government Printing Office, 1880–1901), pp. 720–725.

6. Civil War Centennial Commission, pp. 233–242.

Chapter 2

1. Charles O. Paullin, *Paullin's History of Naval Administration 1775–1911* (Annapolis: Naval Institute Press, 1968), p. 191.

2. *Ibid.*, p. 194.

3. Henry B. Sturdy, "The Establishment of the Naval School at Annapolis," *U.S. Naval Institute Proceedings* 72, 1946, p. 4.

4. Charles Todorich, *The Spirited Years: A History of the Antebellum Naval Academy* (Annapolis: Naval Institute Press, 1984), pp. 14–18.

5. *Journal of the Congress of the Confederate States of America, 1861–1865*, vol. I, p. 547.

6. Tom H. Wells, *The Confederate Navy: A Study in Organization* (Birmingham: University of Alabama Press, 1971), p. 67.

7. *Official Records of the Union and Confederate Navies in the War of the Rebellion*, series II, vol. II (Washington, D.C.: Government Printing Office, 1894–1927), p. 533.

8. *Ibid.*, p. 635.

9. *Civil War Naval Chronology, 1861–1865*, section VI (Washington, D.C.: Department of the Navy, Naval History Division, 1971), pp. 318–319.

10. William H. Parker, *Recollections of a Naval Officer* (1883; new edition, Annapolis: Naval Institute Press, 1985), p. 344.

11. Wells, p. 46.

12. *Ibid.*, p. 342.

13. J. Thomas Scharf, *History of the Confederate States Navy* (New York: Rogers & Sherwood, 1877), p. 774.

14. *Extracts from the Regulations of the Navy School*, Department of the Navy, CSA, December 15, 1863 (Special Collections Library, Duke University, Durham, North Carolina), p. 1.

15. *Ibid.*

16. Hubbard T. Minor, Diary, U. S. Army Military Research Collection, Carlisle, Pennsylvania.

17. G. Melvin Herndon, "The Confederate States Naval Academy," *Virginia Magazine of History and Biography*, July 1961, p. 306.

18. *Regulations for the Interior Police of the School-Ship* Patrick Henry, Department of the Navy, CSA, 1863 (Manuscript Collection, Yale University, New Haven, Connecticut), pp. 3–16.

19. *Regulations for the Confederate States School Ship* Patrick Henry, Department of the Navy, CSA, 1863 (Manuscript Department, Eleanor S. Brockenbrough Library, Museum of the Confederacy, Richmond, Virginia), pp. 1–30.

20. William H. Parker, *Questions on Practical Seamanship* (Richmond: Macfarland and Furgusson, 1863), pp. 1–92.

21. *Official Records ... Navies*, series II, vol. II, pp. 550–551.

22. Wells, pp. 69–70, 162–163.

23. *Regulations of the Confederate States School-Ship* Patrick Henry, pp. 9–10.

24. Scharf, p. 774.

25. *Regulations of the Confederate States School-Ship* Patrick Henry, pp. 10–11.

Chapter 3

1. Craig I. Symonds, Introduction to the 1985 edition of William H. Parker, *Recollections of a Naval Officer, 1841–1865* (originally published 1883; new edition, Annapolis: Naval Institute Press, 1985), pp. ix.

2. J. Thomas Scharf, *History of the Confederate States Navy* (New York: Rogers & Sherwood, 1877), p. 773.

3. Symonds, pp. ix–x.

4. *Ibid.*, p. xii.

5. *Ibid.*, p. xv.

6. Scharf, p. 773.

7. William H. Parker, *Recollections of a Naval Officer, 1841–1865* (1883; new edition, Annapolis: Naval Institute Press, 1985), p. 216.

8. Charles E. Clark, *My Fifty Years in the Navy* (Boston: 1917), p. 11.

9. Parker, p. 220.

10. *Ibid.*, p. 221.

11. *Ibid.*, p. 232.

12. William R. Trotter, *Ironclads and Columbiads* (Winston Salem, N.C.: John F. Blair, 1989), pp. 70–71.

13. *Official Records of the Union and Confederate Navies in the War of the Rebellion*, series I, vol. IV (Washington, D.C.: Government Printing Office, 1897–1927), p. 595.

14. Parker, pp. 260–261.

15. *Ibid.*, p. 272.

16. *Official Records ... Navies*, series I, vol. VII, p. 23.

17. *Ibid.*, pp. 56–57.

18. Parker, p. 299.

19. Tom H. Wells, *The Confederate Navy: A Study in Organization* (Birmingham: University of Alabama Press, 1971), p. 67.

20. Letter to R. Thomas Campbell from the Navy Register, United States Naval Academy, Nimitz Library, May 12, 1997.

21. Thomas T. Moebs, *Confederate States Navy Research Guide* (Williamsburg,Va.: Moebs, 1991), p. 234.

22. *Official Records ... Navies,* series I, vol. VII, p. 598.

23. John M. Coski, *Capital Navy* (El Dorado, Calif.: Savas Woodbury, 1996), p. 80.

24. *Official Records ... Navies,* series I, vol. II, pp. 822–828.

25. Scharf, p. 774.

26. *Ibid.,* p. 774.

27. *Register of Officers of the Confederate States Navy, 1861–1865* (Richmond: Department of the Navy, CSA, 1864).

28. Scharf, pp. 702–703.

29. Moebs, p. 227.

30. *Official Records ... Navies,* series I, vol. X, pp. 367–368.

31. Moebs, p. 227.

32. Coski, pp. 221–222.

33. Beverly Lyall (archivist, Nimitz Library, U.S. Naval Academy), letter to R. Thomas Campbell, April 24, 1997.

34. "Confederate Navy Record." State of Alabama, Department of Archives and History.

35. *Official Records ... Navies,* series I, vol. X, pp. 724–725.

36. Moebs, p. 204.

37. Eileen A. Ielmini (Georgia Historical Society), letter to R. Thomas Campbell dated April 29, 1997.

38. *Official Records ... Navies,* series II, vol. II, p. 135, 141.

39. *Ibid.,* series II, vol. I, p. 292.

40. Coski, pp. 195–210.

41. *Official Records ... Navies,* series I, vol. IX, pp. 669–674.

42. Moebs, p. 215.

43. Wells, p. 19.

44. *Civil War Naval Chronology* (Washington, D.C.: Department of the Navy, Naval History Division, 1971), p. vi–297.

45. Moebs, p. 201.

46. *Ibid.,* p. 248.

47. *Ibid.,* p. 191

48. *Ibid.,* p. 186.

49. *Ibid.,* p. 224.

50. *Ibid.,* p. 249.

51. Parker, p. 344.

52. Moebs, p. 202.

Chapter 4

1. John M. Coski, *Capital Navy* (El Dorado, Calif.: Savas Woodbury, 1996), p. 13–14, 153.

2. Thomas T. Moebs, *Confederate States Navy Research Guide* (Williamsburg, Va.: Moebs 1991), p. 242.

3. W. P. Trent, *Southern Writers: Selections in Prose and Verse* (New York: Macmillan, 1905), pp. 295–296.

4. National Park Service, Richmond National Battlefield, Richmond, Virginia.

5. "Confederate Forces Afloat," Appendix II in *Dictionary of American Fighting Ships,* vol. II (Washington, D.C.: Department of the Navy, 1971), p. 275.

6. J. Thomas Scharf, *History of the Confederate States Navy* (New York: Rogers & Sherwood, 1887), p. 773.

7. *Register of Officers of the Confederate States Navy, 1861–1865* (Richmond: Department of the Navy, CSA, 1864).

8. *Official Records of the Union and Confederate Navies in the War of the Rebellion*, series II, vol. II (Washington, D.C.: Government Printing Office, 1894–1927), pp. 630–645.

9. R. Thomas Campbell, *Academy on the James* (Shippensburg, Pa.: Burd Street, 1998), pp. 97–98.

10. *Ibid.*, p. 101.

11. *Official Records of the Union and Confederate Navies in the War of the Rebellion*, series I, vol. XV (Washington, D.C.: Government Printing Office, 1894–1927), pp. 501–502.

12. Ezra J. Warner, *Generals in Gray* (Baton Rouge: Louisiana State University Press, 1959), pp. 53–54.

13. Thomas Lawrence Connelly, *Autumn of Glory: The Army of Tennessee, 1862–1865* (Baton Rouge: Louisiana State University Press, 1971), pp. 504–506.

14. James M. Morgan, *Recollections of a Rebel Reefer* (New York: Houghton Mifflin, 1917), pp. 212–218.

15. *Official Records of the Union and Confederate Navies in the War of the Rebellion*, series I, vol. II (Washington, D.C.: Government Printing Office, 1894–1927), pp. 822–828.

16. James M. Morgan, "A Realistic War College," *U. S. Naval Institute Proceedings*, March 1916, pp. 549–550.

17. William H. Parker, *Recollections of a Naval Officer* (1883; new edition, Annapolis: Naval Institute Press, 1985), pp. 372–379.

Bibliography

Campbell, R. Thomas. *Academy on the James*. Shippensburg, Pa.: Burd Street, 1998.

Civil War Centennial Commission of Tennessee. *Tennesseans in the Civil War*, Vol. 1. Nashville: Civil War Centennial Commission of Tennessee, 1964.

Civil War Naval Chronology, 1861–1865. Washington, D.C.: Department of the Navy, Naval History Division, 1971.

Clark, Charles E. *My Fifty Years in the Navy*. Boston: 1917.

"Confederate Forces Afloat." Appendix II in *Dictionary of American Fighting Ships*, Vol. II. Washington, DC: Department of the Navy, 1971.

"Confederate Naval Cadets." *Southern Historical Society Papers*, vol. XXXII.

"Confederate Navy Record." State of Alabama, Department of Archives and History.

Connelly, Thomas Lawrence. *Autumn of Glory: The Army of Tennessee, 1862–1865*. Baton Rouge: Louisiana State University Press, 1971.

Coski, John M. *Capital Navy*. El Dorado Hills, Calif.: Savas Woodbury, 1996.

Extracts from the Regulations of the Navy School. Department of the Navy, CSA, December 15, 1863. Special Collections Library, Duke University, Durham, North Carolina.

Herndon, G. Melvin. "The Confederate States Naval Academy." *The Virginia Magazine of History and Biography*, July 1961.

Ielmini, Eileen A. (Georgia Historical Society). Letter to R. Thomas Campbell. April 29, 1997.

Journal of the Congress of the Confederate States of America, 1861–1865. Vol. 1.

Letter to R. Thomas Campbell from the Navy Register, Nimitz Library, United States Naval Academy. May 12, 1997.

Lyall, Beverly (archivist, Nimitz Library, U. S. Naval Academy). Letter to R. Thomas Campbell. April 24, 1997.

Minor, Hubbard T. Diary. 3 vols. U. S. Army Military Research Collection, Carlisle, Pennsylvania.

Moebs, Thomas T. *Confederate States Navy Research Guide*. Williamsburg, Va.: Moebs, 1991.

Morgan, James M. "A Realistic War College." *U.S. Naval Institute Proceedings*, March 1916.

_____. *Recollections of a Rebel Reefer*. New York: Houghton Mifflin, 1917.

"Muster Roll, Co. E, 42nd Tennessee Inf." Washington, D.C.: National Archives.

Official Records of the Union and Confederate Armies in the War of the Rebellion. Washington, D.C.: Government Printing Office, 1880–1901.

Official Records of the Union and Confederate Navies in the War of the Rebellion. Washington, D.C.: Government Printing Office, 1894–1927.

Parker, William H. " The Gold and Silver in the Confederate States Treasury." *Southern Historical Society Papers*. Vol. XXI. 1893.

_____. *Questions on Practical Seamanship*. Richmond: Macfarland and Furgusson, Printers, 1863.

_____. *Recollections of a Naval Officer* (1883). New edition, Annapolis: Naval Institute Press, 1985.

Paullin, Charles O. *Paullin's History of Naval Administration 1775–1911*. Annapolis: U.S. Naval Institute, 1968.

Register of Officers of the Confederate States Navy, 1861–1865. Richmond: Department of the Navy, CSA, 1864.

Regulations for the Confederate States School Ship Patrick Henry. Department of the Navy, CSA, 1863. Manuscript Department, Eleanor S. Brockenbrough Library, Museum of the Confederacy, Richmond, Virginia.

Regulations for the Interior Police of the School-Ship Patrick Henry. Department of the Navy, CSA, 1863. Manuscript Collection, Yale University, New Haven, Connecticut.

Scharf, J. Thomas. *History of the Confederate States Navy*. New York: Rogers & Sherwood, 1877.

Sturdy, Henry B. "The Establishment of the Naval School at Annapolis." *U.S. Naval Institute Proceedings* 72, 1946.

Todorich, Charles. *The Spirited Year: A History of the Antebellum Naval Academy*. Annapolis: Naval Institute Press, 1984.

Trent, W. P. *Southern Writers: Selections in Prose and Verse*. New York: Macmillan, 1905.

Trotter, William R. *Ironclads and Columbiads*. Winston Salem, N.C.: John F. Blair, 1989.

Warner, Ezra J. *Generals in Gray*. Baton Rouge: Louisiana State University Press, 1959.

Wells, Tom H. *The Confederate Navy: A Study in Organization*. Birmingham: University of Alabama Press, 1971.

Index